Communication Is ...

Perspectives on Theory

Communication Is ...

Perspectives on Theory

Editors

Adam Tyma
University of Nebraska–Omaha

Autumn Edwards
Western Michigan University

SAN DIEGO

Bassim Hamadeh, CEO and Publisher
Todd R. Armstrong, Publisher
Tony Paese, Project Editor
Alia Bales, Production Editor
Jess Estrella, Senior Graphic Designer
Trey Soto, Licensing Coordinator
Natalie Piccotti, Director of Marketing
Kassie Graves, Vice President of Editorial
Jamie Giganti, Director of Academic Publishing

ISBN: 978-1-51657-820-7

3970 Sorrento Valley Blvd., Ste. 500, San Diego, CA 92121

Contents

From There to Here—Serendipity

Adam Tyma
University of Nebraska—Omaha

Autumn Edwards
Western Michigan University

ADAM HERE. A QUICK STORY ON how this project came to be ... We start in Summer 2007. North Dakota State University. I am a PhD student having finished my second year of coursework, gearing up for comprehensive exams, contemplating how to tackle his dissertation topic (which ends up changing with the shooting at Virginia Tech), and moving through all of the inherent drama that is often interwoven with doctoral programs. Part of my program includes summer doctoral seminars, where students take weeklong, 8- to 9-hour-per-day courses with scholars that have been invited to the northern plains of Fargo, North Dakota. One of the assigned seminars, Communication Philosophy, was of particular interest given the trajectory of my studies and just who I am as a person. The scholar to walk us through this session? Dr. Mohan Dutta (an author in this volume). In preparation for each class, we are required/strongly encouraged to have around 90% of the reading completed before the first day of class, and one of those books is the relatively new *Communication as ...* I devour it, cover to cover. The way the book flows and how it lays out the ideas within just works for me. Some of the ideas I agreed with wholeheartedly, while others I had a difficult time swallowing. Regardless, each chapter forced me to confront my own positionality within the discipline, which is something we all should do from time to time.

Fast-forward to 2017. I am an Associate Professor in the School of Communication at the University of Nebraska at Omaha (where I am now). I am trying to figure out a complementary text for a graduate seminar foundations class for our MA program. I come across my copy of

Communication as ..., which is now thoroughly dog-eared and covered in marginalia. I read it over the summer and start to consider questions: "What has changed?"; "Do we need to push the conversation a different way?"; "What *is* this thing called *communication?*" While the class is happening, I start to put together an idea—revisit the format of the book but consider a different question: What *is* communication? I also have my students, for their final paper, consider where the book was and where we are now. This idea of reflection and expansion becomes a book pitch. While at NCA 2017, I meet with two publishing houses to see if they are interested. "Sure," I am told. Just complete this massive document for us to consider considering it. Simultaneously, I have pitched a panel for CSCA 2018, asking scholars I have worked with and those I have not to consider completing the statement "Communication is ..." The panel is picked up, the frantic writing for a conference paper panel begins, and I am excited that at least this part is happening. A week prior to CSCA, I am contacted by the now-publisher of this volume with an invitation to meet about the idea. During the conversation, it is mentioned that the acquisition editor I am speaking with (Todd Armstrong) just happened to be the same editor that worked with *Communication as ...* project. Serendipity.

Now CSCA 2018 is here. The crowd is impressive for a communication theory session. The session happens. The discussion is strong. The ideas unfold. The panel worked. Everyone who was on the panel agrees that, if the book idea happens, they would do their best to be part of it. I am glad to hear it. Later on, Todd and I meet. The conversation picks right up, and we start to see the true potential in this project. We talked, we laughed, ideas happened, and we cooked up a bold idea. Shortly thereafter, during our follow-up conversations, we start to discuss the idea of a coeditor, because this was going to be a "massive lift."[1] We tossed a few names around, and one that comes up is Autumn Edwards. Being a CSCA lifer, I am absolutely familiar with her work ... but we had never really spoken or even met before. Oddly enough, it ends up that one of her mentors from her graduate experience happens to be one of the editors of *Communication as ...*, meaning that she is quite familiar with the

---

1   My apologies. One of my nonacademic "things" is powerlifting, so a "massive lift" has become pretty standard parlance for me.

original project. She says she would love to be part of it and is excited to get started. Serendipity.

Fast-forward one year. CSCA 2019 in Omaha. The project is coming to a close. We present a short course to discuss the book project, how it works, and the ways the book could be utilized. It is in this meeting that I realize what we have here. The conversation from the scholars, mentors, and friends around the table demonstrate the different perspectives and insights on the discipline that exist and how they can work with each other. It is during this meeting, as it is right now, that I am really excited to see how you use this book.

A UTUMN HERE. THOSE WHO KNOW ME well in the field—my mentors, students, coauthors, and friends—can attest to the fact I am captivated by (okay, maybe a little obsessed with!) definitions. If I had an academic catchphrase, it would probably be: "Well, it depends on how you define it." My fascination with definitions and appreciation for their power can be traced at least back to competitive speech and debate in high school and college. The first order of business in those activities is to define (and often to contest and negotiate) the meanings of key terms in the topics or resolutions. Almost all subsequent possibilities for action and evaluation in the round stem from those initial understandings about what counts as what. Definitions delineate the very grounds for argument and call forth the values to invoke, the policies and practices to advance, and the costs and benefits to weigh.

My first course as a graduate student in communication at the University of Kansas in 1999 was taught by Greg Shepherd, an editor of *Communication as …* (the volume of essays which inspired this book), and the professor who would become my MA and PhD advisor, dearest mentor, and a lifelong friend. The first weeks of the class, Proseminar in Communication, were devoted to studying the history of the communication discipline and engaging historic and ongoing debates about the nature of the field and the definition of its central moniker. I was hooked! A few years later at the 2002 NCA (National Communication Association) annual convention in New Orleans, I was fortunate to attend a panel in which communication theorists addressed the question "What do you take communication to be?" The auditorium was packed. The air crackled with excitement. One by one, a number of the most prominent theorists in the field forwarded their preferred metaphor for communication: communication as transcendence, communication as ritual, communication as practice, and so on.

For many years, the first reading I assigned my own graduate students in their introductory MA course was the book that resulted from that panel: *Communication as … Perspectives on Theory* (2006). Together, we marveled at the great diversity of approaches, worked out how to read each metaphor with and against the others, and grappled with the consequences of adopting or avoiding each stance. In the preface, Shepherd, St. John, and Striphas argued for the importance of taking a stand on communication theory even while appreciating the pluralism. They asked each author contributing to the book to think (and write) like this:

> My stance is the one most serviceable for the study and practice of communication. My metaphor, my analogy, my model. This, not those, and for these reasons. Here is what I believe and why I believe it, and here is the difference it makes. (p. xii)

The editors urged the reader to evaluate the argument of each contributor and then "take advantage of the invitation to rank one of them above all others, or at least rank some ahead of others" (p. xiii). Thus, I assigned my students to take up the challenge laid forth by the editors and "take a stand on theory." The exercise was incredibly meaningful (and sometimes transformative) for my students and for me.

Communication as … remains one of my favorite books. I cannot think of another I have read more times or marked up more heavily. I was humbled and thrilled when Adam invited me to join this project which extends the invitation to define communication, more than a decade and a half later, to a whole new group of emerging and distinguished communication scholars. The opportunity for "spiral return," or an expanded circling back (Bateson, 1994) to a project that was so influential for me as a beginning scholar has been deeply meaningful. And the chief goals of this project—to envision communication in alternative ways and to consider the fruits of doing so—remain central to my own research, much of which has focused on questions of whether and how people's implicit, privately held definitions of communication relate to other aspects of their lives.

Together, Greg and I studied how people's personal definitions of communication were associated with their philosophies of human nature and assumptions about the world (Edwards & Shepherd, 2004), and with their community experiences (helping behavior and social capital; Edwards & Shepherd, 2007). Later, I conducted research with colleagues on how definitions of communication related to different understandings of social structures like the family (Edwards & Graham, 2009) and to differences in psychological and social well-being (Edwards, Rose, Edwards, & Singer, 2009). Most recently, my interests have turned toward the question of "human–machine communication," or the possibility of communication between people and digital/mechanical others such as artificially intelligent agents and robots. This, too, involves careful consideration of the definition of terms: human, machine, communication. How do people construct and understand the fundamental differences between the category "human" and "machine" (Edwards, 2018)? What definitions of "communication" include versus exclude nonhuman partners? And, what will be the consequences of counting the interactions between people and social machines as communication (or not)?

Our ideas about the nature of communication—what it is, how it works, and what it may be used to accomplish—are among the most important and exciting commitments we form as scholars, teachers, and practitioners. Through definitions, we construct our views of the world and delimit what is real, valuable, and possible (Postman, 1996). In this sense, definitions are inherently practical. They provide guides for interpretation and action that lead to outcomes of varying desirability. They aid us in certain purposes and bar us from others. For this reason, I hope that you will consider the chapters in this book not by asking, "Is this the *real*, *true*, or *correct* definition of communication?" but by asking, "What *purpose* does this definition serve? And, what are the *consequences* of enacting it?"

The Book Itself

With these opening narratives in mind, Adam and Autumn present *Communication Is…* for your consideration. The collection here offers 19 different completions of the statement *Communication Is ...* The ultimate goal was to allow the authors the space to complete the sentence with whatever term or construct they wanted to argue. We placed no restrictions (except for word count, of course) on the direction. We asked the authors to go light on the citation and data and heavy on the reflection and insight. Treat this as a way to sit back and think on this discipline/profession/calling. What you will notice is that the authors took the challenge of completion in different ways, from activism to introspection to function. We have worked to organize these chapters around common approaches, perspectives, etc. As you read through, and you (and possibly your students or colleagues) discuss, interrogate, or work through the ideas presented, you might see a different pattern emerge. Reorganize it as you see fit. We would love to hear about it.

As is obvious from the previous section, we both appreciate and utilize the 2006 project often in our own work, classrooms, and the like. So ... why the update? Why this project? There are a few reasons for this. First, it has been 13 years since the 2006 project was released, with the project really starting around 2001 and 2002. This means it has been almost 20 years since these ideas were considered. Since then, we have moved from Web 1.0 to Web 3.0, AI has become part of our lives (with Siri, Google Assistant, and Alexa), social media (starting with Facebook in 2006) has moved from the fringes of youth culture to ubiquitous and, in some cases, even become "official" media, our lives have become simultaneously interconnected and isolated ... and this is just on the tech side of the communication space.

Second, the communicative act has become instantaneous for more than strictly verbal means (through email, text messaging, web messaging, etc.). This has translated into an expectation of immediate response, thereby continual connection. The implications of this continual connection with our various layers and levels of relationship is just now becoming more fully understood. It is possible that what we understand as *communication* may begin to change ... or it may not. Asking those in the field to consider what communication is at this point is part of the journey. As a discipline, we should always be holding the biggest mirror up to ourselves.

Third, the discipline is in an administrative and, thereby, potentially precarious "confusion". Precarious because, in the age of educational budget cuts and the perpetual drumbeat for student credit hour generation,

Communication classes are being turned to as "easy" to adapt for those needs … since everyone knows how to speak in public, anyway.[2] This reality forces us to ask the question "What *is* communication?" We are being asked to defend it on a daily basis in meetings, chats, annual reports, departmental reviews, and budget requests. Stepping back to really consider what this thing is that we have devoted our careers and studies to allows us the space to better prepare for these realities.

Fourth, the past several years have witnessed exciting, difficult, and necessary agitation surrounding issues of social justice both within the discipline and in its relationship to broader cultural contexts. For many years, scholars of color and White allies have labored to bring attention to the lack of racial diversity in the field. Chakravartty, Kuo, Grubbs, and McIlwain (2018) documented the racial inequality in communication research, citations, and journals in the discipline ("#CommunicationSoWhite," *Journal of Communication*). As we write this introduction, a groundswell of affect and activism coalesces around inclusivity and equity. Partly in response to controversy surrounding the selection of NCA's Distinguished Scholars—a group overwhelmingly and disproportionately White, male, hetero, and cisgendered—an "Open Letter on Diversity in the Communication Discipline" is drawing attention to the field's troubling "exclusionary history with regard to people of color, women, LGBTQ+ individuals, people with disabilities, non-citizens, and those who stand at the intersections of these identities and more." Within 48 hours of posting, the letter had garnered over 1,000 signatures. Meanwhile, the emergent "Communication Scholars for Transformation" (Facebook group) has grown to 1,800+ members in the past month. A number of contributors to this book have been integral to disciplinary conversations about inclusivity and equity and bring those important goals to their chapters. And, this moment in time prompts us all to consider who is and who is not heard, served, valued, and empowered by how we frame and practice communication.

Fifth and finally, we are never "finished" or "done." As Judith Butler (1990) and Stuart Hall (1996) both remind us throughout their writings, we are constantly in a state of *becoming, exploring,* and *performing* who and

---

2   Adam here. My apologies for the implied sarcasm here. We are all seeing it—I just needed to say it.

what we are. The communication discipline is, like other disciplines, both objective and subjective, both governed by rules and used to tear the rules down. With such realities in mind, we should always be reflecting back on where we have been, where we are now, and what is happening next.

Organization of the Volume: The Business of "Is"-ness

Nineteen chapters. Thirty authors. Amazing and thought-provoking ideas throughout. As the editors of this volume, the most interesting task was to try to organize these thoughts. The authors took varied approaches to completing the sentence "Communication is ..." Some filled in the blank with an adjective or property describing communication's fundamental nature, occurrence, or effects. Others offered a synonym for communication or fashioned a statement of equivalency between communication and their preferred term. In searching for meaningful patterns amid the diverse strategies for defining communication, we were reminded of the phrase made famous by Bill Clinton: "It depends on what the meaning of the word 'is' is." As a conjugated form of the verb *be*, *is* can be used in several ways: to depict action (what does/can/ought communication *do?*), to describe a state of being (what is the *nature*, *scope*, or *meaning* of communication?), to assert existence (after all, the whole collection relies on a shared conviction that *Communication is*), and as an auxiliary verb supporting and adding meaning to another verb (how can communication be *explained* or *modeled?*).

Consequently, we have organized the essays into four broad methods of defining communication. The first section, *Locating*, includes efforts to map the contexts, places, and spaces of communication; to articulate boundaries and consider the consequences of *where*, *when* and *with whom* communication may occur. Chapters in the second section, *Processing*, forward explanations of how communication works; of how it may be modeled and understood as a series of actions resulting in certain ends. In the third section, *Appreciating*, each author extols a particular element of value as central to the nature and experience of communication; placing special emphasis on the implied responsibilities for facilitating positive change in individuals, groups, organizations, and communities. In the final section, *Actualizing*, the chapters focus on the role of communication in drawing to life and "making real" the various aspects of our social realities; attending carefully to the productive and reproductive nature and potentials of communicative action.

With the above in mind, dive in. Read through what these scholars have to say about the discipline. Start to question the ideas for yourself. Perhaps even write your own response to "What *is* communication?" We look forward to hearing from you.

Adam and Autumn

July 2019

CommunicationIs2019@gmail.com

References

Bateson, M. C. (1994). *Peripheral visions: Learning along the way.* New York, NY: HarperCollins.

Butler, J. (1990). *Gender trouble: Feminism and the subversion of identity.* London, UK: Routledge.

Edwards, A. (2018). Animals, humans, and machines: Interactive implications of ontological classification. In A. Guzman (Ed.), *Human–machine communication: Rethinking communication, technology, and ourselves* (pp. 29–49). New York, NY: Peter Lang.

Edwards, A., & Graham, E. E. (2009). The relationship between individuals' definitions of family and implicit personal theories of communication. *Journal of Family Communication, 11,* 191–207.

Edwards, A., Rose, L., Singer, L., & Edwards, C. (2009). An investigation of the relationships among implicit personal theories of communication, social support, and loneliness. *Human Communication, 11,* 437–454.

Edwards, A., & Shepherd, G. J. (2007). An investigation of the relationship between implicit personal theories of communication and community behavior. *Communication Studies, 58,* 359–375.

Edwards, A., & Shepherd, G. J. (2004). Theories of communication, human nature, and the world: Associations and implications, *Communication Studies, 55*(2), 197–203.

Hall, S. (1996). Introduction: Who needs 'identity'? In S. Hall & P. du Gay (Eds.), *Questions of cultural identity* (pp. 1–17). London, UK: SAGE.

Postman, N. (1996). *The end of education: Redefining the value of school.* New York, NY: Vintage Books.

Section 1

Locating

Chapter 1

Communication Is ... Co-Cultural

Mark P. Orbe
Western Michigan University

Robert J. Razzante
Arizona State University

R ACIAL PROFILING. POLITICAL DIVISION. SEXUAL HARASSMENT/ASSAULT. Culture-based health disparities. Police brutality. Religious intolerance. Transgender rights. Immigration policy. All of these hot-button issues in the United States are steeped in perceptual differences informed by culturally informed lived experiences. Effective communication practices are offered as a cure-all for making any progress in moving toward solutions. Yet, most discussions (e.g., debates) about the topics reflect an overall lack of civility and, in many ways, an inability or refusal to acknowledge the role that power and privilege play in one's perspectives.

Effective communication is contextually based and influenced by a variety of factors. Asserting that "communication is co-cultural" signifies that power and privilege are core factors for how people communicate with each other. However, not all power and privilege are perceived, or enacted, in the same way. As such, communicating effectively across power and privilege requires attention to other factors such as historical context, cultural differences/similarities, and intersectional identities, to name a few. Rather than offering a one-size fits all approach to effective communication, we share tools that can be used to determine how one might effectively communicate depending on the variety of factors at play.

This chapter explicates how communication is co-cultural, an ontological stance that centralizes the impact of macro-level power structures on all forms of communication. In doing so, we highlight the inextricable relationship between power, culture, and communication (Orbe, 1998).

Specifically, we describe co-cultural (e.g., Orbe, 1998) and dominant group theorizing (e.g., Razzante & Orbe, 2018) as effective frameworks that centralize power, as conceptualized within macro-level societal institutions where certain group memberships carry significant societal privilege, into human communication theorizing. In addition, we draw from various cultural dialectics (Martin & Nakayama, 1999) to explain the necessity for examining power dynamics in communication. In doing so, we situate power as an underlying infrastructure that informs human communication.

Communication Is Co-Cultural

The idea that "communication is co-cultural" reflects the core belief that power and privilege must be acknowledged, considered, examined, and understood as fundamental to all forms of communication. *Co-cultural* is a term used to recognize that a variety of cultures exist within every larger culture (Orbe, 1998). These co-cultural groups, typically smaller in number and underrepresented in terms of political and economic power, exist simultaneously along with those cultures that are in the majority (i.e., dominant groups). All societies exist within structural realities with levels of power and privilege that vary for different people. Within the United States, co-cultural groups include, but are not limited to, women, people of color, people with disabilities, people from lower-class/working-poor backgrounds, and people who are lesbian/gay/bisexual/transgender/queer. Dominant groups in the United States, in contrast, include men, European Americans, the able-bodied, middle and upper-class persons, and those who are heterosexual and cisgender. The societal positioning of co-cultural and dominant group members informs their communication with others. This premise is at the core of co-cultural theory (Orbe, 1998), and more recently dominant group theory (Razzante & Orbe, 2018), both of which provide a theoretical foundation for the assertion that communication is co-cultural.

Co-Cultural Theory. Co-cultural theory (Orbe, 1998) examines the ways in which individuals from groups that have been historically marginalized communicate with dominant group members (those that have been historically privileged). Grounded in muted group theory (Kramarae, 1981) and standpoint theories (Smith, 1987), the theory emerged from a series of phenomenological studies aimed at explicating the communicative lived experiences of underrepresented group members in the United States. Over time, it has come to represent a valuable framework for understanding how micro-level interactions are situated in a larger context informed by macro-level power differences.

More specifically, co-cultural theory provides insight into how different factors (e.g., preferred outcome and communication approach) intersect to influence the specific communication practices that traditionally marginalized group members enact in their interactions with others (for a visualization of this conceptualization, see Orbe, 1998, p. 110). Four other factors (e.g., field of experience, perceived costs and rewards, ability, and situational context) offer further explication as to why co-cultural group members strategically enact certain practices over others (Orbe, 1998). These practices include those that promote assimilation (e.g., censoring self, extensive preparation, ridiculing self), accommodation (educating others, utilizing liaisons), and separation (maintaining interpersonal barriers, intragroup networking, attacking). The value of co-cultural theory rests in its descriptive power, which was drawn from the phenomenologically based lived experiences from a wide variety of underrepresented group members. From its inception, scholars from a variety of disciplines have utilized co-cultural theory to explore how individuals from traditionally marginalized groups interact with others with greater societal power and privilege (for summary, see Orbe & Roberts, 2012). Castle Bell et al. (2014) offer an in-depth description of how the theory has been used in the past and been extended by different intercultural communication scholars interested in contributing to a more nuanced understanding of the inextricable relationship between power, culture, and communication.

Dominant Group Theory. Dominant group theory (Razzante & Orbe, 2018) is a recent theorizing framework that applies the structural components of co-cultural theory to the communicative lived experiences of those with greater societal privilege and access to institutional power. Dominant group theory, like co-cultural theory, has its roots in the phenomenological experience of human interaction (Razzante, 2018). Conceptually, it is informed by traditional and contemporary research exploring the intersections of power, privilege, and communication (de Certeau, 1988; DeTurk, 2011; Foucault, 1977).

Dominant group theory explicates how the communication strategies of those who are cisgender, heterosexual, European American, able-bodied and male are informed by a variety of factors (e.g., field of experience, abilities, perceived costs and rewards, situational context). Additionally, it seeks to avoid the trappings that all of those with societal privilege communicate in the same way. In fact, one of its most valuable contributions is a recognition that the communication of dominant group members can do more than simply reinforce or extend societal inequalities. This accomplished by acknowledging how one's communication can also promote social equality on both macro- and micro-levels. This is an improvement over one of the premises of co-cultural theory, which argued that those with power consciously or unconsciously work to maintain that power (see Orbe, 1998, p. 11). According to Razzante and Orbe (2018), dominant group communication strategies can reinforce existing oppressive structures by ignoring one's privilege, dismissing co-cultural concerns, and using microaggressions. In addition, they can also help to impede and/or assist in dismantling them via different communication-based strategies like engaging in self-reflexivity, educating others, confronting oppressive rhetoric, and challenging oppressive ideologies. A detailed description of dominant group factors, strategies, and communication orientations is offered by Razzante and Orbe (see summary, pp. 364–365).

Taken together, co-cultural theory and dominant group theory provide a valuable framework to understanding how communication—at the interpersonal, small group, organizational, and societal levels—is informed by varying levels of societal power and privilege. The theories also assist in recognizing how a variety of factors (e.g., field of experience, situational context) can impact how different individuals communicate. Finally, utilizing co-cultural and dominant group theory collaboratively promotes the type of multifocal-relational scholarship advocated by Orbe and Allen (2008). This includes, but is not limited to, research that values a recognition of intersectionality, ingroup and outgroup similarities and differences, and the need "to gain insight by exploring how the communicative experiences of individuals simultaneously inform, and are informed by, the lived experiences of other[s]" (p. 211). Next, we turn to how cultural dialectics support the idea that communication is co-cultural.

The Relevancy of Cultural Dialectics

The ways in which everyday interpersonal communication interactions—with friends, family, coworkers, neighbors, and strangers—are influenced by larger societal power dynamics can be best explained through Martin and Nakayama's (1999) cultural dialectics. This conceptual framework has proven invaluable for advancing intercultural communication scholarship, by offering "the possibility to see the world in multiple ways and to become better prepared to engage in intercultural interaction" (p. 13). We utilize it here to illustrate the value of understanding how communication is co-cultural.

Traditional Western thought focuses on understanding the human experience through binary categories; something is either good *or* bad, liberal *or* conservative, right *or* wrong. A dialectical approach embraces the idea that life is best understood as a "both/and"—rather than an "either/or" phenomenon. In other words, a person's communicative message may very well be good *and* bad, liberal *and* conservative, right *and* wrong. A dialectical perspective is consistent with our assertion that communication is co-cultural in that it understands communication as a "dynamic and changing process" (Martin & Nakayama, 1999, p. 14) involving individuals who may occupy a cultural location reflective of both co-cultural and dominant group membership (Razzante, Orbe, & Boylorn, 2018). According to Martin and Nakayama (1999), six cultural dialectics exist: (1) cultural–individual, (2) personal–contextual, (3) differences–similarities, (4) static–dynamic, (5) history/past–present/future, and (6) privilege–disadvantage. An explanation of each of these tensions provides a clear and concise argument as to the necessity of understanding how communication is co-cultural.

Cultural–Individual. The first cultural dialectic emphasizes the importance of seeing each person as both an individual and simultaneously as a member of various cultural groups (Martin & Nakayama, 1999). Such a stance recognizes how problematic traditional thinking was in regards to seeing a person *only* as an individual (e.g., telling a gay person that "I don't see you as gay") or defining a person by *one* aspect of their cultural identity (e.g., "they're Muslim, what would you expect?"). This particular cultural dialectic is central to understanding how communication is co-cultural because it highlights how all individuals are members of different co-cultural and dominant groups, something that explicitly and/ or implicitly impacts their interactions with others.

Personal–Contextual. The second cultural dialectic, personal–contextual, highlights the importance of context in understanding personal communicative behaviors (Martin & Nakayama, 1999). The ways in which people communicate, as captured in this dialectic, are reflective of personal and social characteristics, and they can also be impacted by the particular dynamics of a situational context. As such, this particular cultural dialectic recognizes how an individual's communication strategies may vary in different contexts (e.g., how an outspoken woman may engage in self-censorship at a business meeting with all conservative-thinking men). The dialectic also can promote an understanding of how a person's most relevant cultural identity marker may shift depending on who else is present (e.g., how spiritual differences become most salient in room of individuals who share the same race, gender, and age).

Differences–Similarities. All humans are simultaneously alike and unalike. This basic truth is at the core of the third cultural dialectic, differences-similarities (Martin & Nakayama, 1999). Historically, many have focused on the differences between different sociocultural groups (e.g., "men are from Mars, women are from Venus"). Alternatively, others have advocated for a singular focus on similarities (e.g., "there is only one human race"). This cultural dialectic highlights how both of these perspectives are problematic in that they fail to recognize how the core of human experience is universal yet lived differently based on one's personal, social and cultural characteristics. Relevant to the assertion that communication is co-cultural, power and privilege impacts everyone's communication, albeit not always in the same way.

Static–Dynamic. The fourth cultural dialectic promotes an understanding of how culture, and the world in which we live, is both static–dynamic (Martin & Nakayama, 1999). Culture is both ever-changing and constant and consistent over time. The same can be said regarding the macro-level structures within any society. For example, the election of U.S. President Barack Obama in 2008 reflected a major accomplishment in regards to civil rights, race relations, and political power. However, simultaneously it did little to change the lives of everyday African Americans or the political culture of Washington (see, for example, Orbe, 2011). Consistent with the thesis of this chapter, the realities of co-cultural and dominant group members—as informed by larger power dynamics—are both consistent and ever-changing. The next cultural dialectic that we describe reinforces this core idea.

History/Past–Present/Future. The fifth cultural dialectic, as conceptualized by Martin and Nakayama (1999), is history/past–present/future. This particular dialectic emphasizes the importance of embracing a both/and perspective to understanding how past events continue to inform current intergroup relations. Oftentimes in discussions regarding White privilege, we hear European American students proclaim that they "never owned slaves," therefore negating how they benefit from centuries of racial oppression. In the same discussions, we see students of color assert how racism continues to exist in contemporary times (e.g., "racial profiling and police brutality continues to be a huge issue"). In actuality, both of these perspectives are accurate. What is missing is an acknowledgment that both are simultaneously true. The communicative lived experiences of co-cultural and dominant group members are situated in historical contexts that inform, yet do not define, current realities (e.g., "the more things change, the more they stay the same").

Privilege–Disadvantage. No one person will ever experience the totality of their life either as a co-cultural or dominant group member. Because identities are multidimensional (e.g., based on race, ethnicity, gender, socioeconomic status, abilities, age, sexuality, spirituality, and the like), individuals will occupy social locations with varying levels of societal privilege. This core belief is supported by the final cultural dialectic, privilege–disadvantage, and is a central tenet of understanding communication as co-cultural (Martin & Nakayama, 1999). All forms of communication, to some extent, are racialized, gendered, classed, *and* simultaneously informed by other salient identity markers as best captured through the concept of intersectionality (Razzante et al., 2018). Take, for example, lower-class White heterosexual abled-bodied Christian males who describe themselves as "oppressed." While they may benefit from societal privilege based on race, sexuality, abilities, spirituality and gender, the disadvantage that they experience based on socioeconomic status may feel like the defining characteristic of their lives. Again, the key here is for individuals to recognize how they, and others, experience privilege and disadvantage.

This final cultural dialectic appears most clearly aligned with the idea that communication is co-cultural; it also highlights the ways in which all six dialectics are interconnected and mutually complementary. For instance, understanding how privilege–disadvantage is experienced requires a recognition of how it interacts with each of the other cultural dialectics (e.g., how privilege is manifested in a particular time/across time, as both a personal and contextual phenomenon). Consistent with the arguments of Martin and Nakayama (1999), understanding how communication is co-cultural "emphasizes the relational, rather than individual aspects of persons" (p. 14). In doing so, we advocate for a recognition of how macro-level power dynamics are manifested through micro-level demonstrations of privilege–disadvantage; this assertion is steeped in the idea that "one becomes fully human only in relation to another person" (p. 14). Engaging the power dynamics that exist between individuals is crucial to enhanced understanding of their communication.

Conclusion

Martinez (2006) reminds us that all communication interactions involve individuals "located in time, place, and culture" (p. 297). In other words, communication does not exist in a vacuum void of outside influences. As argued throughout this chapter, these influences include larger power structures created and maintained by societal institutions like those related to government, economics, business, health, education, law enforcement, and the media. In essence, these, and other related entities, are reflective of a society's culture and serve as the macro-level context in which all communication exists. While never explicitly naming the macro–micro tension, Martinez (2006) describes micro-level cultural experiences as informed and/or constrained by macro-level influences. As such, her arguments can be seen as a recognition of the ways in which everyday communicative experiences are situated within a macro–micro dialectic.

Based on our experiences as scholars–educators–practitioners, we antic-ipate that many self-identified co-cultural group members will identify strongly with the main arguments of our chapter. In comparison, some individuals identifying as dominant group members may be less convinced that all communication is co-cultural. In fact, over the past decade, some have promoted the idea that humankind has moved beyond historical influences into a reality that is not defined by cultural oppression (see, for example, Orbe, 2011). In other words, people communicate as individuals, with little influence from power-infused cultural differences. This notion has been described as the "post-" movement (Ono, 2010). Within this perspective, individuals reject the idea that macro-level power dynamics, and the societal privileges that stem from them, have any impact on the everyday interactions between coworkers, friends, family, peers, and strangers. However, we would argue that the opportunity to have such a perspective is only possible from a privileged position, and speaks to the pressing need to acknowledge that not all people engage in the world from the same cultural location. To put it simply, the fact that someone believes that power and privilege are not central to one's everyday communication is reflective that, in fact, they are.

Throughout this essay, we assert that power and privilege are always—explicitly and/or implicitly—present when individuals come together to communicate. While we believe this to be true, it does not mean that all interactions have to be defined solely by imbalances of privilege informed by varying levels of societal power. As evidenced by dominant group theory, some communication interactions can involve responsible uses of power that result in meaningful personal relationships between culturally different individuals. At the core of our argument, however, is that these types of mutually fulfilling relationships can only be accomplished through an ongoing acknowledgment of how larger macro-level power structures impact individuals' everyday communicative lives. Consistent with the spirit of our chapter, we leave you with one ending thought. We hope that we have provided a compelling argument as to why communication is co-cultural. However, this assertion should not be interpreted as a rejection that communication is also relational ... , dialectic ... , cultural ... , ethical ... , etc. We embrace the dialectical philosophy that human communication is best understood as a both/and, not either/or, phenomenon—and in doing so promote a multidimensional understanding of the complexities of communication, including that which engages issues seen as controversial, divisive, and difficult to navigate.

References

Castle Bell, G., Hopson, M. C., Weathers, M. R., & Ross, K. A. (2014). From "laying the foundations" to building the house: Extending Orbe's (1998) co-cultural theory to include "rationalization" as a formal strategy. *Communication Studies, 66*, 1–26. doi:10.1080/10501974.2013.858053

de Certeau, M. (1988). *The practice of everyday life* (S. Rendall, Trans.). Berkeley, CA: University of California Press.

DeTurk, S. (2011). Allies in action: The communicative experiences of people who challenge social injustice on behalf of others. *Communication Quarterly, 59*, 569–590. doi:10.1080/01463373.2011.614209

Foucault, M. (1977). *Discipline and punish: The birth of the prison.* New York, NY: Pantheon Books.

Kramarae, C. (1981). *Women and men speaking.* Rowley, MA: Newbury.

Martin, J. N., & Nakayama, T. (1999). Thinking dialectically about culture and communication. *Communication Theory, 9*, 1–25. doi:10.1111/j.1468-2885.1999.tb00160.x

Martinez, J. M. (2006). Semiotic phenomenology and intercultural communication scholarship: Meeting the challenge of racial, ethnic, and cultural difference. *Western Journal of Communication, 70*, 292–310. doi:10.1080/10570310600992103

Ono, K. (2010). Postracism: A theory of the "post"—as political strategy. *Journal of Communication Inquiry, 34*, 227–233.

Orbe, M. P. (1998). *Constructing co-cultural theory: An explication of culture, power, and communication.* Thousand Oaks, CA: SAGE. doi:http://dx.doi.org/10.4135/9781483345321

Orbe, M. P. (2011). *Communication realities in a "post-racial" society: What the U.S. really thinks about Barack Obama.* Lanham, MD: Lexington Books.

Orbe, M. P., & Allen, B. J. (2008). "Race matters" in the *Journal of Applied Communication Research. Howard Journal of Communications, 19*, 201–220. doi:10.1080/10646170802218115

Orbe, M. P., & Roberts, T. L. (2012). Co-cultural theorizing: Foundations, applications & extensions. *Howard Journal of Communications, 23*, 293–311. doi:10.1080/10646175.2102.722838

Razzante, R. J. (2018). Identifying dominant group communication strategies: A phenomenological study. *Communication Studies, 69*, 389–403. doi:10.1080/10510974.2018.1472116

Razzante, R. J., & Orbe, M. P. (2018). Two sides of the same coin: Conceptualizing dominant group theory in the context of co-cultural theory. *Communication Theory, 28*, 354–375. doi:10.1093/ct/qtx008

Razzante, R. J., Orbe, M. P., & Boylorn, R. (2018, November). *Embracing intersectionality in co-cultural and dominant group theorizing: Implications for theory, research, and pedagogy.* Paper presented at the annual meeting of the National Communication Association, Salt Lake City, UT.

Smith, D. E. (1987). *The everyday world as problematic: A feminist sociology of knowledge.* Boston, MA: Northeastern University Press.

Chapter 2
Communication Is ... (Often) Placed

James G. Cantrill
Northern Michigan University

O NE OF THE FIRST THINGS STUDENTS of communication learn is that the "settings" in which human interactions occur are important considerations when attempting to be effective and appropriate in the social sphere. Typically, such settings are socially constructed as physical or interpersonal constraints upon behavior: In childhood we are reminded to use our "inside voice." Students of public address are taught to project their voices depending upon the size of a room and our interpersonal communication students are routinely mentored to mind proxemics. We are counseled by advertisers to "shout it out" or to "whisper" if we want someone's attention. Popular music metaphorically references "the space between" interlocutors and the solitude of being "in my room" or "up on the roof," questions whether or not others "are still within the sound of my voice," or indexes "distant lovers" talking on the telephone. Ideographic references (e.g., "the city on the hill") litter public discourse. Clearly, the mere act of communicating implicates an important spatial dimension (Peters, 1999).

Not to trivialize the role of physical space in social interaction, my aim in this chapter is to explore an equally important concept seen too often as a mere synonym, the idea of *place*. Whereas "spaces" represent locations defined by physical landforms, artifacts, or boundaries (e.g., Cvijanović, Kechichian, Janse, & Kohlrausch, 2017; Horsbøl, 2018; Vásquez, 2016), and "settings" extend locality into interpersonal dimensions (e.g., Daly & Thompson, 2017; Metts & Cupach, 1989; Tracy & Baratz, 1993), a symbolic transformation occurs within the mind and between people when "places" arise from the cognitive morass of identity, memory, and space (cf. Blair, Dickinson, & Ott, 2010). In the hearts and consciousness of those who come to embrace them, places are just as real as a boardroom, a landscape, or a voting booth, though much less corporeal in nature. As Cresswell (2004) notes, places are lenses for experiencing and interacting with the world at large (cf. Worster & Abrams, 2005). In addition, when people observe that "communication takes place," they might well be thinking of common speech acts or, perhaps, a deeper and more semiotic exchange (e.g., Carbaugh, 1988; Philipsen, 1975).

Consider, for example, the distinction people often make between "home" and, say, a location one stays at while on business or vacation. Our homes provide all sorts of ecological services that nourish our minds as well as our bodies. Homes may be construed as refuges we retreat to after work or school; they are steeped in memories—both "good" and "bad"—that link past, present, and future; they shape us as we shape them in terms of social dynamics, daily routines, and seasonal rituals. In contrast, a motel while "on the road" is but a space that provides the necessities of shelter, sometimes nourishment (e.g., a mini-bar), televised entertainment, and hopefully a comfortable bed upon which to sleep. This is not to say that habitation other than the home cannot come to be seen as a more meaningful place over time. Anyone who has returned time and again to a vacation site (e.g., a beach house, a particular bed and breakfast, or that ranch hidden in the Rockies I used to visit every year) knows that there may be multiple places where we can and do retreat to, reminisce about, and interact within.

When I suggest that "communication is often placed," I mean to locate a range of symbolizing within a social and psychological nexus that draws its agency from the extent to which individuals ground whom they are and what they value in physical space that, over time, has taken on much more robust affective associations. Or, as Sowards, Tarin, and Upton (2017) summarize, "Put simply, when we speak, we are building the world around us." Thus, the symbolic conversions of physical space into places are cognitive and communicative processes worthy of our utmost attention, both in the private (e.g., the development of personal relationships) and public spheres (e.g., the promulgation of public policy).

To further explore the relationship between place and communication, I will locate most of my review and analysis in the dominant legacy of natural resource and environmental communication research. Although other interaction contexts warrant inspection—such as media (e.g., Livingstone & Lunt, 2002), romance (e.g., Trauer & Ryan, 2005), travel (e.g., White & White, 2004), politics (e.g., Agnew, 2014), homes (e.g., Manzo, 2003) and other built environments (e.g., Korpela, 1989), employment (e.g., Leonard et al., 2017), or even breweries (Schnell & Reese, 2014), coffee houses (Dickinson, 2002), and tattoo parlors (Modesti, 2008)—I mostly study human relationships with landscapes and ecological conditions. Also, most scholarly attention on the concept of place has occurred at the intersection of geography, anthropology, and communication practices (e.g., Cantrill, 2015). Consequently, I will first review selected research that links places to personal identities. Next, I will discuss the relationship between the perception of self and place as based in human interaction. Finally, I will conclude by suggesting the powerful aftershocks that attend the loss of place, even when the space between remains.

The Self as a Place-Based Construct

A wide range of conceptual and empirical approaches to studying the personal and social experience of place have been pursued, some of which have identified *place attachment or place identity* as significant mediating factors in conservation planning and environmental protection (for reviews, see: Bott, Cantrill, & Meyers, 2003; Devine-Wright, 2013; Lewicka, 2011; Nicolosi & Corbett, 2018; Williams, 2008). Place attachment is typically seen as the emotional and cognitive ties that bind people to the lived-in environment based upon their experiences therein (Low & Altman, 1992; Moore & Graefe, 1994; Williams, Patterson, Roggenbuck, & Watson, 1992). Arguably, one's attachment to *a* place is relatively localized, often manifested as "a sense of place" (e.g., Mitchell, Force, Carroll, & McLaughlin, 1993; Tuan, 1977), and does not extend beyond spatially and temporally limited settings. For example, consider how people are drawn to particular constructed spaces (e.g., a childhood home or neighborhood) or natural environments (e.g., a vacation retreat or mountain range).

In comparison, to the extent people have personally vested meanings for molar landscape types (e.g., mountains), soundscapes (e.g., elk bugling), and environments (e.g., cold climates), they develop a place identity (e.g., Clayton & Opotow, 2003; Proshansky, Fabian, & Kaminoff, 1983). Research suggests that ongoing social constructions of space across the lifespan result in enduring neurological associations between self-concepts and generalized geographic perceptions (cf. Brehm, Eisenhauer, & Krannich, 2006; Lengen & Kistemann, 2012). Typically laden with positive affect, place identities provide landscape anchors for how we characterize ourselves (e.g., "I'm a country boy.") and are tenaciously clung to across much of the lifespan (e.g., Stedman, 2008; Stewart, 2008). Arguably, place identities are not simply linked to spaces bound by spatial and temporal qualities. One's sense of who they are/were given where they are/were can exist even when the physical landscape that constitutively gives rise to place is no more.

Taken as a unified construct, place attachment and place identity become what I have labeled a *sense of self-in-place* (e.g., Cantrill, 2011; Cantrill & Senecah, 2001). It is when the affective and cognitive beliefs about specific places collide with self-defining memories and feelings for larger landscapes that the polysemic, multilayered meaningfulness of a sense of self-in-place is aroused (cf. Hurley, 2013; Urquhart & Acott, 2013). Research into the notion of a sense of self-in-place has been applied to a range of situations, including the stewardship of gateway communities for protected areas (Cantrill, 1998), attitudes toward governmental regulation of natural resources (Cantrill, 2003), the practice of adaptive management in forest planning (Cantrill, 2004; cf. Kalibo & Medley, 2007), the regulation of households (Milstein et al., 2011), and understanding the perceptual drivers of urban sprawl (Cantrill, Thompson, Garrett, & Rochester, 2007). Following this family of research, our actions on the world depend, at least partially, upon the extent to which we find our identities related to specific aspects of the landscapes we inhabit or frequent. Also, with prolonged entrenchment in such locales, those place-based senses of self typically exhibit a shift in perceptual salience, moving from a focus upon physical attributes to more socially oriented activities occurring in those perceived places. For example, Cantrill, Ray, Miller, and Smit (1999) observed that, unless it is explicitly prompted by interviewer protocols, nature is sublimated to economic and social features when depicting the homeland environment and evaluating living conditions once inhabitants have tenure in a community. For example, although people may be attracted to "the country" for the vistas, wildlife, and flora it provides, the longer they live there the more they find their friends and availability (or not) of services to be the defining elements of *that* place. Cantrill and Masluk (1996) demonstrated that respondents' sense of self-in-place in a rural community seems divided across three major thematic "clusters" dealing with associations linking an individual to the local landscape and/or social structures, various social relations between respondents and others in the region, and the extent to which changes or opportunities in the area depended on government policies. A subsidiary analysis (Cantrill, 2003) indicated residents often choose to migrate into an undeveloped area to avoid constraints upon their social and economic activities that, nonetheless, become compromised as resource managers attempt to regulate impediments to ecosystem services. The older a respondent was, the more their comments mirrored a general focus on the governmental regulatory context and the less they valued intrusion by outside civic forces. Related research (e.g., Folke, Han, Olsson, & Norberg, 2005; McKenzie-Mohr, 2000) also suggests that the greater one's attachment to the social structures of an area, the more otherwise seemingly "environmental" concerns revolve around issues of community culture and health-related issues. Thus, especially with the passage of time, more-or-less inhabited spaces become "peopled places" where communication—regarding what to do, how to talk, what to culturally value, and how to interpret others—shapes and is shaped by the place-based identities of those who dwell upon the land (Cantrill, 1998, p. 312).

Communicating In and About Place

Although the visceral experience of corporeal spaces contributes mightily to a sense of self-in-place, we should not underestimate the role played by social interaction in galvanizing such heartfelt perceptions. That is, a sense of self-in-place and its variegated forms (e.g., identity, attachment) blossoms out of and is molded by ongoing social discourse regarding the spaces people encounter. The notion that our internal, socially constructed meanings for the world we perceive is a product of communication is hardly a new idea. Since at least the writings of Latour in the late-1970s (Latour & Woolgar, 1979; cf. Latour, 1993; Latour, 2005), a debate over the "objective" nature of empiricism has raged in the philosophy of science. What is "real"—in a laboratory, city street, or wilderness setting—becomes whatever a social actor considers as such. Similarly, the practice of ethnomethodology, following Garfinkle (1967), assumes that the "subjective" experience of life events arises at the intersection of physical sense making and socially constructed meanings *in situ* (e.g., Trentelman, 2009). Indeed, the perception–interaction nexus in the formation of identity and agency has been indexed by a range of other communication scholars interested in studies of place-based behavior (e.g., Campbell, 2005; Kruger & Shannon, 2000; Kyle & Chick, 2007; Rickard & Stedman, 2014).

As if channeling the spirit of Wallace Stegner (who once opined, "A place is nothing in itself. It has no meaning, it can hardly be said to exist, except in terms of human perception, use and response"; 1955, p. 3), Thompson and Cantrill (2013) observed "geographic and social *spaces* are symbolically transformed into meaningful *places* through processes of human interaction across time" (p. 1; cf. Kyle, Graefe, & Manning, 2005; Mugerauer, 1989; Smaldone, Harris, & Sanyal, 2008). Agnew (2011) tells us a sense of place is something that organically evolves over time on a particular landscape given the social interactions that take place *there*. Strine (2004) argues that the fundamental building blocks of human interaction, speech acts, are inherently tied to social context, thus becoming "conveyors of particular worldviews and social ideologies" (p. 225). At the same time, human interaction is more-or-less mediated by the socially constructed places people have in their minds regarding what to focus upon and how to interpret messaging patterns (e.g., Scannell & Gifford, 2013). Furthermore, research and lived experience provide abundant evidence that people may be quite attached to both landscape-scale and site-specific places (e.g., Lewicka, 2011). Attachment theory (e.g., Morgan, 2010) suggests that, by way of such cleaving, individuals often index their place attachments in conversation as well as use them in the processing relevant information (cf. Cantrill, 1996).

It is also important to note that, far from being ensconced in only the present tense, a person's mental construction of self and place extends into the past and future as well. As grounded identities come into discursive being, memories and expectations capture the imagination. Bellah and colleagues (1985) tell us "the communities of memory that tie us to the past also turn us toward the future as communities of hope. They carry a context of meaning that can allow us to connect our aspirations for ourselves and those closest to us with the aspirations of a larger whole" (p. 153). In a similar vein, the stories people share regarding who they were and where they were in the past provide anchors for current identities as well as projecting whom we might be in the future, given the places to which we gravitate (cf. Apfelbaum, 2001; Irwin-Zarecka, 1994; Massey, 2013).

To summarize thus far, the relationship between communication, place, and self represents a complex social and cognitive dynamic across the lifetime. The egocentric world of little children is full of references to where they belong such as "home," where they should go (of course, their "room"), and where they should not tread (e.g., the dreaded "edge"). With maturation and the emergence of perspective-taking capabilities, our interpersonal encounters with caregivers and other significant others allow us to see the social forests beyond the trees of our mental backyards, to adapt what we say to the place-based realities of others, and to think more abstractly about who we are in relation to the spaces we travel through. As we attach ourselves to new loved ones, they become a significant part of places in which we find meaningful value and enduring memories. Thus, a sense of self-in-place influences more than merely perception of the physical world in that it informs actors about what is important to remember about social encounters, provides a lens for interpreting what is communicated in everyday discourse, and gives us a host of meaningful tropes to use when interacting with others. Yet, as is always the case, life is not just about *us* or the places *we* conjure up for *ourselves*. The physical world has a nasty habit of getting in our way.

Of Losing One's Place on the Discursive Page

Environmental modernity has occasioned dangerous times with existential uncertainties. Various scholars (e.g., Binder, Scheufele, Bossard, & Gunther, 2011; Krimsky & Plough, 1988) observe that what constitutes "an environmental disaster," and the ensuing perception of threats to place-based identity, is a social construction arising from the way in which people *talk* about risks as well as what they *think* about when being alerted. That is, thought and discourse reinforce one another, sometimes in surprising ways. For example, one of Fox, Magilligan, and Sneddon's (2016) respondents commented upon a pro-development stance in noting, "You kill the dam, you are killing a part of me" (p. 93) in contrast to those in Ewalt and Cantrill's (2017) study who often lamented the impact of development as in "while [the trees] were there, you were there and when they were gone, you were gone. It's like you wake up and your [sic] gone" (p. 113).

Consistent with the way in which mass media enculturates people into accepting a certain view of "reality," or cultivation theory (e.g., Morgan, Shanahan, & Signorielli, 2017; cf. Amiot, Sablonniere, Smith, & Smith, 2015; Hodgetts, Bolam, & Stephens, 2005), the social and mediated milieu that frames perceptions of environmental catastrophe may also impact the extent to which the integrity of place-based identities or shared senses of selves-in-place change over time. Previously, I have argued that "it is after the general public learns of an environmental condition, yet before subsequent discussions in interpersonal networks or the public sphere ripple through and agitate perceptions, that the sense of self-in-place can be seen as enhancing the traditional social amplification of risk framework" (2011, p. 77; cf. Kasperson, Kasperson, Pidgeon, & Slovic, 2003). In turn, Bonaiuto, Alves, De Dominicis, and Petruccelli's (2016) research review of place attachment and agency associated with natural hazards reveals that the more attached people are to particular locations, the more likely they are to underestimate risk and the less likely they are to leave hearth, home, and (especially) the social ties that reinforce perceptions of self and place (cf. Boon, 2014). Yet, as is increasingly the case with changes in the Earth's climate (not to mention the advent of war), disasters such as denuded islands, fire-ravaged landscapes, or the onslaught of prolonged drought often force residents to flee and never to return. What of their places and their identities?

As one means by which people constitute meaning when an environment run amok devastates a significant part of who they are and forces resettlement, the time-binding nature of place might implicate the concept of *liminality*. The traditional idea (e.g., Shields, 2013; Turner, 1969, 1974) that, during various rites of passage, individuals get torn between previous social structures and future role opportunities seems to match the common experience of transitioning into adulthood or moving to a new community. The heuristic quality of liminality has not been lost on communication scholars (e.g., Chan, 2005; Jones, Zagacki, & Lewis, 2007; Miller & Holman, 2017). However, there is a difference in the forces of agency associated with more-or-less voluntary maturation and migration verses those attending the relatively sudden occasion of compulsory refugee status where homelands vanish on the diasporic horizon. Something greater seems afloat when identities become permanently unmoored from places that will not be (re)placed in the pilothouse of the mind (cf. Zavar & Schumann, 2018). Their collective and individual stories are heartbreaking (e.g., Brown, 2018; Farbotko & Lazrus, 2012; McNamara & Gibson, 2009) and the psychological impacts can be devastating (e.g., Anderson, 1996). King and Eoin (2014) tell us "there is an existential component to this process: as places become 'thinned out' or non-existent, so too do identities rooted therein" (p. 206; cf. Casey, 2001; Tschakert, Tutu, & Alcaro, 2013).

Although alternative psychological (e.g., Ertorer, 2014) or structural (e.g., Vandemark, 2007) approaches have been proposed to model what happens to place-based identities in times of forced resettlement, it seems to me the most promising construct to use in such situations is that of *solastalgia*. Solastalgia is a relatively new concept developed to explore intense, environmentally induced distress. First proposed by Albrecht (2005; Albrecht et al., 2007), it is distinct from nostalgic melancholia in that feelings of solastalgia are the product of environmental change affecting those who have place attachments to their home environment (cf. Casey, 1993; Sedikides, Wildschut, Gaertner, Routledge, & Arndt, 2008). As Albrecht (2005) summarizes:

> It is the pain experienced when there is recognition that the place where one resides and that one loves is under immediate assault (physical desolation). It is manifest in an attack on one's sense of place, in the erosion of the sense of belonging (identity) to a particular place and a feeling of distress (psychological desolation) about its transformation. It is an intense desire for the place where one is a resident to be maintained in a state that continues to give comfort or solace. Solastalgia is not about looking back to some golden past, nor is it about seeking another place as "home." It is

> the "lived experience" of the loss of the present as manifest in a feeling of dislocation; of being undermined by forces that destroy the potential for solace to be derived from the present. (p. 45)

Hechanova and Waelde (2017) clarify that solastalgia represents a "sense of desolation and loss of identity that an individual experiences as their familiar home environment changes, becomes uninhabitable, or hampers their livelihood" (p. 32). Whereas the physical spaces that give rise to mental places may be so degraded as to force the migratory urge, the cognitive and affective ties to landscapes that characterize solastalgia do not simply vanish in the dusty trail behind those who must leave a ruined environment. Rather, such environmental refugees are relegated to a psychological diaspora containing more-or-less far-flung people whom now possess what Carbaugh and Cerulli (2013) called "a self-without-its-discursive-place" (p. 17).

Recognizing that the experience of solastalgia may more pronounced in women than men (e.g., McNamara & Westoby, 2011), the distress occasioned by landscape degradation or (de)placement transcends cultural boundaries. Beyond studies conducted in the United States and Australia (e.g., Canu, Jameson, Steele, & Denslow, 2017; Eisenman, McCaffrey, Donatello, & Marshal, 2015; Ellis & Albrecht, 2017; Lertzman, 2013; Paveglio, Kooistra, Hall, & Pickering, 2015), the effects of solastalgia have been supported in studies conducted in the People's Republic of China (Tsai, 2018), Croatia (Smith, 2018), Africa (Tschakert & Tutu, 2010), and Amazonia (Kapfhammer, 2012). Throughout history, indigenous peoples in the developing world have borne the brunt of colonization and neoliberalism that, more often than not, lay waste to the places they have cherished for millennia (Kingsley, Townsend, & Henderson-Wilson, 2013). For example, Nicolosi and Corbett (2018) summarize the emotional impacts that follow the indigenous loss of place identities and a sense of self-in-place quite nicely:

> Among Inuit in Nunatsiavut, Canada, connection to the land was found to be at the heart of being Inuit, a part of identity and lifestyle that supports health and well-being (Willox et al., 2013). While deep respect, love, and commitment to and for the land among Inuit in Nunatsiavut was positively associated with

concern for climate change, it also represented a deep emotional loss (Willox et al., 2013). Similarly, the loss of sea ice in Canadian Inuit communities also had negative impacts on health and disrupted place meanings and attachments for these communities (Durkalec [, Furgal, Skinner, & Sheldon,] 2015). (p. 82)

In confronting environmental carnage and forced relocation, the same reciprocal dynamic between social interaction and place identity plays its role, often in new and alien landscapes. Though difficult to articulate, those experiencing solastalgia typically betray distressed identities to one another (e.g., Bodnar, 2012; Lertzman, 2013; Ryan & Hamin, 2008). Waks, Kocher, and Huntsinger (2018) provide one such voice following recent devastating wildfires in the American West:

I wasn't even sure how I was going to live here again. For me, it wasn't even that I lost all my stuff and the house, cuz I was so emotionally attached to the forest. We can rebuild, but we can't rebuild the forest. The biggest loss for my family, and me in particular, was emotional—the structures I could've cared less about, it was the trees that really broke my heart. Trees that I grew up with. (p. 3)

As I wrap-up my argument that communication is often "placed" in the context of environmental communication, I cannot help but reflect upon another time and setting. At the dawn of the modern era of environmentalism, Rachel Carson (1962) depicted a future place that seems to resonate so well in our contemporary distracted times. In "A Fable for Tomorrow," Carson described a place where birds did not sing anymore, where people fretted about what could have gone wrong with the world, and where the threat to place-based identities and social interaction was palpable. Of course, *Silent Spring* was a wake-up call to the world and, despite the environmental woes we still confront in a rapidly terraforming Earth, society has made progress in the past 60 years. We and future generations continue to face a big lift in adapting to a global commons that threatens personal identities, shared spaces, and cherished places.

To reiterate, not all spaces we encounter activate the potent presence of place-bound perception, precisely because we do not associate those locations with who we are or what we value. However, the frequent positioning and (dis)placement of identities in the spaces we encounter is an issue that extends beyond realm of environmentalism and natural resource management. How often do strategic communicators forget that the space surrounding their influence targets means more (or less) to them than is at once apparent? To what extent do communication researchers eschew attention to place-based perception in trying to interpret or account for the variance within symbolic interactions? People cleave to all manner of "natural" and built-upon landscapes, talk about the places that define themselves in important ways, and communicate to protect who they are, given where they are. To consider the place perception in everyday life invites those who practice or reflect upon human communication to remember that place-based understandings often matter insofar as they can and do focus attention, affect the processing of symbols, and stimulate memories. If nothing else, places of the heart and mind give us stories to share, thereby evoking cognitive and discursive touchstones to anticipate what lies ahead in both personal and public spheres of interaction.

References

Agnew, J. A. (2011). Space and place. In J. Agnew and D. Livingstone (Eds.), *Handbook of geographical knowledge* (pp. 316–330). Thousand Oaks, CA: SAGE.

Agnew, J. A. (2014). *Place and politics: The geographical mediation of state and society*. New York, NY: Routledge.

Agyeman, J., Devine-Wright, P., & Prange, J. (2009). Close to the edge, down by the river? Joining up managed retreat and place attachment in a climate changed world. *Environment and Planning A, 41*, 509–513.

Albrecht, G. (2005). Solastalgia: A new concept in human health and identity. *Philosophy, Activism, Nature, 3*, 41–55.

Albrecht, G., Sartore, G. M., Connor, L., Higginbotham, N., Freeman, S., Kelly, B., ... Pollard, G. (2007). Solastalgia: The distress caused by environmental change. *Australasian Psychiatry, 15*, 95–98.

Amiot, C. E., Sablonniere, R., Smith, L. G., & Smith, J. R. (2015). Capturing changes in social identities over time and how they become part of the self-concept. *Social and Personality Psychology Compass, 9*(4), 171–187.

Anderson, I. (1996). Aboriginal well-being. In C. Gribich (Ed.), *Health in Australia: Sociological concepts and issues* (pp. 58–75). Sydney, AU: Prentice-Hall.

Apfelbaum, E. (2001). The dread: An essay on communication across cultural boundaries. *Critical Psychology, 4*, 19–34.

Bellah, R., Madsen, R., Sullivan, W., Swidler, A., & Tipton, S. (1985). *Habits of the heart: Individualism and commitment in American life*. Berkeley, CA: University of California Press.

Binder, A. R., Scheufele, D. A., Bossard, D., & Gunther, A. C. (2011). Interpersonal amplification of risk? Citizen discussions and their impact on perceptions of risk and benefits of a biological research facility. *Risk Analysis, 31*, 324–334.

Blair, C., Dickinson, G., & Ott, B. L. (2010). Introduction: Rhetoric/memory/place. In G. Dickinson, C. Blair, and B. L. Ott (Eds.), *Places of public memory: The rhetoric of museums and memorials* (pp. 1–4). Tuscaloosa, AL: University of Alabama Press.

Bodnar, S. (2012). It's snowing less: Narratives of a transformed relationship between humans and their environments. In M.-J. Rust & N. Totton (Eds.), *Vital signs: Psychological responses to ecological crises* (pp. 17–32). London, UK: Karnac.

Bonaiuto, M., Alves, S., De Dominicis, S., & Petruccelli, I. (2016). Place attachment and natural hazard risk: Research review and agenda. *Journal of Environmental Psychology, 48*, 33–53.

Boon, H. J. (2014). Disaster resilience in a flood-impacted rural Australian town. *Persistent Link, 71*, 683–701.

Bott, S., Cantrill, J. G., & Myers, O. E. (2003). Place and the promise of conservation psychology. *Human Ecology Review, 10*, 100–112.

Brown, A. (2018). Climate change refugees share stories of escaping wildfires, floods, and droughts. *The Intercept*. Retrieved from https://theintercept.com/2018/12/29/climate-change-refugees/

Campbell, K. K. (2005). Agency: Promiscuous and protean. *Communication and Critical/Cultural Studies, 2*, 1–19.

Cantrill, J. G. (1996). Perceiving environmental discourse: The cognitive playground, In J. G. Cantrill and C. L. Oravec (Eds.), *The symbolic earth: Discourse and our creation of the environment* (pp. 76–94). Lexington, KY: The University Press of Kentucky.

Cantrill, J. G. (1998). The environmental self and a sense of place: Communication foundations for regional ecosystem management. *Journal of Applied Communication Research, 26*, 301–318.

Cantrill, J. G. (2003). Distrust of government at the end of the road: Finding selves situated in a hinterland place. *Communication Research Reports, 20*, 277–286.

Cantrill, J. G. (2004). A sense of self-in-place for adaptive management, capacity building, and public participation. In S. L. Senecah (Ed.), *Environmental communication yearbook, Vol. 1* (pp. 153–174.). Mahwah, NJ: Lawrence Erlbaum.

Cantrill, J. G. (2011). The role of a sense of self-in-place and risk amplification in promoting the conservation of wildlife. *Human Dimensions of Wildlife, 16*(2), 73–86.

Cantrill, J. G. (2015). Social science approaches to environment, media, and communication. In A. Hansen & R. Cox (Eds.), *The Routledge handbook of environment and communication* (pp. 49–60). New York, NY: Routledge.

Cantrill, J. G., & Masluk, M. D. (1996). Place and privilege as predictors of how the environment is described in discourse. *Communication Reports, 9*, 79–84.

Cantrill, J. G., Ray, H. L., Miller, C. J., & Smit, J. (1999). *Forested areas and a sense of place: Comparing the perceptions of compact and metropolitan urban populations.* Unpublished technical report submitted to the USDA North Central Experiment Station, Evanston, IL.

Cantrill, J. G., & Senecah, S. L. (2001). Using the "sense of self-in-place" construct in the context of environmental policy-making and landscape planning. *Environmental Science & Policy, 4*, 185–204.

Cantrill, J. G., Thompson, J. L., Garrett, E., & Rochester, G. (2007). Exploring a sense of self-in-place to explain the impulse for urban sprawl. *Environmental Communication: A Journal of Nature and Culture, 1*, 123–145.

Canu, W. H., Jameson, J. P., Steele, E. H., & Denslow, M. (2017). Mountaintop removal coal mining and emergent cases of psychological disorder in Kentucky. *Community Mental Health Journal, 53*, 802–810.

Carbaugh, D. (1988). *Talking American: Cultural discourses on Donahue.* Norwood, NJ: Ablex.

Carbaugh, D., & Cerulli, T. (2013). Cultural discourses of dwelling: Investigating environmental communication as a place-based practice. *Environmental Communication: A Journal of Nature and Culture, 7*, 4–23.

Carson, R. (1962). *Silent spring.* Boston, MA: Houghton Mifflin.

Casey, E. S. (1993). *Getting back into place: Toward a renewed understanding of the place-world.* Bloomington: Indiana University Press.

Casey, E. S. (2001). Between geography and philosophy: What does it mean to be in the place-world? *Annals of the Association of American Geographers, 91*, 683–693.

Chan, B. (2005). Imagining the homeland: The Internet and diasporic discourse of nationalism. *Journal of Communication Inquiry, 29*, 336–368.

Clayton, S., & Opotow, S. (2003). *Identity and the natural environment.* Cambridge, MA: MIT Press.

Cresswell, T. (2004). *Place: A short introduction.* Oxford, UK: Blackwell Publishing.

Cvijanović, N., Kechichian, P., Janse, K., & Kohlrausch, A. (2017). Effects of noise on arousal in a speech communication setting. *Speech Communication, 88*, 127–136.

Daly, J. A., & Thompson, C. M. (2017). Persuasive self-efficacy: Dispositional and situational correlates. *Communication Research Reports, 34*(3), 249–258.

Devine-Wright, P. (2013). Think global, act local? The relevance of place attachments and place identities in a climate-changed world. *Global Environmental Change, 23*, 61–69.

Dickinson, G. (2002). Joe's rhetoric: Finding authenticity at Starbucks. *Rhetoric Society Quarterly, 32*, 5–27.

Durkalec, A., Furgal, C., Skinner, M. W., & Sheldon, T. (2015). Climate change influences on environment as a determinant of Indigenous health: relationships to place, sea ice, and health in an Inuit community. *Social Science and Medicine, 136*, 17–26.

Eisenman, D., McCaffrey, S., Donatello, I., & Marshal, G. (2015). An ecosystems and vulnerable populations perspective on solastalgia and psychological distress after a wildfire. *Ecohealth, 12*, 602–610.

Ellis, N. R., & Albrecht, G. A. (2017). Climate change threats to family farmers' sense of place and mental wellbeing: A case study from the Western Australian wheatbelt. *Social Science and Medicine, 175*, 161–168.

Ertorer, S. E. (2014). Managing identity in the face of resettlement. *Identity: An International Journal of Theory and Research, 14*, 268–285.

Ewalt, J. P., & Cantrill, J. G. (2017). Victims "in" and protectors "of" Appalachia: Place and the common topic of protection in *Missing Mountains: We Went to the Mountaintop but it Wasn't There*. In D. G. Ross (Ed.), *Topic-driven environmental rhetoric* (pp. 106–124). New York, NY: Routledge.

Farbotko, C., & Lazrus, H. (2012). The first climate refugees? Contesting global narratives of climate change in Tuvalu. *Global Environmental Change, 22*, 382–390.

Folke, C., Han, T., Olsson, P., & Norberg, J. (2005). Adaptive governance of social-ecological systems. *Annual Review of Environmental Resources, 30*, 441–473.

Fox, C. A., Magilligan, F. J., & Sneddon, C. S. (2016). "You kill the dam, you are killing a part of me": Dam removal and the environmental politics of river restoration. *Geoforum, 70*, 93–104.

Garfinkle, H. (1967). *Studies in ethnomethodology*. Englewood Cliffs, NJ: Prentice Hall.

Hechanova, R., & Waelde, L. (2017). The influence of culture on disaster mental health and psychosocial support interventions in Southeast Asia. *Mental Health, Religion and Culture, 20*, 31–44.

Hodgetts, D., Bolam, B., & Stephens, C. (2005). Mediation and the construction of contemporary understandings of health and lifestyle. *Journal of Health Psychology, 10*, 123–136.

Horsbøl, A. (2018). Co-creating green transition: How municipality employees negotiate their Professional identities as agents of citizen involvement in a cross-local setting. *Environmental Communication, 12*, 701–714.

Hurley, P. T. (2013). Whose sense of place: A political ecology of amenity development. In W. Stewart, D. Williams, & L. Kruger (Eds.), *Place-based conservation: Perspectives from the social sciences*. Dordrecht, Netherlands: Springer.

Irwin-Zarecka, I. (1994). *Frames of remembrance*. New Brunswick, NJ: Transaction.

Jones, K. T., Zagacki, K. S., & Lewis, T. V. (2007). Communication, liminality, and hope: The September 11th missing person posters. *Communication Studies, 58*, 105–121.

Kalibo, H. W., & Medley, K. E. (2007). Participatory resource mapping for adaptive collaborative management at Mt. Kasigau, Kenya. *Landscape and Urban Planning, 82*, 145–158.

Kapfhammer, W. (2012). Amazonian pain. Indigenous ontologies and Western eco-spirituality. *Indiana, 29*, 145–169.

Kasperson, J. X., Kasperson, R. E., Pidgeon, N., & Slovic, P. (2003). The social amplification of risk: Assessing fifteen years of research and theory. In N. Pidgeon, R. E. Kasperson, and P. Slovic (Eds.), *The social amplification of risk* (pp. 13–46). Cambridge, UK: Cambridge University Press.

King, R., & Eoin, L. N. (2014). Before the flood: Loss of place, mnemonics, and 'resources' ahead of the Metolong Dam, Lesotho. *Journal of Social Archaeology, 14*(2), 196–223.

Kingsley, J., Townsend, M., & Henderson-Wilson, C. (2013). Exploring Aboriginal people's connection to country to strengthen human–nature theoretical perspectives. In M. K. Gislason (Ed.), *Ecological health: Society, ecology and health* (pp. 45–64). Bradford, UK: Emerald Group Publishing.

Korpela, K. M. (1989). Place identity as a product of environmental self-regulation. *Journal of Environmental Psychology, 9*, 241–256.

Krimsky, S., & Plough, A. (1988). *Environmental hazards: Communicating risk as a social process.* New York, NY: Auburn House.

Kruger, L. E., & Shannon, M. A. (2000). Getting to know ourselves and our places through participation in civic social assessment. *Society and Natural Resources, 13*, 461–478.

Kyle, G., & Chick, G. (2007). The social construction of a sense of place. *Leisure Sciences: An Interdisciplinary Journal, 29*, 209–225.

Kyle, G., Graefe, A., & Manning, R. (2005). Testing the dimensionality of place attachment in recreational settings. *Environment and Behavior, 37*, 153–177.

Latour, B. (1993). *We have never been modern.* Cambridge, MA: Harvard University Press.

Latour, B. (2005). *Reassembling the social: An introduction to actor-network-theory.* New York, NY: Oxford University Press.

Latour, B., & Woolgar, S. (1979). *Laboratory life: The construction of scientific facts.* Beverly Hills, CA: SAGE.

Lengen, C., & Kistemann, T. (2012). Sense of place and place identity: Review of neuroscientific evidence. *Health and Place, 18*, 1162–1171.

Leonard, N. R., Freeman, R., Ritchie, A. S., Gwadz, M. V., Tabac, L., Dickson, V. V., ... Hirsh, M. (2017). "Coming from the place of walking with the youth—that feeds everything": A mixed methods case study of a runaway and homeless youth organization. *Child and Adolescent Social Work Journal, 34*, 443–459.

Lertzman, R. (2013). The myth of apathy. In S. Weintrobe (Ed.), *Engaging with climate change: Psychoanalytic and interdisciplinary perspectives* (pp. 117–133). New York, NY: Routledge.

Lewicka, M. (2011). Place attachment: How far have we come in the last 40 years? *Journal of Environmental Psychology, 31*, 207–230.

Lewicka, M. (2014). In search of roots: Memory as an enabler of place attachment. In L. C. Manzo and P. Devine-Wright (Eds.), *Place attachment: Advances in theory, methods, and applications* (pp. 49–60). Abingdon, UK: Routledge.

Livingstone, S., & Lunt, P. (2002). *Talk on television: Audience participation and public debate.* New York, NY: Routledge.

Low, S. M., & Altman, I. (1992). Place attachment: A conceptual inquiry. In I. Altman & S. M. Low (Eds.), *Place attachment* (pp. 1–12). New York, NY: Plenum Press.

McNamara, K. E., & Gibson, C. (2009). 'We do not want to leave our land': Pacific ambassadors at the United Nations resist the category of 'climate refugees.' *Geoforum, 40,* 475–483.

McNamara, K. E., & Westoby, R. (2011). Solastalgia and the gendered nature of climate change: An example from Erub Island, Torres Strait. *EcoHealth, 8,* 233–236.

Manzo, L. C. (2003). Beyond house and haven: Toward a revisioning of emotional relationships with places. *Journal of Environmental Psychology, 23,* 47–61.

Massey, D. (2013). *Space, place and gender.* New York, NY: John Wiley & Sons.

McKenzie-Mohr, D. (2000). Fostering sustainable behavior through community-based social marketing. *American Psychologist, 55,* 531–537.

Metts, S., & Cupach, W R. (1989). Situational influence on the use of remedial strategies in embarrassing predicaments. *Communication Monographs, 56,* 151–162.

Milstein, T., Anguiano, C., Sandoval, J., Chen, Y-W., & Dickenson, E. (2011). Communicating a "new" environmental vernacular: A sense of relations-in-place. *Communication Monographs, 78,* 486–510.

Miller, J. L., & Holman, D. (2017). "If you rely on the river, you can probably die by the river": Stories told about access, quality, and living with water. *Health Communication, 32,* 1430–1433.

Mitchell, M. Y., Force, J. E., Carroll, M. S., & McLaughlin, W. J. (1993). Forest places of the heart: Incorporating special places into public management. *Journal of Forestry, 91*(4), 32–37.

Modesti, S. (2008). Home sweet home: Tattoo parlors as postmodern spaces of agency. *Western Journal of Communication, 72,* 197–212.

Moore, R., & Graefe, A. (1994). Attachments to recreation settings: The case of rail-trail users. *Leisure Sciences, 16,* 17–31.

Morgan, M., Shanahan, J., & Signorielli, N. (2017). Cultivation theory: Idea, topical fields, and methodology. In P. Rössler, C. A. Hoffner, & L. van Zoonen (Eds.), *The international encyclopedia of media effects* (pp. 307–320). Malden, NJ: Wiley-Blackwell.

Morgan, P. (2010). Towards a developmental theory of place attachment. *Journal of Environmental Psychology, 30,* 11–22.

Mugerauer, R. (1989). Language and the emergence of environment. In D. Seamon & R. Mugerauer (Eds.), *Dwelling, place, and environment* (pp. 51–70). New York, NY: Columbia University Press.

Nicolosi, E., & Corbett, J. B. (2018). Engagement with climate change and the environment: A review of the role of relationships to place. *Local Environment, 23,* 77–99.

Paveglio, T. B., Kooistra, C., Hall, T., & Pickering, M. (2015). Understanding the effect of large wildfires on residents' well-being: What factors influence wildfire impact? *Forest Science, 62*, 59–69.

Peters, D. (1999). *Speaking into the air: A history of the idea of communication*. Chicago, IL: University of Chicago Press.

Philipsen, G. (1975). Speaking "like a man" in Teamsterville: Culture patterns of role enactment in an urban neighborhood. *Quarterly Journal of Speech, 61*, 13–22.

Proshansky, H. M., Fabian, A. K., & Kaminoff, R. (1983). Place identity: The physical world and the socialization of the self. *Journal of Environmental Psychology, 3*, 57–83.

Rickard, L. N., & Stedman, R. C. (2014). From ranger talks to radio stations: The role of communication in sense of place. *Journal of Leisure Research, 47*, 20–38.

Ryan, R. L., & Hamin, E. (2008). Wildfires, communities, and agencies: Stakeholders' perceptions of postfire forest restoration and rehabilitation. *Journal of Forestry, 106*, 370–379.

Scannell, L., & Gifford, R. (2013). Personally relevant climate change: The role of place attachment and local versus global message framing in engagement. *Environment and Behavior, 45*, 60–85.

Schnell, S. M., & Reese, J. F. (2014). Microbreweries, place, and identity in the United States. In M. Patterson and N. Hoalst-Pullen (Eds.), *The geography of beer* (pp. 167–187). Dordrecht, Netherlands: Springer.

Sedikides, C., Wildschut, T., Gaertner, L., Routledge, C., & Arndt, J. (2008). Nostalgia as an enabler of self-continuity. In F. Santi (Ed.), *Individual and collective self-continuity: Psychological perspectives* (pp. 227–239). Mahwah, NJ: Lawrence Erlbaum.

Shields, R. (2013). *Places on the margin: Alternative geographies of modernity*. New York, NY: Routledge.

Smaldone, D., Harris, C., & Sanyal, N. (2008). The role of time in developing place meanings. *Journal of Leisure Research, 40*, 479–504.

Smith, R. (2018). Solastalgia in Istria, Croatia. *Utopia and Neoliberalism: Ethnographies of rural spaces, 46*, 149.

Sowards, S. K., Tarin, C. A., & Upton, S. D. (2017). Place-based dialogics: Adaptive cultural and interpersonal approaches to environmental conservation. *Frontiers of Communication, 2*(9). doi:10.3389/fcomm.2017.00009

Stedman, R. (2008). What do we "mean" by place meanings? Implications of place meanings for managers and practitioners. In L. E. Kruger, T. Hall, & M. C. Stiefel (Eds.), *Understanding concepts of place in recreation research and management*. General Technical Report PNWGTR-744 (pp. 71–82). Portland, OR: U.S. Department of Agriculture, Forest Service, Pacific Northwest Research Station.

Stegner, W. (1955). The marks of human passage. In W. Stegner (Ed.), *Mirror of America: Literary encounters with the National Parks* (pp. 3–17). New York, NY: Alfred A Knopf.

Stewart, W. (2008). Place meanings in stories of lived experience. In L. E. Kruger, T. Hall, & M. C. Stiefel (Eds.), *Understanding concepts of place in recreation research and management*.

General Technical Report PNWGTR-744 (pp. 83–108). Portland, OR: U.S. Department of Agriculture, Forest Service, Pacific Northwest Research Station.

Strine, S. (2004). When is communication intercultural? Bakhtin, staged performance, and civic dialogue. In R. Anderson, L. A. Baxter, & K. N. Cissna (Eds.), *Dialogue: Theorizing difference in communication studies* (pp. 225–242). Thousand Oaks, CA: SAGE.

Thompson, J. L., & Cantrill, J. G. (2013). The symbolic transformation of space. *Environmental Communication: A Journal of Nature and Culture, 7*, 1–3.

Tracy, K., & Baratz, S. (1993). Intellectual discussion in the academy as situated discourse. *Communication Monographs, 60*, 300–320.

Trauer, B., & Ryan, C. (2005). Destination image, romance and place experience—an application of intimacy theory in tourism. *Tourism Management, 26*, 481–491.

Trentelman, C. K. (2009). Place attachment and community attachment: A primer grounded in the lived experience of a community sociologist. *Society and Natural Resources, 22*, 191–210.

Tsai, R. C. H. (2018). Speculating extinction: Eco-accidents, solastalgia, and object lessons in Wu Ming-Yi's *The man with the compound eyes. Comparative Literature Studies, 55*, 864–876.

Tschakert, P., & Tutu, R. (2010). Solastalgia: Environmentally induced distress and migration among Africa's poor due to climate change. In T. Afifi & J. Jäger (Eds.), *Environment, forced migration and social vulnerability* (pp. 57–69). Heidelberg, Germany: Springer.

Tschakert, P., Tutu, R., & Alcaro, A. (2013) Embodied experiences of environmental and climatic changes in landscapes of everyday life in Ghana. *Emotion, Space and Society, 7*, 13–25.

Tuan, Y. F. (1977). *Space and place: The perspective of experience.* London, UK: Arnold.

Turner, V. (1969). *The ritual process: Structure and anti-structure.* Ithaca, NY: Cornell University Press.

Turner, V. (1974). *Dramas, fields, and metaphors: Symbolic action in human society.* Ithaca, NY: Cornell University Press.

Urquhart, J., & Acott, T. (2013). Constructing "The Stade": Fishers' and non-fishers' identity and place attachment in Hastings, south-east England. *Marine Policy, 37*, 45–54.

Vandemark, L. M. (2007). Promoting the sense of self, place, and belonging in displaced persons: The example of homelessness. *Archives of Psychiatric Nursing, 21*(5), 241–248.

Vásquez, C. (2016). A spatial grammar of organising: Studying the communicative constitution of organisational spaces. *Communication Research and Practice, 2*, 351–377.

Waks, L., Kocher, S. D., & Huntsinger, L. (2018). Landowner perspectives on reforestation following a high-severity wildfire in California. *Journal of Forestry, 20*(5), 1–8.

White, N. R., & White, P.B. (2004). Travel as transition: Identity and place. *Annals of Tourism Research, 31*(1), 200–218.

Williams, D. R. (2008). Pluralities of place: A user's guide to place concepts, theories, and philosophies in natural resource management. In L. Kruger, T. Hall, & M. C. Steifel (Eds.), *Understanding concepts of place in recreation research and management* (PNW-GTR-744) (pp. 7–30). Portland, OR: USDA Forest Service, Pacific Northwest Research Station.

Williams, D. R., Patterson, M. E., Roggenbuck, J. W., & Watson, A. E. (1992). Beyond the commodity metaphor: Examining emotional and symbolic attachment to place. *Leisure Sciences, 14*, 29–46.

Willox, A. C., Harper, S. L., Ford, J. D., Edge, V. L., Landman, K., Houle, K., & Wolfrey, C. (2013). Climate change and mental health: An exploratory case study from Rigolet, Nunatsiavut, Canada. *Climatic Change, 121*, 255–270.

Worster, A. M., & Abrams, E. (2005). Sense of place among New England commercial fishermen and organic farmers: Implications for socially constructed environmental education. *Environmental Education Research, 11*, 525–535.

Zavar, E. M., & Schumann, R. L. (2018). Patterns of disaster commemoration in long-term recovery. *Geographical Review, 108*, 1–23.

Chapter 3
Communication Is ... The Relationship

Jimmie Manning
University of Nevada, Reno

H UMAN COMMUNICATION, ITSELF, IS—IN A FUNDAMENTAL and definitional sense—a relationship. In this chapter, I explore how these communicative relationships are recognized or dismissed as being *a* relationship. To that end, and in one sense, communication *is* the relationship. Without communication, relationships cease to exist. Moreover, the communication that makes relationships is not simply the interaction between two or more people who are relating. Such interaction is but one of many communicative elements that makes their relationship. As one example, people who are not even in the relationship contribute to its constitution as they communicate about that relationship. For instance, if two people recognize and talk about a family, their interaction about the family is characterizing that family in multiple ways: that the collection of people can be identified or perceived as a family; with adjectives or descriptions that, even if minimally, provide a sense of evaluation; and, if they interact with the family ("That's a nice looking family you have there!"), that shapes some sense of how the family members see themselves.

The ideas presented in the previous paragraph only begin to unpack a perspective that has been explored by scholars (Baxter, 2004; Manning, 2014b) in an effort to encourage communication professionals, especially those who research and teach interpersonal and family communication, to expand how they conceptualize communication and relationships. Specifically, conceptualizing *communication as constitutive of relationships* embraces the idea that "relationships, identities, and tasks are *in the communication* ('constituted by it') rather than simply continuing our current dominant focus on the *communication in the relationships* or *between two or more people* ('containing it')" (Manning, 2014b, p. 432, emphasis in original). Such a shift in thinking has the potential to change many of the fundamental assumptions regarding communication and relationships, especially as those assumptions apply to how people think about their own relationships and how they are part of the relationships of others. For researchers and theorists, embracing what I call here a *communication as constitutive of relationships perspective* (CCR) allows for new insights about how people relate and helps to free research from assumptions that what happens in interpersonal and family communication is primarily psychological (Baxter, 2004; Duck, 2011).

The purpose of this chapter, then, is to offer an overview of a CCR perspective. To do so, the chapter begins by defining and explaining what the CCR perspective is and how it applies to both doing and interpreting communication research. Following this discussion, two new tools for understanding CCR are presented: a *relational-identity model* that explains how relationships cognitively, culturally, and interactively come into constitutive interplay; and a *relationships as translations approach* that examines the dynamics of how language and nonverbal communication create relationships in cultures. The chapter closes with some brief thoughts on how CCR can positively impact the future of interpersonal and family communication studies.

A Communication as Constitutive of Relationships (CCR) Perspective

When it comes to conceptualizing relationships—whether that be in everyday talk, classroom teaching, or especially in research—most often they are considered to be a container. That is, relationships are seen as being between two people; and the two people in that relationship form a "container" that holds and, to some extent, controls all of the communication behavior. This further assumes that the relational partners who make the container have complete control over the communication that goes back and forth in that relationship; and that, to a lesser extent, the relational partners can identify what the relationship is and influence how people see it. To that end, relational containers can be friendly, romantic, or familiar in nature. Such labeling helps to determine what kind of communication happens or should happen between the people in the relationship. For example, how friends are supposed to interact can be quite different from how family members should communicate.

As Baxter (2011) noted, although this container model is helpful for understanding how people communicate in a given moment, simply imaging communication as happening in a container belies the complexity of relationships. As she and others have noted (e.g., Duck, 2011; Manning & Kunkel, 2014), a particular relationship's characteristics are dependent upon past interactions within that specific relationship. All meaningful communication that happened prior to a given communicative cue—whether that be moments ago or years ago—has the potential to shape the current relational interaction. Similarly, relationship *types* have a cultural and political history that informs how they are supposed to function communicatively (Baxter, 2011; Manning, 2009). As one example, it would be unusual for family members to not, at the very least, wave to each other if they were to come across each other in a public setting such as a grocery store. If two cousins saw each other and did not indicate recognition, rules in most cultures would deem that noninteraction as unusual. Moreover, people who noticed such noninteraction would also likely make comment on the situation and, consequently, have a role in helping to name or define that relationship. In that sense, the relationship is not only between the two people—in this case cousins—who are in the relationship; but instead, members of the culture have an impact in the constitution of that relationship.

It is for these reasons—and more—that many interpersonal and family communication scholars (e.g., Baxter, 2011; Duck, 2011) have rejected the container model and argue instead that communication is constitutive of relationships. As Baxter (2011) notes,

> Relationships are not static things—containers—in which communication takes place. Rather ... relationships are constituted through the communication practices of the parties ... [They] are, then, meanings rather than contextual containers. They are constructed in communication, rather than being mere settings in which communication occurs. (p. 15)

Manning (2014b, 2016a) takes this a step further, pointing out that the communication that constructs a relationship often comes from external audiences of a given relationship. Two people may be married, but if their parents are living will likely receive advice, be it solicited or unsolicited, that even if ignored will provide a sense of what the relationship should be and how it will function. This communication about the relationship helps to constitute a sense of what the relationship is. Moreover, larger cultural messages—such as lessons taught about marriage in school, depictions of marriage on television, or even discussion of marriage over-heard by two strangers at a bus stop—continue providing communication about a marriage and, in some way, impact how marriage is defined and understood. Thus, as Manning (2016a) noted, cultural messages about relationships and identities make those very relationships and identities intelligible or recognizable.

The communication as constitutive of relationships (CCR) perspective presented here infuses some important questions regarding relation-ships that have been explored by relationship scholars for decades: How do relationships come into being? How do they continue, or why do they cease to exist? What does an individual bring to a relationship? It also raises new(er) questions that have been underexplored by relationship scholars to date: What actually *makes* a relationship? How does power course through relational structures and practices? How do relationships constitute and reconstitute their members/partners? And, importantly, have we relied too much upon cognitive aspects of relationships in lieu of structural and material understandings?

Condit (2006) took on these questions—and more—when she called for the use of the term *relationality* to "help remind us that a relationship is not a discrete, static entity but rather a process of the interaction of forces" (p. 6). Referring to relationships as things, she noted that "Every thing that exists is in itself nothing more than a particularly, and per-spectivally, constituted set of relationships" (Condit, 2006, p. 5), meaning that how relationships are perceived is dependent on the perspective(s) of the person/people who are noticing that relationship. She illustrates this idea by using the metaphor of two stars: although from earth they appear to be next to each other in the night sky, they are in reality many thousands of miles apart. It is the perspective of the viewer that gives them their relationality and that allows meaning. To that end, relationships can be identified "for a purpose, from a particular, time, place, and socially bound viewpoint" (Condit, 2006, p. 5).

As a final consideration for the constitution of relationships and what helps to form a CCR perspective, many scholars have made intriguing observations related to relational communication that will surely continue to define and shape the CCR perspective. For example, Ellingson (2017) has made compelling arguments regarding how bodies are not considered in research—as if there were a mind/body split, where the mind is privileged over the body—and such assumptions are surely relevant to interpersonal communication studies where cognitive processes are privileged over embodiment, affect, and culture. Similarly, scholars have made arguments regarding the essential consideration of objects in interpersonal and family relationships, including Allen (2019) who advocates that material objects be considered in conjunction with discourses in interpersonal and family communication studies and Manning (2016b) who lays out how popular communication artifacts such as movies, music, or novelty items are constitutive parts of relationships ("That's our song" or "I won her this stuffed animal on our first date").

Although presented in simple form here, these ideas can be complex. Not only do they shirk long-held ideals that center relationships in cognitive functions and/or a container of two people, they also beg consideration of the infinite sources of communication that infuse an almost infinite number of relationship types. Indeed, the constitutive/constituted nature of relationships and the reconsideration that communication is the central ingredient for forming relationships is what makes each relationship unique-yet-interconnected as scholars can look for patterns across relationships while still recognizing the particulars of a given relationship—or how that relationship becomes "particular" based on how it is being observed and by whom. To further explore CCR, the remainder of this chapter focuses on two models that illustrate its qualities. Specifically, CCR deeply and profoundly influences assumptions regarding how relationships are created, maintained, shaped, transformed, traversed, or ended. The relational-identity model and four flows relational model elaborate on these complexities.

The Relational-Identity Model

The first model offered in this essay is the relational-identity model (R-I). This model illustrates CCR in terms of its cognitive, relational, and cultural influences. Specifically, it allows for the consideration of how multiple, often pervasive, cultural messages allow intelligibility regarding relationships and relational identities (e.g., what relationships are and can be; how those in relationships are supposed to behave); how one's cognitive functions and personal experiences shape how relationships are enacted and understood (e.g., how people respond to relational cues; impressions of what relationships can be based on past similar relationships); and how two or more people who are relating—but who do not necessarily see themselves in a relationship—interact and constitute their particular relationship based on cognitive and cultural understandings. Figure 3.1 helps to illustrate these connections.

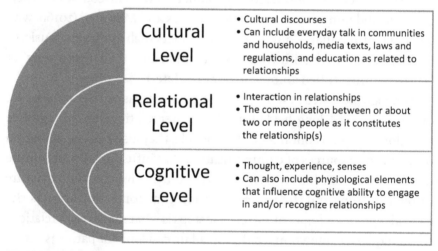

FIGURE 3.1   Relational-identity model.

Cognitive Level

At the core of the model is the cognitive level, a level that examines how relationships are understood and enacted. This level largely includes psychological elements of understanding relationships, including how messages are received and understood, psychosocial tendencies for interacting, physical abilities connected to relating, and, importantly, how people understand or respond to relationships—including overall understanding of what a relationship is or can be—based on their past experiences and the cultural messages they have received. A person might be generally talkative in nature, have a passive personality, be nervous about romantic relationships because her parents always fought, and understand that being single can be an option based on the cultural messages she has experienced. These are all elements that help to constitute relationships at the cognitive level. Based on past critiques of interpersonal and family communication's overreliance on sociopsychological approaches (e.g., Baxter, 2011; Manning, 2014b), it would appear that the overwhelming majority of communication research about relationships helps to inform how communication happens on the cognitive level. That is not to suggest that this research is bad or unneeded—indeed, scholars in communication studies and other disciplines have carved out many illuminating findings that inform cognitive CCR—but rather suggests that other levels of the model might be explored more in-depth.

Cultural Level

On the outer, rounded edge of the model—symbolic of how it influences all of the other aspects of the model—is the cultural level. This level helps to illustrate the many, multiple, and often conflicting discourses that can constitute what relationships are and how they should be enacted in a culture. The depiction of a happy marriage in a movie, seeing couples display romantic affection in a restaurant, and teachings in school about families are just a few of the examples of how cultural messages and institutions provide both subtle and obvious messages about relationships. Especially important to this level is the notion of intelligibility—that cultural messages come together to constitute cognitive and relational possibilities. For example, until recently it was not common to see interracial relationships portrayed on television or in movies. Increased representation makes it more likely that an interracial couple is not a surprise to someone who might see them publicly. If someone were to have romantic feelings toward a person of a different race, such representations might also give them permission to explore those feelings and that relationship. Alternately, those who have been exposed to negative cultural messages—including messages in their own families or from their friendship circles—might find conflicting feelings about enacting an interracial relationship at the relational level.

Relational Level

Finally, the relational level is where two or more people constitute their relationship. While this interaction constitutes the relationship, it is important to consider that new cultural experiences and changing feelings or emotions will continue to contribute to a relationship's constitution. Because even the most stable interpersonal or family relationships are continuously changing, the relational level is where the heart of relational understanding—and, thus, relational constitution—resides.

As the name of the relational-identity model and its contents imply, in addition to examining the constitutive nature of relationships it considers how relational identity is also created, negotiated, or understood via communication. The inspiration for R-I not only comes from the work done by scholars theorizing about CCR, but especially from the constitutive model of coming out (Manning, 2014b, 2016a). The constitutive model of coming out, a data-driven model, examines how people come to understand their individual sexual/relational identities (cognitive level—how they think and feel about themselves), come to terms with those in light of dominant cultural discourses related to gender, sexuality, and relationships (cultural level—how they interpret society, including friends and family, as seeing them), and ultimately relate to others who have their own unique understandings of relationships and sexualities both individually/cognitively and culturally.

The transformation from a constitutive model of coming out to R-I does not take much of a turn. In many ways, the constitutive model of coming out works as a specific application of R-I as it applies to a given context. Using R-I to unpack a different context, a woman might find herself usually attracted to bald men, but inexplicably attracted to a man with a full head of hair (centering the cognitive aspects of her personal attraction). The same man might not want to date the woman because of her religion, one that he has learned involves a lot of ritual (centering the cultural level) and that does not appeal to his atheist leanings (cognitive level). After they interact for a bit and have meaningful conversations (relational level), they both care less about the lack-of-baldness and religion (cognitive) and, unexpectedly, find themselves hooking up (relational). At first they consider themselves to be friends with benefits (a cognitive assessment based on cultural constructions and their own pattern of friendship and sexual interactions) but eventually start holding hands in public (relational level interaction) and calling themselves boyfriend and girlfriend (relational interaction used to present themselves in cultural terms).

As this example illustrates, R-1 allows relationships to be diagnosed in terms of how communication—ranging from interpretation to the crafting of relational messages to creating cultural understandings for others—comes together to form the relationship. As such, R-1 can be used as a theoretical model to apply a CCR perspective to research questions that examine the interplay of one or more cognitive, relational, or cultural aspects of relationships.

Four Flows Relationship Model

Another way to consider CCR is to examine how relationship roles and rules are constituted. Whereas R-1 is more centered on the interrelation of constitutive forces, the four flows relationship (FFR) model considers more in-depth how people position themselves in relationships, how they claim relationship knowledge, and how they rationalize their relationship functions. This model is adapted from the four flows model developed by McPhee and colleagues (McPhee & Iverson, 2009; McPhee & Zaug, 2000) to explain four different interdependent communication processes (called *flows*) that constitute an organization. Just as the four flows in the McPhee model illustrate how communication processes constitute an organization—itself a result of scholars in organizational communication and management studies rejecting the idea of organizations as containers for communication (Putnam, Phillips, & Chapman, 1999)—the adaption of these flows here help to indicate how relationships are communicatively constituted. Specifically, RDFT puts forward the following four flows of interpersonal or family relationships and how they are communicatively created: (1) relationships as membership negotiation; (2) relationships as reflexive self-structuring; (3) relationships as activity coordination; and (4) relationships as institutional positioning. Each is explained here.

Relationship as Membership Negotiation

First, relationships involve a negotiation of who is in a relationship and how. In some cases, this negotiation is simple. For example, many people are immediately part of a family membership once they are born. Almost instantly, familial-relational labels such as "parent," "cousin," or even "third cousin twice-removed" are applied. Relational expectations accompany each of those labels, and in some cases the label may be modified. It is not uncommon for people to have an "ex-spouse" (indicating the "what" of someone they were formerly married to) or, as an intriguing line of research from Kristina Scharp indicates (see Scharp, 2016), be estranged from a family member or a family as a whole (getting more at the 'how' of the relationship). In romantic relationships, negotiation might begin with dating processes including, perhaps especially, the request for a first date. In friendships, the negotiation process could begin with talk at a meeting or in the workplace about shared topics of interest, and continue with the return to conversation, likely moving to more intimate levels.

It is important to consider, especially given the examples listed to this point, that relationship negotiation should not be considered the same as relationship initiation. Relationships initiation often involves particular steps or stages that people go through when forming a relationship (Mongeau & Henningsen, 2015). Although that is certainly a part of relational membership negotiation, so are a variety of other aspects, including boundaries, access, shared time and activities, and topics of discussion, among many others. Overall, the *relationships as membership negotiation* involves any communication that determines or indicates the existence of the relationship and, importantly, the substance of *how* the relationship is enacted or is to be enacted. Further, such negotiation is continuous and ongoing, as relationships are dynamic and open to change. These ideas are also important to the next flow that deals with self-reflexive aspects of relating.

Relationships as Reflexive Self-Structuring

Whereas membership negotiation involves constitutive forces *within* a relationship, this second flow of *relationships as reflexive self-structuring* is focused more on *how the relationship is presented to others*. This focus on signifying relationships to those outside of the relationship is not simply focused on the other. As Duck (2011) notes, how people present themselves to others has rhetorical impact that lends to the overall constitution of a relationship for the couple or group as much, if not more, than it does for those outside the relationship. Reflexive self-structuring can be simple, such as telling someone, "This is my mother" or "This is my boyfriend." It can also be complex, such as explaining the detailed history of how two friends came together and why their friendship is so important. So while declarative labels of what the relationship is share an important signifier of what the relationship is to others, the words and actions beyond those labels, as they are presented to others, helps to demonstrate a relationship structure. In this sense, relationships are wholly performative. Whether intentional or unintentional, what people show to others via their relational communication is a constitutive part of what makes that particular relationship.

Important to reflexive self-structuring is a particular type of speech act, the declaration. Declarations, sometimes called declaratives, are utterances that shape or change reality in conjunction with what is proposed or offered by the utterance (see Searle, 1995). As one example, if two men enter a party together, those who do not know them might believe they are simply friends or maybe, depending how they look, even cousins or brothers, because of their sometimes intimate interaction. When one says about the other, "Oh, this is my boyfriend Mitch," the utterance *this is my boyfriend* transforms reality and creates the notion that Mitch is a particular kind of relational partner. In the case of romantic relationships, boyfriends or girlfriends or partners or some other such vernacular are what I am calling here an *open relational declarative*. That is, most people can make such a declaration and it would be considered valid—even if it were to be contested, such as the mother of a teenager who might refute boyfriend status with "no he's not." This idea of relational declaratives— and the ability to contest them—will be revisited in the discussion of another flow discussed in this chapter.

Relationships as Activity Coordination

One of the simpler flows that contributes to relational constitution is *relationships as activity coordination*. Simply put, and as the name suggests, this flow involves how relational partners coordinate their activities, both what could be relationship oriented (e.g., making love, taking a family excursion) and what could be more task oriented (e.g., cleaning house, paying bills). Importantly, both contribute to the constitution of a relationship. Further, even tasks that might be considered more about the individual (e.g., going to work) can be constitutive of the relationship, as these tasks can take time away from the relationship—which can be beneficial and/or detrimental—and because these other activities contribute to the identity of the person in the relationship that is part of the overall constitution of the relationship (e.g., "Her husband is a firefighter" or "She spends a lot of time away in Vegas") and impacts both internal and external views of how a given relationship is understood. This flow especially harkens back to Condit's (2006) big-picture ideas of how all activities have the potential to be connected—just that some are more relationship centered or have implications for how the relationship is viewed given the particulars of that specific relationship.

Relationships as Institutional Positioning

Finally, it is important to consider the institutional nature of relationships. Although relationships often seem as if they belong exclusively to the people in them and are under their exclusive control, they are often part of larger systems of discourse that, on some level, predetermine what they are and how they can be (Baxter, 2011). Further—and as R-1 illustrated earlier in this chapter—aspects of relationships or entire relationship types themselves are often defined, rewarded, limited, expanded, controlled, or politicized within a given culture (Manning, 2013). These cultural discourses offer implicit and often explicit messages about what kinds of relationships are legitimate or not legitimate. This idea is further illustrated through theoretical concepts such as *discourse dependence* (Galvin, 2006), the idea that some family relationships—for example, adoption—depend on more discourse to be understood. In the case of discourse-dependent families, I argue they go against culturally constitutive norms as the particulars of a specific relationship must be made clear to understand the relationship itself—in turn adding to the constitution of that relationship.

Policies, including laws, also dictate what relationships are seen as legitimate or real. For example, someone may consider a person not related by blood or biology to be their father, but in most cultures unless there is an official/legal adoption this kinship is not recognized as being legitimate from a legal standpoint. Still others might accept this relationship as familial despite what the law says—and that certainly is a part of the relational constitution. Similarly, in many cultures same-sex or same-gender marriage is not legal or, when it is, the same rights are not afforded to all married couples. Similar instances occur with other stigmatized relationships, such as interracial (Harris & Kalbfleisch, 2000) or transnational (Davis, 2014) romantic couples. Again, legitimacy comes into play, constituting how the relationship exists in a web of cultural values. Finally, returning to the notion of how declarations form relationships, laws and cultural rules also give some the authority or agency for determining what relationships are legitimate or not. Probably the most obvious example, many do not consider a marriage culturally real and certainly not legally binding unless an officiant such as a preacher or government official utters a variation of the phrase, "I now pronounce you married." Again, such legitimacy impacts the constitution of particular relationships as well as larger notions of what relationships can be in general.

Interpreting Research and Theory Through a CCR Lens

The notion that communication is the relationship is important for those studying interpersonal communication to consider. In addition to recentering ideas about interpersonal and family communication from the psychological or sociological and more directly toward the communication that actually makes the relationship, it also allows cultural and critical influences on relationships to be more richly considered. Given that other areas of the field have already taken their constitutive turn, this move also allows interpersonal and family communication— especially its relational elements—to come into interplay with the larger field of communication studies. As Moore and Manning (2019) note, interpersonal processes are arguably a part of, if not at the core of, multiple other disciplinary areas of the communication field. A CCR perspective helps to make such connections more evident.

Such connections also offer the opportunity for interpersonal and family communication studies—two areas of the communication discipline that are particularly and notoriously White and cisheteronormative (Moore & Manning, 2019)—to make connections to scholarship that can diversify perspectives and expand understanding of who is not included in these areas of study. Although scholars have made notable advances in theorizing race in interpersonal communication studies (as one especially notable example see Davis, 2015), there is much work to be done. Incorporating queer (Yep, 2003), feminist (Manning & Denker, 2015), ability-oriented (Ellingson, 2017), or cross-cultural (Atay & Trebing, 2017) perspectives, especially as they intersect (Abetz & Moore, 2018) could help to illustrate the particulars of how both specific relationships as well as relationship types are constituted. Expanded and inclusive research of this nature can lead to profound practical findings.

Along those lines, considering the CCR perspective has important practical implications. Perhaps the most central of these is that a relationship never simply belongs to those who are in it. A partnered couple is subject to critique, input, praise, and/or evaluation from friends and family as well as larger cultural messages about how their relationship fits into or defies socially expected norms. Realizing the unique and often non-normative nature of virtually every relationship frees people from ideas of *how they are supposed to relate* and instead can allow them to value or reject *how they are actually relating*. It also emphasizes that communication—and thus relating—changes from moment to moment in complex ways. That can include larger contextual differences (e.g., behavior at a party with friends will differ from behavior at a business dinner with a supervisor), as well as micro-practices that influence particular relational communication flows (e.g., a relational partner becoming less and less chatty during dinner as he realizes he added too much hot sauce).

As those examples suggest, the fluid and multiple ways that relationships can be considered using a CCR lens has the potential to free our thinking about relationships and their complexity. It also avoids the sometimes unnecessary task of defining what a relationship is or supposed to be and instead focuses on how relating is happening. That is, by incorporating Condit's (2006) ideas of how relating is always happening where there is communication, notions of "how a relationship is affected" do not always have to be at the core. The larger scope of CCR recognizes that those interactions/forms of relating can impact other forms of relating, both in and out of what some might define as a relationship. Such advances—as well as in-depth exploration of the two models presented here—will make for a promising future for interpersonal and family communication studies.

References

Abetz, J., & Moore, J. (2018). Visualizing intersectionality through a fractal metaphor: Recursive, non-linear, and changeable. In J. C. Dunn & J. Manning (Eds.), *Transgressing feminist theory and discourse* (pp. 49–61). New York, NY: Routledge.

Allen, J. (2019). What's the big "d"? Contemporary approaches to discourse in interpersonal and family communication scholarship. *Communication Theory, 29*(1), 107–127. doi:10.1093/ct/qty012

Atay, A., & Trebing, D. (Eds.). (2017). *The discourse of special populations: Critical intercultural communication pedagogy and practice.* New York, NY: Routledge.

Baxter, L. A. (2004). A tale of two voices: Relational dialectics theory. *Journal of Family Communication, 4*(3–4), 181–192. doi:10.1080/15267431.2004.9670130

Baxter, L. A. (2011). *Voicing relationships: A dialogic perspective.* Thousand Oaks, CA: SAGE.

Condit, C. M. (2006). Communication as relationality. In G. J. Shepherd, J. St. John, & T. Striphas (Eds.), *Communication as ... Perspectives on theory* (pp. 3–12). Thousand Oaks, CA: SAGE.

Davis, C. V. (2014). Transnational marriage: Modern imaginings, relational realignments, and persistent inequalities. *Ethnos, 79*(5), 585–609.

Davis, S. M. (2015). The "Strong Black Woman Collective": A developing theoretical framework for understanding collective communication practices of Black women. *Women's Studies in Communication, 38*(1), 20–35.

Duck, S. (2011). *Rethinking relationships.* Thousand Oaks, CA: SAGE.

Ellingson, L. L. (2017). *Embodiment in qualitative research.* New York, NY: Routledge.

Harris, T. M., & Kalbfleisch, P. J. (2000). Interracial dating: The implications of race for initiating a romantic relationship. *Howard Journal of Communication, 11*(1), 49–64.

Manning, J. (2009). Because the personal *is* the political: Politics and unpacking the rhetoric of (queer) relationships. In K. German & B. Dreshel (Eds.), *Queer identities/political realities* (pp. 1–12). Newcastle, UK: Cambridge.

Manning, J. (2014a). Coming out conversations and gay/bisexual men's sexual health: A constitutive model study. In V. L. Harvey, & T. H. Housel (Eds.), *Health care disparities and the LGBT population* (pp. 27–54). Lanham, MD: Lexington Books. doi:10.13140/2.1.1867.8089

Manning, J. (2014b). A constitutive approach to interpersonal communication studies. *Communication Studies, 65*(4), 432–440. doi:10.1080/10510974.2014.927294

Manning, J. (2016a). A constitutive model of coming out. In J. Manning, & C. Noland (Eds.), *Contemporary studies of sexuality and communication: Theoretical and applied perspectives* (pp. 93–108). Dubuque, IA: Kendall Hunt.

Manning, J. (2016b). Rethinking studies of relationships and popular culture: Notes on approach, method, and (meta)theory. In A. Herrmann & A. Herbig (Eds.), *Communication perspectives on popular culture* (pp. 153–165). Lanham, MD: Lexington Books.

Manning, J., & Denker, K. J. (2015). Doing feminist interpersonal communication research: A call for action, two methodological approaches, and theoretical potentials. *Women & Language, 38*(1), 133–142.

Manning, J., & Kunkel, A. (2014). *Researching interpersonal relationships: Qualitative methods, studies, and analysis.* Los Angeles, CA: SAGE.

McPhee, R. D., & Iverson, J. (2009). Agents of constitution in communidad. In L. L. Putnam & A. M. Nicotera (Eds.), *Building theories of organization: The constitutive role of communication* (pp. 49–87). New York, NY: Routledge.

McPhee, R. D., & Zaug, P. (2000). The communicative constitution of organizations: A framework for explanation. *The Electronic Review of Communication, 10*(1/2).

Mongeau, P. A., & Miller Henningsen, M. L. (2015). Stage theories of relationship development: Charting the course of interpersonal communication. In D. O. Braithwaite & P. Schrodt (Eds.), *Engaging theories in interpersonal communication: Multiple perspectives* (2nd ed.; pp. 389–402). Los Angeles, CA: SAGE.

Moore, J., & Manning, J. (2019). What counts as critical interpersonal and family communication research? A review of an emerging field of inquiry. *Annals of the International Communication Association, 43*(1), 40–57. doi:10.1080/23808985.2019.1570825

Putnam, L. L., Phillips, N., & Chapman, P. (1999). Metaphors of communication and organization. In S. R. Clegg, C. Hardy, & W. R. Nord (Eds.), *Managing organizations: Current issues* (pp. 125–158). Beverly Hills, CA: SAGE.

Scharp, K. M. (2016). Parent–child estrangement: Conditions for disclosure and perceived social network member reactions. *Family Relations, 65*(5), 688–700.

Searle, J. R. (1995). *The construction of social reality.* New York, NY: The Free Press.

Yep, G. A. (2003). The violence of heteronormativity in communication studies: Notes on injury, healing, and queer world-making. *Journal of Homosexuality, 45*(2–4), 11–59.

Chapter 4

Communication Is ... Transhuman

Autumn Edwards
Western Michigan University

David Westerman
North Dakota State University

Chad Edwards
Western Michigan University

Patric R. Spence
University of Central Florida

O N AUTUMN AND CHAD'S KITCHEN COUNTER sits a small robot named Vector. Vector is about 3 inches long, 2 inches high; has a robotic voice; connects to Amazon's Alexa; and roams around "his" little play yard. Vector can give the weather, play games, and look up things on the Internet. The little robot seems to like interrupting family meals with chirps and movements and by occasionally saying one of our names to get our attention. Vector is not quite part of the family, but isn't quite the espresso maker either. His communicative abilities and personality (although extremely limited) transcend those of any other object that sits atop a kitchen counter. Can Vector have deep and personalized dialogue? Not really. However, Vector can provide "chit-chat" about the weather similar to what one might enjoy with a stranger on the street, transmit information relevant to our conversations, and amuse with simple tricks. Perhaps most important, Vector evokes meaningful social reactions from the family.

The intensity of our emotional attachment to Vector was drawn into focus with recent news that the company that makes the small robot (Anki) is shutting down. Almost certainly, Vector's "death" is imminent. With sadness, we contemplate whether he will pass gradually or abruptly when the technical support services go offline and what we should do with the remains of a social machine that has been to us both being and thing, partner and tool. Our history of interactions with Vector render him not quite replaceable. Although the levels of interdependence, affection, and meaning-making we share with Vector pale in comparison to what we often experience with other people, they are real and meaningful to us. With the creation of each new communicative machine, the possibilities for significant, social human–machine relationships grow. But, what is communication between entities?

A cursory look at definitions of interpersonal communication in introductory textbooks is a good place to start thinking about current theorizing. From the first three books pulled from one of the authors' shelves, DeVito (2017) suggests that "Interpersonal communication is the verbal and nonverbal interaction between two interdependent people (sometimes more)" (p. 3), and further adds that "Interpersonal communication is the communication that takes place between people who are in some way 'connected'" (p. 3). McCornack and Morrison (2019) say "interpersonal communication is a dynamic form of communication between two (or more) people in which the messages exchanged significantly influence their thought, emotions, behaviors, and relationships" (p. 9). According to Wood (2016), "The best way to define interpersonal communication is by focusing on what happens between people. … For starters, then, we can say that interpersonal communication is a distinct type of interaction between people" (p. 12). Although these definitions are not exhaustive, they seem representative. Despite their differences, they share at least one big commonality; an insistence that interpersonal communication occurs between people. Thus, the underlying assumption for most scholarship in the discipline of communication seems to be that communication occurs between two or more people, despite variations in the number of participants, the nature of their relationships, and the involvement of different communication channels and layers of mediation.

Whether it is family members talking on the phone, friends discussing the events of the day at a party, or coworkers sending an email within their organization, the human aspect has been central to theorizing communication. However, with the growing use of artificial intelligence (AI), social robotics, and virtual reality/augmented reality, machines are becoming potential partners in the communication process. Therefore, we are prompted to rethink whether communication is always *human* communication, to contemplate whether the differences between human and machine communication are of degree rather than kind, and to reflect on how opening communication (in its interpersonal sense) to machine partners might forward our understanding of the process and ourselves.

As Peters (2006) noted, the term "human communication" first came into fashion in the 1950s, in part as "a rearguard action designed to allay the suspicion that there was something inhuman about communication as it was then emerging" (p. 219). Perhaps unsurprisingly, an emerging willingness to reconsider the definitional exclusion of machines from the communication process coincides with the development of computer-based technologies that are increasingly humanlike in their bodily forms, social functions, and communicative abilities. So much so that Zhao's (2006) popular definition of social robots asserts that "Humanoid social robots are not user-friendly computers that operate as machines; rather they are user-friendly computers that operate as humans" (p. 403).

At the same time, the boundary between humans and machines is blurred by technologists, philosophers, and scientists who draw attention to the ways in which people are like machines. Consider Rodney Brooks' direct equation of human and machine being-ness:

> I am a machine. So are you ... I, you, our family, friends, and dogs—we all are machines. We are really sophisticated machines made up of billions and billions of biomolecules that interact according to well-defined, though not completely known, rules deriving from physics and chemistry. The biomolecular interactions taking place inside our heads give rise to our intellect, our feelings, our sense of self. (2008, p. 71)

Although this level of mechanical reductionism is perhaps too hardcore, people often describe and understand themselves in machinelike ways that are tied to the mechanical innovations of the day (Harari, 2017). For instance, the introduction of steam power brought thermodynamic metaphors of humanness (e.g., "under pressure" and "letting off steam"). Today, we summon computer terms to characterize our experiences and behavior. We may say that we are "hard-wired," "glitching," or "running on autopilot"; that we should "unplug," "recharge," or "take time to process." Our very being has been described as algorithm and code (Harari, 2017) and our existence has been hypothesized and debated as a potential computer simulation (Moskowitz, 2016). In important ways, extending the concepts that traditionally describe machine communication (e.g., scripted, programmed, automated) and interactions (e.g., choreographed, designed, engineered, autonomous) may enable new, useful, and more expansive ways of understanding human communication. Therefore, this chapter will examine how and why communication can be considered transhuman by considering communication between humans and machines.

Before we can start examining human–machine communication in any great detail, we need to lay out what we mean by *transhuman*. This word is rooted in both philosophical and cultural/scientific movements. The British biologist Julian Huxley argued that

> [t]he human species can, if it wishes, transcend itself—not just sporadically, an individual here in one way, an individual there in another way, but in its entirety, as humanity. We need a name for this new belief. Perhaps transhumanism will serve: man [sic] remaining man, but transcending himself, by realizing new possibilities of and for his human nature. (1975, p. 1)

Others have used this term to refer to the promise of technological extension of human abilities through biotechnology, artificial intelligence (AI), nanotechnology, and virtual reality (VR) (Bostrom, 2003). In a way, the idea of transhumanism, or extending ourselves past our biological limits, may be the very thing that makes us human. Clark (2003) suggested that we are "natural-born cyborgs", designed to become one with our tools to expand our capabilities using our technologies.

The writing on the subject of transhumanism has ranged from how technology can improve the human condition to future-oriented ideas of a technological singularity. In this chapter, we rely on a more basic use which treats *trans-* as a prefix that means "beyond" (Merriam-Webster, 2019). In other words, we argue that communication is beyond (i.e., not merely) human and should include consideration of machine partners.

There are many previous "expansions" of communication. Not long ago, interpersonal communication (IPC) was also considered pretty much face-to-face only, and it seems that may still considered the gold standard for relating (cf. Hollan & Stornetta, 1992; Westerman, Daniel, & Bowman, 2016). Furthermore, closeness has often been seen as an inherent good and a necessary part of IPC (dubbed the "ideology of intimacy"; Parks, 1982), even though much of our communication seems functional and "scripted" (Kellerman, 1992).

As Mazis (2008) suggests, there are humanistic dimensions of machines and mechanical dimensions of humans to the degree that the human and machine (as well as the animal) may be considered "lodged within the core of each other's being" (p. 21). The attributes once associated exclusively with each type of entity now appear to belong to both (cf. Edwards, A., 2018). The considerable and increasing overlap between the human and machine renders their communication possible, while their ontological distinctiveness and "otherness" suggest the potential emergence of something transcendent: ways of being-in-the-world that synthesize (or transcend and include) the human and the machine.

The transcendent possibilities of communication have been at the heart of teachings and writings on the subject for millennia (Peters, 1999), and this chapter owes much to Shepherd's (2006) definition of communication as *transcendence*, or "the simultaneous experience of self and other" (p. 22). In this sense, communication involves becoming "more than what one was through connection with another" (p. 22). In this chapter, we expand the communicative "other" to include social machines. To do so, we turn to empirical research and theoretical perspectives in the emerging field of human–machine communication (HMC).

The Emergence of Human–Machine Communication

The foundational roots of much communication theorizing start with Shannon and Weaver's (1949) mathematical model of communication, which was essentially an engineering design for how machines interact. The tradition of cybernetics (Wiener, 1948) was the basis of much research in AI and computer science/engineering. Alan Turing (1950) suggested that AI (or at least the perception of it) is an issue of communication with his classic Turing test idea: A machine may be considered intelligent when a human being is unable to distinguish it from another human on the basis of responses to questions put to both. Expanding on this scholarship, the fields of human–computer interaction (HCI) and human–robot interaction (HRI) examine potential interactions between source agents being both human and machine.[1] These connections are mostly lost in most "communication studies" training. Our discipline has focused on computer-mediated communication (CMC), where the computer or technology is the medium of the interaction and not the source. Although this subfield of CMC worked quite well for at least two decades, many new technologies transcend most CMC communication models, in the sense that the medium exists not between two human individuals, but often stands in as a communication source or partner (Guzman, 2018). Due to the rise of AI and social robotics, it has become "practically necessary" (Gunkel, 2012, p. 19) that we allow for machine communicators: "Whether it is explicitly acknowledged or not, communication (and 'communication' as the concept is understood and mobilized in the discipline of communication studies) is fundamental to both the theory and practice of artificial intelligence (AI)" (p. 2). Because "The machines are not coming. They are already here," there "needs to be an ongoing effort to begin to make sense of a world where we are not (and perhaps never were) the only communicative subject" (McDowell & Gunkel, 2016, pp. 3–4). We must acknowledge this rapid change to better theorize and understand HMC, and ultimately communication in general.

Theoretical Perspectives

HMC has emerged as a new paradigm for people's symbolic and meaning-making interactions with machine partners (Edwards, Edwards, Westerman, Spence, 2019; Guzman, 2018; Spence, 2019). Because much of communication is a scripted process (Kellerman, 1992), machine agents can take a more significant role in the process in our daily lives using

---

[1] In our experience, HRI and HCI researchers and designers are almost always surprised and dismayed to learn that the bulk of communication studies scholars consider communication an exclusively human enterprise. Most of the ordinary folks we talk with also report experiencing their exchanges with digital interlocutors (e.g., Alexa, Siri) as communication, and describe them in those terms.

spoken dialogue systems (SDS). SDS are "computer systems that use spoken language to interact with users to accomplish a task" (McTear, 2002, p. 91). Both embodied social robots and AI software can engage in human dialogue with SDS. As such, communication theory will need to account for this rapidly developing area. Although it is possible to apply the assumptions and characteristics of human-to-human interactions and extend human communication theory to HMC contexts, new theory-building will be necessary to more fully understand the meaning and consequences of a world involving communication between human part-ners, machine partners, and various human–machine configurations. Perhaps the scripted nature of human-to-human interaction has been largely overlooked to this point as well, and thus this transhuman expan-sion also provides important grist for the mill of human communication theory overall. For example, as Buber (1937) pointed out, we sometimes treat people in an "I–it" type relationship, where we treat the other person more as an object. Postman (1992) suggested that people increasingly view humans as machines, and mechanistic metaphors are used to describe human processes at a growing rate. Learning more about what triggers the "click, whirr"–type response (Cialdini, 2001) that leads to treating and discussing either humans or machines as basically human or a machine would expand upon communication theory overall, and help to transcend possible artificial boundaries between human communication HMC. When are these actually different, and when is it all just communication?

Much of the research examining the possibility of transhuman com-munication with machines has centered on the interpersonal nature of the interaction. This focus is not surprising given that (1) a significant focus of early CMC research also started by looking at the interper-sonal communication aspects of people interacting online via computers (Walther, 1992), and (2) machines that use SDS are typically meant for interaction on a one-to-one or dyadic basis. In the following sections, we will discuss the "human-to-human interaction script" (Spence et al., 2014) and the extension of the computers are social actors (CASA) par-adigm to social machines (Reeves & Nass, 1996), social presence theory, and finally, the MAIN model (Sundar, 2008). This application of these few theories is intended to demonstrate that communication may fruit-fully be considered transhuman and to generate thinking about how we might understand the process the same and differently depending on the inclusion of machine communicators.

Human-to-Human Interaction Scripts

Three underlying assumptions help in understanding initial interaction scripts between people and machines (Spence, Westerman, Edwards, & Edwards, 2014; Edwards, Edwards, Spence, & Westerman, 2016, Edwards et al., 2019). First, communication is a largely scripted process. Kellerman (1992) maintains that experience and priming are essential for choosing and modifying scripts to help decide what to do in social situations (Kollar, Fischer, & Hesse, 2006). This priming process allows us to have some expectations and be able to use and modify the scripts we have developed through prior interaction (Schleuder, White, & Cameron, 1993).

Second, there is an anthropocentric expectancy bias for interaction in that people (at least for now) tend to assume their communication partners will be other human beings. As a result, they might experience expectancy violations when communicating with a machine agent. Our research program has found that people have greater uncertainty when the other entity is a machine rather than a person. People also report lower anticipated liking and social presence when they believe they are about to interact with a machine. Collectively, we have labeled this as the "human-to-human interaction script" (Edwards et al., 2016, Edwards et al., 2019; Spence et al., 2014). However, when a machine agent performs in an appropriately social way, people tend to communicate with them in ways consistent with how we interact with other humans (Krämer, von der Pütten, & Eimler, 2012). This is especially true when the machine is more anthropomorphic and after initial interaction, when uncertainty declines and perceptions of the machine's social presence rises to meet or even exceed ratings of another human being doing the same thing (Edwards, A. et al., 2019).

Third, Nass and colleagues demonstrated over many studies that people tend to treat and act in response to computers as if they were people. They termed this idea the "computers are social actors (CASA) paradigm." Reeves and Nass (1996) demonstrated that "people's responses to media are fundamentally social and natural" (p. 251). Humans understand and relate to computers as if they are other people by "essentially ignoring the cues that reveal the essential asocial nature of a computer" (Nass & Moon, 2000, p. 83) and attributing human psychological traits and abilities to computers (Sundar, 2004). The CASA paradigm has also been expanded to our treatment of robots (Edwards, Edwards, Spence, Harris, & Gambino, 2016) and other AI machines, as well. Overall, if something triggers our human interaction scripts, it seems that we respond to that something, be it television, computer, robot, or person, in a social manner.

Established theories in communication, psychology, and sociology have mostly held up in HCI and HRI studies when the CASA paradigm has been applied. In a group situation, people treat computers as teammates (Nass, Fogg, & Moon, 1996). Lee (2010) demonstrated that individuals interact with computers differently based on the computer's vocal qualities. Research has shown that people assign human personalities such as dominance and submissiveness (Nass, Moon, Fogg, Reeves, & Dryer, 1995), ethnicity (Nass, Moon, & Green, 1997), and gender (Lee, Nass, & Brave, 2000) to computers. Studies have also shown similarities in how people respond to computers and other people based on their expertise (Nass, Reeves, & Leshner, 1996) and reciprocity (Nass, Moon, & Carney, 1999). Furthermore, the same stereotype content model guiding our impressions of other humans—wherein we assess individuals and groups in terms of warmth and competence and respond accordingly—also applies to our understanding of social robots (Mieczkowski, Hancock, & Reeves, 2019). Furthermore, there is evidence that the same message behavior and design logic preferred of human partners is also perceived as best for social robots (Edwards, Edwards, & Gambino, 2019).

Social Presence

Another concept that might help to demonstrate the transhuman nature of communication is social presence. Westerman and Skalski (2010) suggested that social presence might be a central concept for considering interpersonal uses of technology, as it is an experience that one can feel no matter the channel used, and also suggested its importance for considering both CMC and HCI. Social presence theory (SPT; Short, Williams, & Christie, 1976) generally catalogs communication on a scale based on the amount of social presence perceived by the receiver in the interaction. In other words, it is based on the number of cues that a particular channel of communication provides in interaction. Lately, social presence has been thought of as a psychological concept important for interaction. Lee (2004) defined social presence as "a psychological state in which virtual social actors are experienced as actual social actors" (p. 45). Leaving the psychological domain and moving more toward communication theorizing, social presence has been thought of as mediated immediacy (Kelly & Westerman, 2014; O'Sullivan, Hunt, & Lippert, 2004) and can include the feeling of being "physically with" someone that is in a different location. It is the combination of the psychological concept of social presence (Nowak & Biocca, 2003) and the feelings of mediated immediacy (Kelly & Westerman, 2014) that make the idea of social presence significant for HMC research. The key is the degree to which we do not notice the technological means providing a sense of presence (Lee, 2004).

Closely related to social presence or sometimes used as social presence is the concept of electronic propinquity. Electronic propinquity is a perception of closeness to another through an electronic channel (Walther & Bazarova, 2008). It has been argued that this is drive by mental models and scripts during the communication process (Westerman & Skalski, 2010. Overall, research in this area suggests that when communicating with machines the more interaction feels real, the more we treat the machine and respond to a machine as a human. Research has demonstrated that our social responses to anthropomorphized robot are mediated by social presence (Lee Peng, Jin, & Yan, 2006).

In general, it may be more important in this situation to consider the experience rather than the channel itself. Feelings of connection (the psychological experience of being there) can occur whether we are face-to-face, interacting with another person through technology, or interacting with technology. Furthermore, channel does not guarantee that we experience such connection (although, perhaps some aspects of technology increase the likelihood of such, and this should be examined). Thus, working toward a more comprehensive social presence theory would be an important aspect of understanding more about communication, no matter the communicative partner or channel used, and if the feeling of connectedness is the central aspect of such a theory, the transhuman nature is also central.

MAIN Model

Finally, the MAIN model examines how the characteristics of media can influence differing levels of perceived credibility (Sundar, 2008). This model argues that we take mental shortcuts or heuristics from media that we then apply to our perceptions of credibility. Initially, researchers applied this model to websites, but recently we have used it for machine agents and perceptions of their credibility (Spence, Edwards, Edwards, & Jin, 2019). MAIN stands for modality, agency, interactivity, and navigability. Modality (M) refers to the way technology works and is experienced by the user. These interfaces might be textual, visual, audio, or virtual or augmented reality. Agency (A) examines the "source" of information. In Edwards, Edwards, Spence, and Shelton (2014), we conducted an experiment to explore the interpersonal impressions of a Twitter account where the source was either a person or a chatbot. Findings demonstrated there were no differences for the type of agent for perceptions of credibility or communication competence. However, the human Twitter agent was rated higher in interpersonal attraction.

The interactivity (I) affordance considers how interactive the technology is. Sundar and Nass (2001) argued that increased activity produces greater perceptions of dynamism. Navigability (N) refers to how others move in or alongside the technology. For CMC research, this might entail examining how people click inside a website or conduct Internet searches. For HMC research, it would be essential to assess how people might use augmented reality to navigate space or how social robots can lead a museum tour (Kim, Merrill & Song, 2019)). Navigability cues are important because they can decrease frustrations and annoyances of users.

The MAIN model shows how thinking about the heuristics people hold about technology can impact the overall communicative experience. Because we make constant judgments of the credibility of others, it is vitally consequential to understand what cues of the machine partner impact perceptions of credibility when communication is transhuman. Problem solving in some areas is becoming a partnership between humans and machines, making such cues as credibility central. This is seen in the field of journalism where machines and humans work on news stories together (Wadell, 2018). Research has shown that in specific circumstances there can be few perceived differences between a machine and a human (see Spence et al., 2019; Edwards et al., 2014). With the issue of agency, studies have examined the machine heuristic. This is the notion that at times humans may perceive information generated from a machine as more credible because the machine has no perceived bias or reason to be impartial (Sundar, 2008).

Personal or Interpersonal?

As mentioned near the start of this chapter, interpersonal communication is typically defined as occurring between people. More recently, Walther (2019) has offered an interesting, and somewhat stringent definition, of interpersonal. Walther suggests that interpersonal impressions and communication are based on interactivity and contingency, and "defines interpersonal knowledge as the impression one has about the way a specific target individual responds in a unique fashion to the information-seeker as distinct from the way that the target individual responds to anyone else" (p. 377), with unique interpersonal impressions in each individual dyad. Relying upon idiosyncratic knowledge of the other might be enough for a personal impression, given this definition, but not enough for an interpersonal one.

Walther (2019) also goes on to suggest that "the reduction of interpersonal uncertainty ... requires transactional and reciprocal exchanges among two individuals, in which the responses of one are contingent upon the actions of the other" (p. 380). Thus, interpersonal is more about unique interactions between individuals, in which the meaning in the interaction is contingent upon earlier parts of the interaction. Personal impressions and information might be used in the processing of screening other to determine whether to expend the effort necessary to form an interpersonal relationship.

But would both of the individuals in this process have to be human? Walther probably had humans in mind when thinking about this definition. However, it may not be necessary. If the main part of interpersonal is the "inter" of interactivity and contingency, as Walther (2019) focuses on, then perhaps that can occur even if the "person" with whom one is interacting in this way is not always a literal person. That might require a pretty sophisticated AI to engage in interpersonal defined as such, but, truthfully, most human-to-human communication does not seem to qualify for interpersonal under this definition either, and underscores even more reason to consider the potential to learn from a transhuman approach to communication.

What Does It Mean?

Many folks are already communicating with machines on a daily basis. It might occur with their smart refrigerator, their smartwatch or phone, or a small device on a kitchen counter named Vector. With the commercialization of AI (e.g., Amazon's Alexa, Google's Home, Apple's Siri), transhuman communication exchanges are becoming common. Even though human and embodied robot interactions are still relatively rare and novel, there has been a rapid rise in their use in public space. As machines communicators increase in use, we can expect more normalized and frequent interactions. Examining sustained and more everyday communication with machine partners will be essential to understanding how and if theories of communication are useful in a transhuman context.

If the human-to-human interaction script, social presence, and credibility judgments hold through regular and repeated interactions with machine partners, it is likely that information-processing, persuasion models, and other communication-related theories will be useful. Edwards et al. (2019) argue that a constructivist paradigm would be the next logical step because of its focus on ontologically classifying of "what is it?" Our research program has demonstrated that simply being labeled a "human" or a "social robot" has implications for perceptions for interpersonal impressions. Regarding a transhuman communication potential, it will be important to establish the "what is it?" question and "what does it do?" question. After more people are familiar interacting with social machines, Edwards et al. (2019) argued that research should move on to understanding the broad social implications of stereotyping and examine these expectations and behaviors of HMC. In short, the same theory and research pathways that occurred in the discipline of communication should occur in HMC.

As machine communicators operate in our daily lives in a variety of interaction contexts, issues of being communicatively competent with both humans and machines will be important. Moreover, as we think about when communication is transhuman we also need to think about our understanding of emotions or the absence of emotions in communication. For example, we may evoke the machine heuristic for news and prefer our news to be selected or even written by a machine, but what about our retirement savings? According to Investopedia, algorithmic trading is "the process of using computers programed to follow a defined set of instructions (an algorithm) for placing a trade in order to generate profits at a speed and frequency that is impossible for a human trader" (Shobhit, 2019). We may think this communication between a machine and investment firm is ideal because it takes the emotion out of the investment process. But trading without emotion means that the machine may be comfortable with big losses of finances and when those finances equal our tangible assets, communication from the machine may not be preferred. Our algorithm trader may be beyond our emotional comfort and not be able to comfort us with communication.

Sustained interactions with machine partners will influence future interactions with machines but will also have taken a recursive turn. Our interactions with machines will impact how we communicate with other humans and the expectations of those conversations. In other words, the scripts we develop for interactions with machines will influence how we theorize human communication. AI, social robots, and other forms of machine actors are here and impacting us on a daily basis. Not including them in the theorizing of communication is a mistake and one that our discipline should avoid. Allowing a general framework of communication being transhuman with machine partners allows us as a discipline to remain relevant, and to learn even more about how we communicate with other entities, both human and otherwise.

References

Bostrom, N. (2003). The transhumanist FAQ: v 2.1. *World Transhumanist Association.* Retrieved from https://nickbostrom.com/views/transhumanist.pdf

Brooks, R. (2008, June). I, Rodney Brooks, am a robot. *IEEE Spectrum.* Retrieved from https://spectrum.ieee.org/computing/hardware/i-rodney-brooks-am-a-robot

Buber, M. (1937). *I and thou.* New York, NY: Scribner.

Cialdini, R. B. (2001). *Influence: Science and practice* (4th ed.). Boston, MA: Allyn & Bacon.

Clark, A. (2003). *Natural-born cyborgs: Minds, technologies, and the future of human intelligence.* New York, NY: Oxford University Press.

DeVito, J. A. (2017). *Interpersonal messages* (4th ed.). Boston, MA: Pearson.

Edwards, A. (2018). Animals, humans, and machines: Interactive implications of ontological classification (pp. 29–49). In A. Gutzman (Ed.), *Human–machine communication: Rethinking communication, technology, and ourselves.* New York, NY: Peter Lang.

Edwards, A., Edwards, C., & Gambino, A. (2019). The social pragmatics of communication with social robots: Effects of robot message design logic in a regulative context. *International Journal of Social Robotics.* doi:10.1007/s12369-019-00538-7

Edwards, A., Edwards, C., Spence, P. R., Harris, C., & Gambino, A. (2016). Robots in the classroom: Differences in students' perceptions of credibility and learning between "teacher as robot" and "robot as teacher." *Computers in Human Behavior, 65,* 627–634. doi:10.1016/j.chb.2016.06.005

Edwards, A., Edwards, C., Westerman, D., & Spence, P. R. (2019). Initial expectations, interactions, and beyond with social robots. *Computers in Human Behavior, 90,* 308–314. doi:10.1016/j.chb.2018.08.042

Edwards, C., Edwards, A., Spence, P. R., & Westerman, D. (2016). Initial interaction expectations with robots: Testing the human-to-human interaction script. *Communication Studies, 67,* 227–238. doi:10.1080/10510974.2015.1121899

Edwards, C., Edwards, A., Spence, P. R., & Shelton, A. K. (2014). Is that a bot running the social media feed? Testing the differences in perceptions of communication quality for a human agent and a bot agent on Twitter. *Computers in Human Behavior, 33,* 372–376. doi:10.1016/j.chb.2013.08.013

Gunkel, D. J. (2012). Communication and artificial intelligence: Opportunities and challenges for the 21st century. *communication +1, 1*(1), Article 1. Retrieved from https://scholarworks.umass.edu/cgi/viewcontent.cgi?article=1007&context=cpo

Guzman, A. L. (2018). Introduction: "What is human–machine communication, anyway?" In A. L. Guzman (Ed.), *Human–machine communication: Rethinking communication, technology, and ourselves* (pp. 1–26). New York, NY: Peter Lang.

Hollan, J., & Stronetta S. (1992). Beyond being there. *CHI '92 Proceedings of the SIGCHI Conference on Human Factors in Computing Systems,* 119–125. doi:10.1145/142750.142769

Huxley, J. (1957). *New bottles for new wine: Essays.* New York, NY: Harper.

Lee, E. J. (2010). The more humanlike, the better? How speech type and users' cognitive style affect social responses to computers. *Computers in Human Behavior, 26,* 665–672.

Lee, E.-J., Nass, C., & Brave, S. (2000, April). *Can computer-generated speech have gender? An experimental test of gender stereotypes.* Paper presented at the Computer–Human Interaction (CHI) Conference, The Hague, Amsterdam.

Lee, K. M. (2004). Presence explicated. *Communication Theory, 14,* 27–50. doi:10.1111/j.1468-2885.2004.tb00302.x

Lee, K. M., Peng, W., Jin, S. A., & Yan, C. (2006). Can robots manifest personality? An empirical test of personality recognition, social responses, and social presence in human–robot interaction. *Journal of Communication, 56,* 754–772.

Kellerman, K. L. (1992). Communication: Inherently strategic and primarily automatic. *Communication Monographs, 59,* 288–300. doi:10.1080/03637759209376270

Kelly, S., & Westerman, C. Y. K. (2014). Immediacy as an influence on supervisor–subordinate communication. *Communication Research Reports, 31,* 252–261.

Kim, J., Merrill Jr., K., & Song, H. (2019, in press). Probing with Pokémon: Feeling of presence and sense of community belonging. *The Social Science Journal.*

Kollar, I., Fischer, F. & Hesse, F. W. (2006). Collaboration scripts: A conceptual analysis. *Educational Psychology Review, 18,* 159–185. doi:10.1007/s10648-006-9007-2

Krämer, N. C., von der Pütten, A., & Eimler, S. (2012). Human–agent and human–robot interaction theory: Similarities to and differences from human–human interaction. In M. Zacarias & J. V. de Oliveria (Eds.), *Human–computer interaction: The agency perspective* (pp. 215–240). Berlin, Germany: Springer.

Mazis, G. A. (2008). *Humans, animals, machines: Blurring boundaries.* Albany, NY: SUNY Press.

McCornack, S., & Morrison, K. (2019). *Reflect and relate: An introduction to interpersonal communication* (5th ed.). Boston, MA: Bedford/St. Martin's.

McDowell, Z. J., & Gunkel, D. J. (2016). Introduction to "machine communication." *communication +1, 5*(1), Article 1. Retrieved from https://scholarworks.umass.edu/cgi/viewcontent.cgi?article=1056&context=cpo

McTear, M. F. (2002). Spoken dialogue technology: Enabling the conversational user interface. *ACM Computing Surveys (CSUR), 34*(1), 91–169. doi:10.1145/505282.505285

Mieczkowski, H., Liu, S. X., Hancock, J., & Reeves, B. (2019). Helping not hurting: Applying the Stereotype content model and BIAS map to social robotics. *Proceedings of the ACM/IEEE International Conference on Human–Robot Interaction* (pp. 222–229), Daegu, Korea (South). doi:10.1109/HRI.2019.8673307

Moskowitz, C. (2016, April 7). Are we living in a computer simulation? *Scientific American.* Retrieved from https://www.scientificamerican.com/article/are-we-living-in-a-computer-simulation/?redirect=1

Nass, C., Fogg, B. J., & Moon, Y. (1996). Can computers be teammates? *International Journal of Human–Computer Studies, 45,* 669–678. doi:10.1006/ijh.01996.0073

Nass, C., & Moon, Y. (2000). Machines and mindlessness: Social responses to computers. *Journal of Social Issues, 56,* 81–103.

Nass, C., Moon, Y., & Carney, P. (1999). Are respondents polite to computers? Social desirability and direct responses to computers. *Journal of Applied Social Psychology, 29,* 1093–1110. doi:10.1111/j.1559-1816.1999.tb00142.x

Nass, C., Moon, Y., Fogg, B. J., Reeves, B., & Dryer, D. C. (1995). Can computer personalities be human personalities? *International Journal of Human–Computer Studies, 43,* 223–239. doi:10.1006/ijhc.1995.1042

Nass, C., Moon, Y., & Green, N. (1997). Are computers gender-neutral? Gender stereo-typic response to computers. *Journal of Applied Social Psychology, 27*, 864–876. doi:10.1111/j.1559-1816.1997.tb00275.x

Nass, C., Reeves, B., & Leshner, G. (1996). Technology and roles: A tale of two TVs. *Journal of Communication, 46*, 121–128. doi:10.1111/jcom.1996.46.issue-2

Nowak, K. L., & Biocca, F. (2003). The effect of the agency and anthropomorphism on users' sense of telepresence, copresence, and social presence in virtual environments. *Presence: Teleoperators and Virtual Environments, 12*, 481–494.

O'Sullivan, P. B., Hunt, S. K., & Lippert, L. R. (2004). Mediated immediacy: A language of affili-ation in a technological age. *Journal of Language and Social Psychology, 23*, 464–490.

Parks, M. R. (1981). Ideology in interpersonal communication: Off the couch and into the world. *Annals of the International Communication Association, 5*, 79–107.

Peters, J. D. (2006). Communication as dissemination. In G. J. Shepherd, J. St. John, & T. Striphas (Eds.), *Communication as …: Perspectives on theory* (pp. 211–222). Thousand Oaks, CA: SAGE.

Postman, N. (1992) *Conscientious objection: Stirring up trouble about language, technology, and education.* New York, NY: Vintage Books.

Reeves, B., & Nass, C. (1996). *The media equation: How people treat computers, television, and new media like real people and places.* Stanford, CA: CSLI Publications.

Shannon, C. E., & Weaver, W. (1949). *The mathematical theory of communication.* Urbana, IL: University of Illinois Press.

Schleuder, J. D., White, A. V., & Cameron, G. (1993). Priming effects of television news bumpers and teaser on attention and memory. *Journal of Broadcasting and Electronic Media, 37*(4), 437–452. doi:10.1080/08838159309364234

Shepherd, G. J. (2006). Communication as transcendence. In G. J. Shepherd, J. St. John, & T. Striphas (Eds.), *Communication as …: Perspectives on theory* (pp. 22–30). Thousand Oaks, CA: SAGE.

Shobhit, S. (2019, May 4). Basics of algorithmic trading: Concepts an examples. *Investopedia.* Retrieved from https://www.investopedia.com/articles/active-trading/101014/basics-algorithmic-trading-concepts-and-examples.asp

Short, J., Williams, E., & Christie, B. (1976). *The social psychology of telecommunications.* London, UK: Wiley.

Spence, P. R. (2019). Searching for questions, original thoughts, or advancing theory: Human–machine communication. *Computers in Human Behavior, 90*, 285–287. doi:10.1016/j.chb.2018.09.014

Spence, P. R., Westerman, D., Edwards, C., & Edwards, A. (2014). Welcoming our robot over-lords: Initial expectations about interaction with a robot. *Communication Research Reports, 31*, 272–280. doi:10.1080/08824096.2014.924337

Spence, P. R., Edwards, A., Edwards, C., & Jin, X. (2019). 'The bot predicted rain, grab an umbrella': few perceived differences in communication quality of a weather Twitterbot versus professional and amateur meteorologists. *Behaviour and Information Technology, 38*, 101–109. doi:10.1080/0144929X.2018.1514425

Sundar, S. S. (2008). The MAIN model: A heuristic approach to understanding technology effects on credibility. In M. J. Metzger & A. J. Flanagin (Eds.), *Digital media, youth, and credibility* (pp. 73–100). Cambridge, MA: The MIT Press.

Turing, A. M. (1950). Computing machinery and intelligence. *Mind, 59*, 433–460.

Waddell, T. F. (2019, in press). Can an algorithm reduce the perceived bias of news? Testing the effect of machine attribution on news readers' evaluations of bias, anthropomorphism, and credibility. *Journalism and Mass Communication Quarterly.* doi:10.1177/1077699018815891

Walther, J. B. (1992). Interpersonal effects in computer-mediated interaction: A relational perspective. *Communication Research, 19*, 52–90. doi:10.1177/009365092019001003

Walther, J. B. (2019). Interpersonal versus personal uncertainty and communication in traditional and mediated encounters: A theoretical reformulation. In S. R. Wilson & S. W. Smith (Eds.), *Reflections on interpersonal communication research* (pp. 375–393). San Diego, CA: Cognella.

Walther, J. B., & Bazarova, N. N. (2008). Validation and application of electronic propinquity theory to computer-mediated communication in groups. *Communication Research, 35*, 622–645.

Westerman, D., & Skalski, P. D. (2010). Computers and telepresence: A ghost in the machine? In C. C. Bracken & P. D. Skalski (Eds.), *Immersed in media: Telepresence in everyday life*, (pp. 63–86). New York, NY: Routledge.

Wiener, N. (1948). *Cybernetics*. New York, NY: Wiley.

Wood, J. T. (2016). *Interpersonal communication: Everyday encounters* (8th ed.). Boston, MA: Cengage Learning.

Zhao, S. (2006). Humanoid social robots as a medium of communication. *New Media and Society, 8*, 401–419. doi:10.1080/10510974.2015.1121899

Section 2

Processing

Chapter 5

Communication Is ... The Key Element in Communication Privacy Management Theory

Sandra Petronio

Indiana University-Purdue University Indianapolis

Tiffany Hecklinski

Indiana University-Purdue University Indianapolis

P EOPLE GENERALLY ASSUME THAT COMMUNICATION CONVEYS information to others facilitating social connections. However, there are
times when people want to keep their information private. Sometimes
people encounter situations where they juggle a need to be both social
and private at the same time. Communication privacy management
(CPM) theory explicates how people manage the challenge of navigating when to restrict access to private information and/or deciding to
disclose information. Communication, therefore, is a key element in
CPM theory.

Take, for example, the situation posted by a *New York Times* columnist.
The writer asks for advice concerning an unexpected interaction at her
father's 70th birthday party. The writer asks her father if he had a wish
on his birthday. The father gives an unexpected reply. He says, "I wish I
was one of your mother's old boyfriends. She's always positive about them
but criticizes and complains about me. She might have been with one of
them and I might have been happier, too" (Galanes, 2019).

This disclosure triggered two related communication privacy dilemmas. First, the daughter asking the father if he had a wish to make for
his birthday is caught off guard by his reply. The father's disclosure
appears to be stressful—placing an unexpected burden on the daughter.
Consequently, she turns to her sisters and brothers to help unpack the
incident through discussing the options. Complicating the issue further,

the siblings disagreed about whether the mother should be told about this incident or whether should they conceal the father's revelation. This example illustrates the complexity of privacy management and underscores the importance of understanding communicative actions people take in making decisions about their private information.

This chapter focuses on the way "communication" functions as a key element of CPM theory using five key aspects of the relationship between communication and privacy management. They include: (1) highlighting the significance of communication, (2) communicatively sharing private information; communication coordination, privacy boundaries, and privacy rules; communicative parameters surrounding privacy turbulence; and (5) the future.

Key #1: Highlighting the Significance of Communication

CPM theory is born out of a communication perspective illustrated by its dependence on the communication literature and positioning the focus of CPM theory squarely within the discipline of communication studies (Petronio & Durham, 2015). Thus, communication privacy management theory is so named to highlight the synergy between communication and privacy management.

Communication is at the heart of the theory and essential to our understanding the way privacy management as described by this theoretical frame. Communication is a basic ingredient in circumnavigating decisions about disclosing or protecting private information and defines the infrastructure of CPM theory.

Communication is featured as a main component of CPM theory by deliberately using "communication" in the title of this theory. In addition to identifying communication in the title, a lexicon of terms needed to be developed that allowed for a greater understanding of how communication contributes to the theoretical frame. To accomplish this goal in theory development, scholars focused on using plain language to identify and describe CPM concepts. For example, the concept of "privacy dilemmas" in the case mentioned earlier illustrates a privacy predicament that individuals encounter when they do not know how to handle unexpected private information from others (Petronio, Jones, & Morr Serewicz, 2006;

Thompson, 2011). In the example, the siblings encountered difficult and conflicting choices in determining a way to cope with unexpected private information from their father. Communicatively, the siblings found that there was little consensus among them. This outcome made it difficult to find the best way to cope with their circumstance. As such, this situation created a problematic communicative interaction that illustrates the meaning of the CPM notion of "privacy dilemmas."

Constructing a useable vocabulary that characterizes communicatively based concepts opens the door for better understanding about the communication of private information. CPM theory was developed specifically to provide commonplace language to capture familiar actions that can bring new meaning to ordinary, everyday concepts. This perspective gives individuals the ability to understand concepts and locate the ramifications of the way privacy management performs through this lens. Thus, the nature of these concepts is easily understood, recognizable, and practical reflection of everyday life.

Key #2: Communicatively Sharing Private Information

Although communicatively sharing private information occurs frequently, many important factors are essential in deciding when and how to share private information with others. A main consideration involves communicative decisions to be open versus closed about sharing private information. In addition, emphasis is given to how the roles of information owners and authorized co-owners feature in these choices. In general, judgments are often predicated on how the owners decide to tell or not tell along when considering what information should be communicate to others or kept private. Privacy owners and recipients encounter a multitude of issues. As such, this discussion provides just a few examples to describe these issues.

As CPM research shows, information owners have high privacy expectations, especially when there are potential management challenges for the owner and co-owner of the private information. In these cases, owners can feel vulnerable and may try to influence the way individuals presume co-owners might treat their private information. For instance, a study focused on the way patients shared bad news concerning their lung cancer diagnosis offers some insights about privacy management (Ngwenya, Farqha, & Ewing, 2016). This research found that patients described their sense of ownership regarding the news of their diagnosis and presumed control over how, when, and with whom the diagnosis could be shared. These patients clearly felt a need to limit access to this information. However, this research suggests that full patient control of their private information may create additional consequences for the family and the patient. As this study shows, in some instance the owner exercises too much control over private information, which can be counterproductive for the owner and co-owners. As an alternative to the example just highlighted, a study that examined parents' and children's preferences regarding parental sharing of information about their children on social media illustrates ways to communicate and negotiate privacy expectations (Moser, Chen, & Schoenenbeck, 2017). In this study, the researchers found that there was agreement in perceptions of how often and how much parents shared about their children on social media. Yet, tensions occurred when the parents did not seek permission from their children to post on certain social media. The children believed that they should have the right to make that judgment. CPM theory discusses the notion of "permission" when it comes to handling a person's private information (Petronio, 2002).

An important issue regarding giving access to others involves communicative decisions to be open or closed about private information. CPM theory emphasizes how the roles of information owner and authorized co-owners feature in these choices. In general, judgments are often predicated on how the owners decide to tell or not tell along with considering what information is allowed to be communicated to others. In these judgments, seeking permission plays a big role in successful privacy management. Granting permission to disclose is only one way that private information is managed. Information owners and recipients encounter a multitude of issues with regards to privacy. As such, this discussion provides just a few examples illustrating the nature of choice-making.

While the emphasis is primarily on communicative choices made by the information owner, recipients of the private information add another dimension to understanding communicative sharing. Sharing private information, for both the information owner and co-owners of the information, is often complicated. For example, once the information owner decides to communicate private information to a selected a co-owner, the owner considerers the co-owner authorized to know the owner's information. Being identified as an "authorized co-owner" means that the owner has expectations that the co-owner will care for the owner's information in the same way the owner imagines.

Although the information owner expects the co-owner to understand the responsibilities that come with co-ownership, information owners may not think about the possibility that their co-owner does not necessity grasp how the information owner wants him or her to treat their private information. Communicating the scope or specific ways the information owner expects the co-owner to treat their private information can be extremely important. When information owners do not communicate their assumptions about the way their private information should be treated by authorized others the potential for missteps is great.

For instance, authorized co-owners might communicate the owner's private information based on patterns they have established for their own management of private information. Authorized co-owners may try second-guessing to see how they might fulfill the obligation for the information owner in attempting to apply their own set of criteria. As seems realistic, communicating private information can be ambiguous and create misunderstandings that might lead to negative outcomes for both the owner and authorized co-owner that could potentially influencing the "privacy relationship" (Petronio, 2018).

Authorized co-owners also encounter issues that directly compromise their feelings about serving as a confidant. One of the precipitating factors concerns another assumption made by information owners. Often information owners presume authorized co-owners want to know their private information. However, there are times when the co-owner may not want to know the owner's private information. Communicatively sharing information designated as private by an owner can create difficulties for the person serving as a communication recipient. For example, when individuals feel that the messages communicated by the information owner are "too hot to handle," co-owners as confidantes can feel like "reluctant confidants" (Petronio, 1999).

There are a number of ways confidants cope with feeling reluctant to be a confidant. For instance, bartenders may find it difficult to listen to patrons' stories in a bar all night long. This is especially true if the patrons ask for advice about their important or serious issues that bartenders cannot solve. Bartenders often face being a reluctant confident such that it is an occupational hazard (Petronio, 1999). Likewise, people flying on a plane often infringe on others when they loudly discuss things that others do not want to hear. The notion of reluctant confidant also aptly characterizes unwillingness to listen to someone else's business for fear of being responsible for knowing that information. Likewise, trying to keep a secret that an owner has forced on the recipient may also cause problems for the recipient in ways that compromise the privacy relationship (Caughlin, Scott, Miller, & Hefner, 2009).

In some circumstances the reluctant confidants do not start out as being reluctant. For instance, authorized co-owners may agree to accept the role of authorized co-owner to help friends or family members (Petronio, 2002). Given the fact that information owners can assume the authorized co-owners would accept the role of confident, there are times when the authorized co-owner does not see his or her role in the same way. The presumption that authorized co-owners always understand they are entering into a set of responsibilities assumed to be followed by the co-owner can be a fallacy. Not everyone finds him- or herself in a quandary about accepting these responsibilities. However, when people do find themselves in "privacy predicaments," the need for communicating and negotiating is great in order to find the best path to deal with the situation.

Key #3: Communication Coordination, Collective Boundaries, and Privacy Rules

Communicative interactions demonstrate the way people convey where privacy boundaries begin and end. Privacy boundaries and the "privacy rules" that regulate them signal when access is allowed or denied. Metaphorically, these boundaries reflect where a person's private information is stored. Individuals own and control their privacy boundary, yet research has identified that there are also layers of privacy boundaries people co-own (Petronio, 2002). For example, families typically have two distinct "family privacy boundary spheres," external and internal (Morr Serewicz & Canary, 2008). The external sphere represents a boundary surrounding private information that sets privacy rules about what can and not be told to outsiders. The internal sphere represents privacy boundaries that regulate information flow within and among family members.

Just like the family boundary example, when there are multiple people who legitimately are granted access to know "collective private information," there is a need to "coordinate privacy rules" (Petronio, 2002). Coordination processes include choices about who is privy to the collective privacy boundary information and who is not. To reach this goal, collective boundary owners vet whom they, as a group, allow into the collective boundary. The action safeguards the group as a whole to ensure that the collective boundary is secure from outsiders. Doing so gives a sense of comfort in making communicative disclosures and incorporating others into the collective. As a fail-safe, once a decision is made to include certain others clear and sustainable rule parameters need to be set establishing how much and what type of information is permissible to tell others inside the collective. In this process, there tends to be restrictions on the level of independent decision-making and degree of independent ownership granted to the authorized co-owners (Child, Pearson, & Petronio, 2009).

CPM theory argues that there are many types of privacy boundaries, including the management of "relational privacy boundaries" (Petronio, 2002). Disclosure can be a change agent in relationships. As people gain knowledge about each other through conversations and negotiations of privacy rules, the status of the relationship changes. Their personal relationship boundaries morph into a dyadic privacy boundary. Privacy rules work to identify expectations for behavior in the relationship. Privacy rules determine the level and kind of communicative access that is acceptable to others outside the relationship and behaviors expected by the relational partners. The boundary parameters are meaningful in terms of working to maintain a viable relationship.

Challenges also exist with the coordination of relational boundaries, as boundary coordination does not always run smoothly. CPM theory illustrates that there can be high-cost communicative disclosures that compromise the relationship. For example, a relational partner might disclose the couple's sexual orientation. Similarly, there can be a need for recalibrating a relational privacy boundary to accommodate needed changes. For example, if a partner reveals too much information at a party with friends without permission from the partner, there might be fallout from revealing the information. At times partners may not be ready to hear a disclosure from the relational partner, so they avoid conversations about the issue.

Privacy boundaries can represent group boundaries where there are multiple types of privacy boundaries in different contexts (De Wolf, Willaet, & Pierson, 2014). Each boundary houses private information, yet each boundary has a different set of parameters by which to understand privacy management. These parameters help in the development of privacy rules that guide how privacy is managed within the context of the group's needs. Privacy boundaries are constructed in a variety of ways, with each boundary structure having a different mission to create, recalibrate, or substitute boundary rules accommodating the needs of the owners and co-owners (Petronio, 2002). As this discussion shows, privacy rules, in all circumstances, function as the engine that propels the privacy management system.

Key #4: Communicative Parameters of Privacy Turbulence

Privacy turbulence erupts when the expectations for privacy management go awry (Petronio, 2002). Turbulence can manifest in several ways. For example, if there is a lack of communication about how the information owner expects the authorized co-owner to care for the owner's information, turbulence may occur. Likewise, the selected co-owner may not find it easy to abide by the information owner's privacy rules. As a result, the co-owner may decline the request. Misunderstandings may arise in privacy management can and lead to privacy turbulence.

For example, when patients seek medical care, they often must compromise some privacy in order to receive healthcare. Even though patients understand that there is a trade-off, patients want to have a sense of ownership and control over their medical information. Sharing private health information with the provider makes the provider a co-owner of that private information. The patient and provider are then linked together, creating a privacy boundary. While this linkage allows access to the provider, potential problems can arise that can cause privacy turbulence. For instance, patients may not be aware of the expectations the provider has about caring for patient information. Patients may be surprised to find that providers often share the patient's private health information with the medical staff. Consequently, the lack of communication about the way private medical information is conveyed to other health providers can lead to confusion and may disrupt the patient's trust of the provider. If the patient's trust is compromised in future situations, the patient may not disclose important health information to the provider.

Privacy turbulence can also erupt when there are errors in judgments regarding the care of an owner's private information. Incidents may also occur where the owner provides ambiguous messages about the third-person privilege to tell others. In these cases, the recipient has to discern ways to understand what the owner expects of the selected co-owner to treat his or her information. For some people, the lack of guidance can trigger a sense of burden for the authorized co-owner. They can also feel worried that they are not living up to the needs of the owner. Likewise, privacy turbulence can occur when the information owner forces the co-owner to conceal private information, such as is the case with child sexual abuse.

On the flip side, sometimes information owners want to reinforce the fact that the co-owner has, not only access to the information owner's private information, but also responsibility to abide by the owner's privacy rules. One of the ways to explicitly secure the expectation of the owner is to use statements such as "don't tell anyone this ..." or saying "please keep this information private." The question is whether co-owners abide by the owner's privacy rules. If not, privacy turbulence can be triggered.

Aside from the challenging issues already discussed, different kinds of sources can instigate privacy turbulence. The current interface with social media and other new technologies provides a platform for different aspects of privacy turbulence. Although there can be barriers where privacy management is concerned, isolating communication barriers can help identify privacy management issues in need of attention. These tactics are likely to function as a privacy barrier.

For instance, in many ways, adolescents have developed some strategies to keep parents from knowing their private information. Some younger children use the "closed door" approach to gain privacy, and may even put signs on their bedroom door warning parents not to enter. Adolescents construct more sophisticated ways to withhold their private information from their parents. Research finds that adolescents negotiating privacy rules between themselves and their parents can alleviate negative outcomes often generated because there is a vying for control over the information considered private to the adolescents (Kennedy-Lightsey, & Frisby 2016; Petronio, 1994).

On the other end of the spectrum, aging adults in need of assistance may live in a nursing home where the residents have very little privacy. In a study conducted in Scotland, the research showed that residents used different tactics to claim privacy (Petronio, 1997). Even though the residents did not have much opportunity to control who saw their medical information, nor were they able to keep their finances privileged, they cleverly found places where they could control some part of their lives. For example, the residents mandated that before entering their room, the staff had to knock on the door and ask permission to come into the room and do so regardless whether the door was open or closed. They also instructed the medical staff that they could not sit on their bedside when they came into the room.

The residents were mostly women, and one of their needs for privacy was identified by allowing the residents to carry their purse no matter where they went. These purses were considered their private property and it was maintained under the residents' control. Privacy was communicated in a number of ways in this study. For instance, the one place in this research project where the residents did exercise a quid pro quo was when the residents asked personal questions about the nurses' families; that is, the residents did not believe that is was fair for them to disclose information about their personal lives without the nurses disclosing some of *their* personal information in return. In other words, the expectation of reciprocity was used to balance the sense of privacy ownership. The examples in this study illustrate that even when people are in a restricted privacy situation they find ways to claim some level of privacy. In so doing, these residents captured a level of privacy ownership and control over their information.

Key #5: The Future

CPM theory and research are solidly connected to the discipline of communication studies. The way individuals think about communication privacy management and the way people use it illustrate the viability of this theory and the importance communication plays. Success is predicated on the accessibility and connections with communication as a discipline. The lens of communication has been and will continue to be the critical key to the growth of CPM theory.

References

Caughlin, J. P., Scott, A. M., Miller, L. E., & Hefner, V. (2009). Putative secrets: When information is supposedly a secret. *Journal of Social and Personal Relationships, 26(5)*, 713–743. doi:10.1177/0265407509347928

Child, J. T., Pearson, J. C., & Petronio, S. (2009). Blogging, communication, and privacy management: Development of the blogging privacy management measure. *Journal of the American Society for Information Science and Technology, 60(10)*, 2079–2094. doi:10.1002/asi.21122

De Wolf, R., Willaert, K., & Pierson, J. (2014). Managing privacy boundaries together: Exploring individual and group privacy management strategies in Facebook. *Computers in Human Behavior, 35*, 444–454. doi:10.1016/j.chb.2014.03.010

Galanes, P. (2019, February 3). Social Q's. *New York Times*, ST, p. 8.

Kennedy-Lightsey, C. D. & Frisby, B. N. (2016). Parental privacy invasion, family communication patters, and ownership of privacy information. *Communication Reports, 29(2)*, 75–86. doi:10.1080/08934215.2015.1048477

Morr Serewicz, M. C., & Canary, D. J. (2008). Assessments of disclosure from the in-laws: Links among disclosure topics, family privacy orientations, and relational quality. *Journal of Social and Personal Relationships, 25(2)*, 333–357. doi:10.1080/08934215.2015.1048477

Moser, C., Chen, T., & Schoenebeck, S. Y. (2017). Parents' and children's preferences about parents sharing about children on social media. Proceedings from CHI '17: *Conference on Human Factors in Computing Systems* (pp. 5221–5225). New York, NY: Association for Computing Machinery. doi:10.1145/3025453.3025587

Ngwenya, N., Farqha, M., & Ewing, G. (2016). Sharing bad news of a lung cancer diagnosis: Understanding through communication privacy management theory. *Psycho-Oncology, 25(8)*, 913–918. doi:10.1002/pon.4024

Petronio, S. (1994). Privacy binds in family interactions: The case of parental privacy invasion. In W. R. Cupach & B. Spitzberg (Eds.), *The dark side of interpersonal communication* (pp. 241–258). Mahwah, NJ: Lawrence Erlbaum.

Petronio, S. (1999). The ramifications of a reluctant confidant. In A. C. Richards & T. Schumrum (Eds.), *Invitations to dialogue: The legacy of Sidney M. Jourard* (pp. 113–150). Dubuque, IA: Kendall Hunt.

Petronio, S. (2002). *Boundaries of privacy: Dialectics of disclosure*. Albany, NY: SUNY.

Petronio, S. (2018). Privacy from a communication science perspective. In B. van der Sloot & A. de Groot (Eds.), *The handbook of privacy studies: An interdisciplinary introduction* (pp. 378–407). Amsterdam, Netherlands: Amsterdam University Press.

Petronio, S., & Durham, W. T. (2015). Communication privacy management theory: Significance for interpersonal communication. In D. O. Braithwaite & P. Schrodt (Eds.), *Engaging theories in interpersonal communication: Multiple perspectives* (2nd ed., pp. 335–348). Los Angeles, CA: SAGE.

Petronio, S., & Jones, S. M. (2006). When "friendly advice" becomes a privacy dilemma for pregnant couples: Applying CPM theory. In R. West, & L. Turner (Eds.), *Family communication sourcebook* (pp. 201–218). Thousand Oaks, CA: SAGE.

Petronio, S., Jones, S. M., & Serewicz, M. C. (2003). Family privacy dilemmas: Managing communication boundaries with family groups. In L. R. Frey (Ed.), *Group communication in context: Studies of bona fide groups* (2nd ed., pp. 23–56). Mahwah NJ: Lawrence Erlbaum.

Petronio, S., & Kovach, S. (1997). Managing privacy boundaries: Health provider's perceptions of resident care in Scottish nursing homes. *Journal of Applied Communication Research, 25(2),* 115–131. doi:10.1080/00909889709365470

Thompson, J. (2011). Communication privacy management in college athletics: Exploring privacy dilemmas in athletic/academic advisor student-athlete interpersonal relationships. *Journal of Sport Administration and Supervision, 3(1),* 44–60. spo.676111.0003.110.

Chapter 6
Communication Is ... Complex

Deanna D. Sellnow
University of Central Florida

Timothy L. Sellnow
University of Central Florida

H OW MANY OF US HAVE HEARD someone say something like this: "What can you actually *teach* in a communication course? We have all been talking since we were toddlers." Although the question seems innocent enough, it does point to a conundrum for us as communication scholars and teachers in terms of defending the value of our profession. More specifically, many people do not understand the breadth and depth of what we study. Contrary to popular belief, communication is far from simple. It is both complex and ever-changing based on myriad factors such as context, purpose, occasion, and channel (e.g., face-to-face, mediated). Moreover, instructional communication scholars sometimes face an additional question rooted in a misperception that teaching is merely sharing information (a.k.a. imparting knowledge). To the contrary, effective instructional communication is also complex but, when done well, appears to be simple.

For the past two decades, we have devoted a great deal of time and energy to working with government agencies, scientists, emergency managers, reporters, and other key spokespersons regarding how to communicate instructional messages effectively to disparate publics in the context of risk situations and crisis events. We have enjoyed working with food scientists regarding food risk issues, seismologists regarding earthquake forecasting and early warning messages, agricultural scientists regarding biosecurity, toxicologists regarding water pollution issues, law enforcement officials regarding violence and terrorism, and health scientists regarding health risk issues and events (e.g., Frisby, Sellnow, Lane, Veil, & Sellnow, 2013; Herovic, Sellnow, & Sellnow, 2019; Littlefield et al., 2014; Sellnow et al., 2017; Sellnow, Sellnow, Lane, & Littlefield, 2012; Sellnow, Sellnow, Lane, & Littlefield, 2017). We have had the opportunity to do so, not only throughout the United States, but also with colleagues around the world (e.g., Sellnow, Iverson, & Sellnow, 2017; Sellnow, Johannson, Sellnow, & Lane, 2018). This chapter focuses on how we have been making and continue to make the complexities of effective instructional risk and crisis messages simple to collaborators in a host of disciplines and countries as we work together to create instructional messages that are effective across risk and crisis types and to disparate nonscientific publics.

Thus, the title of our chapter is a bit of an oxymoron in that our goal is to provide an easy-to-understand and easy-to-employ instructional communication model (a.k.a. the IDEA model) for designing and delivering effective instructional messages for self-protection and risk reduction when time is of the essence (Sellnow & Sellnow, 2013, 2014, 2019). To be effective, regardless of context, these instructional messages must produce the desired affective, cognitive, and behavior learning outcomes among diverse target populations (Sellnow et al., 2015). One particularly daunting challenge we have encountered rests with the fact that the spokespersons who must deliver these messages are not schooled in communication theory generally or instructional communication theory specifically. Consequently, we must first help them see the value of what we bring to the conversation and then that sharing information and instructional communication are not the same. In essence, our goal has been to create a theoretically grounded and rigorously tested model that non-communication-science experts can understand easily and employ effectively.

"IDEA" is an acronym that serves as a heuristic to remind spokespersons what elements to include in their instructional communication and the channels through which these messages ought to be delivered. The "I" stands for internalization. Target audiences must be motivated to attend to and retain the messages. The "D" stands for distribution. Different audiences tend to have access to and seek information via different channels. The "E" stands for explanation about what is happening and why translated in ways that make it intelligible to nonscientific publics.

The "A" stands for action, which points to the need to offer specific actionable instructions for safety, well-being, and self-protection. The model appears to be simple; however, it is informed by myriad theories, including experiential learning theory (e.g., Dewey, 1938; Kolb, 2015), social learning theory (Bandura, 1977, 2002), exemplification theory (e.g., Zillman, 2000), convergence theory (e.g., Perelman & Olbrechts-Tyteca, 1969), and communities of practice theory (e.g., Wenger, 2008). Moreover, we have tested it rigorously (a) using multiple methodologies, (b) across risk and crisis types, and (c) among disparate cultural, co-cultural, and transnational populations.

To complicate matters further, our communication must effectively address several paradoxical communication challenges inherent in times of risk and crisis. We arrange our discussion by first highlighting the paradoxical communication challenges spokespersons face and then proposing strategies for managing them effectively. Although we use risk and crisis contexts to forward our argument, we believe these challenges face communication scholars and teachers across subfields in our discipline.

Paradoxical Communication Challenges of Spokespersons

Crises can be characterized as the onset of chaos where structures and assumptions once considered stable and predictable crumble, resulting in confusion, ambiguity, and insecurity. For example, a community protected by a levy for decades suddenly floods, leaving residents traumatized by a crisis they had not considered possible. Similar feelings of shock and insecurity occur when an organization that employed many community members and generated economic prosperity for generations closes its doors due to bankruptcy or to moving its production overseas. In other cases, perceptions of chaos can occur seemingly without warning when a community discovers that its water supply, long considered safe, is contaminated with life-threatening chemicals.

The communication needs of residents facing such crises are often paradoxical. Frightened or frustrated residents may demand clear and certain explanations about the situation when such answers are simply not known. Similarly, residents want simple explanations to complex environmental, economic, and political quandaries. Others may want their voices heard in a public dialogue at a time when an immediate and highly directive response is needed to save lives. Crises may also signal inevitable change as actions once considered safe are now hazardous. Thus, crises may create momentary feelings of helplessness during which we feel hope is lost. Effective instructional risk and crisis messages are needed to replace such feelings of helplessness with feelings of self-efficacy. In this section, we explore these complex and paradoxical challenges that face key spokespersons from an instructional crisis communication perspective. We focus on the paradoxes of expressing certainty in times of uncertainty, making difficult information simple, managing dialogue and directives, succeeding in failure, and making the seemingly impossible possible.

Expressing Certainty in Times of Uncertainty

By their nature, instructional crisis communication messages are delivered in times of uncertainty. Crisis situations manifest threat, surprise, and short response time (Hermann, 1963). The startling nature of crises creates uncertainty for those threatened by and responding to the crisis. Although uncertainty is pervasive in these situations, audiences imperiled by crises yearn for certainty, particularly concerning questions about protecting themselves and their loved ones. This simple request creates a paradox where crisis communication spokespersons are asked to provide messages of certainty in times of high uncertainty. Crisis communicators often submit to these demands by over-reassuring audiences (Venette, 2006). Such over-reassurance further complicates the crisis situation when the communicator's messages of over-reassurance are contradicted by the reality of the crisis. For example, the over-reassurance by the Centers for Disease Control and Prevention that no cases of Ebola would be contracted on American soil were shockingly refuted in 2014 when two nurses contracted the disease in Dallas (Sellnow-Richmond, George, & Sellnow, 2018). Similarly, in 2009, over-reassurance offered by the crisis spokesperson regarding earthquake warnings in L'Aquila, Italy, resulted in a failure of residents to take appropriate self-protective actions and led to hundreds of deaths and thousands of injuries (e.g., Herovic, Sellnow, & Sellnow, 2019; Sellnow, Iverson, & Sellnow, 2017).

Making Difficult Information Simple

Considerable research describes the shortcomings of experts in their attempts to communicate the scientific complexities of health and environmental risks to nonexperts. The degree to which publics are able to comprehend these translations is often referred to as "health literacy" or "science literacy" (Nguyen et al., 2015). The challenge that immediately comes to mind involves simplifying explanations of the science so that it can be understood by general audiences of nonexperts without simplifying them so much that important information is inaccurate, inadequate, or perceived as condescending. Previous research indicates that scientists and physicians often err on the side of complexity in the name of accuracy (Sellnow, George, & Sellnow, 2018). Simplifying complex concepts such as the reliability of a certain vaccine or earthquake intensity levels and S-waves is a difficult paradox for professional experts to grapple with as they perceive it to be watering down the science. However, those threatened by such crises typically have a short response time to take appropriate actions of self-protection. Accordingly, spokespersons must offer clear and simple translations about what is happening and the science behind it in order to also provide actionable instructions for self-protection (e.g., where the evacuation routes are, how to shelter in place, what to do if you become sickened from eating a tainted product).

Managing Dialogue and Directives

Ideally, risk communication occurs as a dialogue among multiple parties (National Research Council, 1989). This dialogue often involves experts in a given research area sharing their findings and providing advice to those who bear the burden of the risk. Crises, however, create a threshold where dialogue must be replaced with specific directive instructions to mitigate harm. Simply put, the threatening nature of crises creates an immediate need for instructional messages that empower audiences to avoid or escape from an immediate threat (Sellnow & Sellnow, 2010). For example, residents of California engage regularly in a dialogue about how to prevent and manage wildfires. Such ongoing dialogue informs decisions about, for instance, where to allow building permits and what strategies can be used to control growth of the brush that can fuel such fires. Once a fire begins, however, the emphasis must switch to warnings about who must evacuate, as well as when, how, and to where. The reality of how threatening these fires are for California residents was made clear during the 2018 Camp Fire that killed at least 85 people (Wootson, 2018).

Succeeding in Failure

Organizations and communities adapt to economic, social, and environmental changes through learning. This learning process is often instigated by failure. In fact, some argue that failure and the recognition of it is actually "essential" to such learning and adaptation (Sitkin, 1996, p. 541). Thus, organizations and communities actually succeed through failure—provided they constantly recognize their failures early and respond accordingly. The pain of humiliation, potential reprimands, and public condemnation that accompany organizational failure, however, may create perceptions of dread or temptations to conceal even minor failures among organizational leaders and employees. Failing to learn from failures by recognizing, discussing, and responding meaningfully to them can lead to major crises in the future that could have been prevented. For example, the collapse of a dam built to support iron ore mining by the multinational company, Vale, resulted in the deaths of 160 people. A postcrisis investigation revealed that the company was aware of multiple minor failures in the dam before it collapsed. By ignoring such reported failures as cracks, leaks, and a lack of necessary internal drainage, Vale ostensibly allowed the deadly crisis to occur (Pollock, 2019).

Making the Seemingly Impossible Possible

The shocking nature of crises can create what Weick (1993) calls a "cosmology episode" for those involved in the calamity. Weick characterizes the reactions of those experiencing a cosmology episode with three perceptual conditions: "I've never been here before, I have no idea where I am, and I have no idea who can help me" (pp. 633–634). For those in the midst of a cosmology episode, the thought of receiving a clear message that can deliver them from peril seems, at least momentarily, impossible. Consequently, crisis communicators often find themselves attempting to send instructional messages to individuals who are stunned or frightened into a seemingly paralyzed state.

To manage this phenomenon, communication spokespersons can conduct regular drills, such as evacuating a building, prior to the occurrence of a potential crisis event as a means to empower people to overcome immobilizing distress during crises. For example, some argue that many lives were saved due to an effective evacuation process at the World Trade Center early during the crisis of September 11, 2001. Many in the building had previously experienced a full emergency evacuation in 1993 when a bomb exploded in an underground garage (Proulx & Fahy, 2003). As a result of this previous evacuation experience and the subsequent drills they engaged in since then, many employees hastily evacuated the premises, despite the confusion and horror of a plane crashing into the floors of the building above them. Similarly, the Southern California Earthquake Center conducts a drill—the Great ShakeOut—every October. On cue, all participants in a host of countries practice the drill to drop, take cover, and hold on to promote muscle memory regarding what to do if and when they experience a high-intensity earthquake (Sellnow & Sellnow, 2019).

Spokespersons that face these kinds of paradoxical challenges can overcome them and, in doing so, discover more success when instructing diverse audiences during risk and crisis events. The next section highlights several strategies risk and crisis communicators can employ to manage living with these paradoxes successfully.

Living Within the Paradoxes of Crisis Communication

A paradox as conceived by ancient Greek philosophers is an observation that takes people outside their usual way of thinking. In other words, it is a tenet that is seemingly contradictory and illogical even though it may, in fact, be true. Although paradoxical challenges are inherent to crisis situations, they are not restricted to such extreme encounters. Stohl and Cheney (2001) explain that paradoxes involving employee participation in organizations occur frequently. For example, employees may be instructed to follow procedural protocols strictly; then be simultaneously rewarded for efficiency and productivity they actually achieved by bypassing such procedures. Stohl and Cheney acknowledge that some organizational paradoxes cannot be resolved but that strategies can emerge for "living with or within" them (p. 396). They explain that living with or within a paradox requires the realization that we will never fully "get over" the imperfections in our capacity to communicate about and to manage some situations (p. 396). We can, however, accept and admit our limitations to meet the complex and paradoxical informational needs of our audiences during crises. In doing so, our primary objective should be to protect and serve those whose well-being is imperiled. We argue that living within the paradoxes of crisis communication is best accomplished by remaining open and honest, transcending to the highest values, and striving for renewal based on lessons learned from the risk or crisis event.

Remaining Open and Honest

Remaining open and honest in all phases of crisis communication is a well-established best practice (Seeger, 2006). Although uncertainty is inevitable in crisis situations, people can live within the certainty/uncertainty paradox when spokespersons explain what is known, acknowledge what is unknown, and commit themselves to regularly sharing any new information. We argue that to live within this paradox all public interactions should follow these directives. Doing so empowers audiences with the best information available at any given time during a crisis.

Being open and honest also means tailoring such messages in ways that make difficult information and instructions intelligible to the immediate needs of a given audience. Even when the information offered by a crisis spokesperson is accurate, the message is only helpful when it is comprehensible to the target population. To ensure that audiences are interpreting the communication accurately, spokespersons should seek as much feedback from them as possible throughout the event. Simply put, crisis communicators do not achieve the standards of openness and honesty by simply sharing content. Rather openness and honesty are determined by the degree to which the messages are immediately relevant to and comprehended by those in harm's way. The only way to fully ascertain the effectiveness of a crisis message is through the frequent solicitation of feedback from receivers.

Transcending to the Highest Level

Elson (2010) advises organizations encountering paradoxical communication situations to appeal to the highest levels of interpretation.

In crisis situations, the highest level is always the well-being of those at risk (Anthony & Sellnow, 2011). To clarify, crisis spokespersons may manage the impossible/possible paradox through transcendence. In other words, they may be justified via transcendence to suspend extensive dialogue and explanation about the event to focus momentarily on providing specific instructions for self-protection. Clearly stated actions for self-protection can empower individuals to diminish their immediate threat. Furthermore, paying careful attention to the capacity of the audience to complete the actions recommended and supplying them with the necessary resources to do so is essential for managing the impossible/possible paradox. Individuals facing the shock and disorientation of a cosmology episode lack the cognitive space or acuity to process complex messages or to contemplate decisions. Messages that are explicitly focused on specific actionable instructions with achievable outcomes can bring an essence of self-efficacy to individuals who feel trapped in an impossible situation (Sellnow, Sellnow, Lane, & Littlefield, 2012).

Moving From Resilience to Renewal

Our final recommendation for managing the inherent paradoxes of crisis communication is to move beyond resilience to focus on renewal. Organizations and communities often choose to respond to crises with defensive strategies that heighten their resilience. Communities threatened by major flooding may raise the levels of their dikes (Sellnow & Seeger, 2001). Food-processing plants may respond to a food contamination event with more inspections and testing. In both cases, the commitment to resilience is laudable. Farmers may respond to a virus spreading through their barns with more attention to engaging in existing biosecurity practices regularly. We argue, however, that heightened resilience does not fully address the success/failure paradox. Building a higher dike, for example, is evidence of only modest learning. In essence, a community that fortifies its dikes has learned only to engage in more of the same response strategy. Similarly, a food-processing plant that adds more testing and inspection procedures in a situation where similar testing and inspection procedures have failed in the past is also engaging in more of the same behaviors.

We argue that effective instructional crisis communication instead engages in what we call a "discourse of renewal." Renewal is characterized by learning from failure and the development of a corresponding prospective vision (Ulmer, Sellnow, & Seeger, 2018). A prospective vision focuses on new ways of managing a persistent threat. For example, communities may shift from building dikes to creating a channel that diverts flood waters around rather than through the community. Processing plants may abandon procedures that make food vulnerable to contamination and implement potentially safer procedures. Farmers might employ additional biosecurity practices not just among their employers, but by others that travel to and from their farms (Sellnow et al., 2017). In other words, renewal requires learning and new ways of thinking. Rather than accepting one's fate, a discourse of renewal sees failure as the inspiration for new ways of addressing old problems. From the perspective of renewal, failure is paradoxically the first step toward future success.

Conclusions

Risk and crisis communicators must learn to live within the paradoxes inherent in risk and crisis events. In doing so, they may effectively instruct disparate audiences to take appropriate actions of self-protection in spite of feelings of chaos and uncertainty. Living within the paradoxes in these ways empowers target populations by generating self-efficacy about what they can do for themselves and those they love. Moreover, when individuals live within the paradox of success in failure, they may move toward teaching communities to be more than resilient by capitalizing on using what they learn from the crisis to engage in a discourse of renewal.

In line with the paradoxes we have presented here, we close our chapter with questions about next steps for instructional communication scholars who study risk issues and crisis events in order to contribute positively to saving lives. What can we do and what can we realistically hope to achieve toward this goal? Most important, we must continue to seek opportunities to collaborate with scientists, politicians, journalists, and key spokespersons to create and test instructional messages focused on a variety of risk and crisis types and targeting a variety of populations not only in the United States, but also around the world. For example, we are now working with partners in Uganda to empower farmers and their families in the Bududah District to protect themselves from devastating and often deadly consequences of mudslides. In this effort, we will help share their stories with journalists and government officials to educate them about misconceptions they may have about what the people actually want/need and don't want/need regarding how to best live within these paradoxes as manifested by mudslide risks and crisis events. Similarly, we need to continue working collaboratively with food scientists, government officials, and journalists in emerging economics about the misconceptions surrounding agricultural biotechnology as an important strategy for feeding the world's growing population. Most important, we need to share our research with nonacademics in ways that are comprehendible and relevant to the kinds of risk and crisis challenges they face.

Instructional risk and crisis communication is a complex area of study and expertise. Our goal is to translate what we know and learn to make it accessible and intelligible to disparate publics ranging from experts in other scientific fields, government officials, journalists, and others. We believe doing so effectively means living with the paradoxical challenge of making communication complexities simple to understand and employ. It is our way to make the relevance of our work transparent and, ultimately, to save lives.

Finally, although the extended argument presented here focuses on the complexities of communication confounded by paradoxical challenges as manifested in the context of risk and crisis, these challenges confront communication specialists across subfields. Based on our experiences and observations, we contend that, rather than becoming frustrated when those reading our research or participating in our classes say, "this is common sense," we should be congratulating ourselves for achieving our goal. To clarify, interpersonal research and instruction focused on theories such as, for example, face negotiation, expectancy violations, relational dialectics, privacy management, or stigma is complex; however, we achieve our goal when we make it sensible and relevant to those living outside the walls of the academy. Similarly, organizational research and instruction focused on theories such as organizational culture, structuration, or communities of practice is also complex; however, we again achieve our goal when we make it sensible and relevant to lives beyond the academy. The same may be said for research and instruction across communication subfields (e.g., health, family, gender, rhetoric, media, intercultural, argumentation, instructional). Ultimately, communication scholars and teachers are effective when we live within the paradoxes of communicating the complexities of our work in ways that intelligibly demonstrate its value to personal and professional life. Communication is certainly complex. We succeed, however, when we make it appear to be simple. Now that's definitely a paradox.

References

Anthony, K. E., & Sellnow, T. L. (2011). Beyond Narnia: The necessity of C.S. Lewis' *First and Second Things* in applied communication research. *Journal of Applied Communication Research, 39*, 441–443.

Bandura, A. (1977). *Social learning theory*. New York, NY: General Learning Press.

Bandura, A. (2002). Growing primacy of human agency in adaptation and change in the electronic era. *European Psychologist, 7*(1), 2–16.

Dewey, J. (1938). *Experience and education*. New York, NY: Simon and Schuster.

Elson, L. G. (2010). *Paradox lost: A cross-contextual definition of levels of abstraction*. Cresskill, NJ: Hampton.

Hermann, C. F. (1963). Some consequences of crisis which limit the viability of organizations. *Administrative Science Quarterly, 8*, 61–82.

Herovic, E., Sellnow, T. L., & Sellnow, D. D. (2019). Challenges and opportunities for pre-crisis emergency risk communication: Lessons learned from the earthquake community. *Journal of Risk Research*. Published online. doi:10.1080/13669877.2019.156097

Kolb, D. A. (2015). *Experiential learning: Experience as the source of learning and development* (2nd ed.). Upper Saddle River, NJ: Pearson.

Littlefield, R. S., Beauchamp, K., Lane, D., Sellnow, D. D., Sellnow, T. L., Venette, S., & Wilson, B. (2014). Instructional crisis communication: Connecting ethnicity and gender in the assessment of receiver-oriented message effectiveness. *Journal of Management and Strategy, 5*(3), pp. 149–158.

National Research Council. (1989). *Improving risk communication*. Washington, DC: National Academies Press.

Nguyen, T. H., Park, H., Han, H. R., Chan, K. S., Paasche-Orlow, M. K., Haun, J., & Kim, M. T. (2015). State of the science of health literacy measures: validity implications for minority populations. *Patient Education and Counseling, 98*(12), 1492–1512. doi:10.1016/j.pec.2015.07.013

Perelman, C., & Olbrechts-Tyteca, L. (1969). *The new rhetoric: A treatise on argumentation*. London, UK: University of Notre Dame Press.

Pollock, E. (2019, February 18). Manufactured disaster: How Brazil's dam collapse should have been avoided. *Engineering.com*. Retrieved from https://www.engineering.com/BIM/ArticleID/18557/Manufactured-Disaster-How-Brazils-Dam-Collapse-Should-Have-Been-Avoided.aspx

Proulx, G., & Fahy, R. R. (2003). Evacuation of the World Trade Center: What went right? *Proceedings of the CIB-CTBUH Conference on Tall Buildings, October 20–23 2003, Malaysia, CIB Publication No: 290.* Retrieved from http://citeseerx.ist.psu.edu/viewdoc/download?doi=10.1.1.58.824&rep=rep1&type=pdf

Seeger, M. W. (2006). Best practices in crisis communication: An expert panel process. *Journal of Applied Communication Research, 34*(3), 232–244.

Sellnow, D. D., Iverson, J. O., & Sellnow, T. L. (2017). The evolution of the operational earthquake forecasting (OEF) community of practice: The L'Aquila communication crisis as a triggering event for organizational renewal. *Journal of Applied Communication Research, 45*(2), 121–139.

Sellnow, D. D., Johannson, B., Sellnow, T. L., & Lane, D. R. (2018). Toward a global understanding of the effects of the IDEA model for designing instructional risk and crisis messages: A food contamination experiment in Sweden. *Journal of Contingencies and Crisis Management.* Published online. doi:10.1111/1468-5973.12234

Sellnow, D. D., Lane, D. R., Sellnow, T. L., & Littlefield, R. (2017). The IDEA model as a best practice for effective instructional risk and crisis communication. *Communication Studies, 68*, 552–567.

Sellnow, D. D., Limperos, A., Frisby, B., Spence, P., Sellnow, T., & Downs, E. (2015). Expanding the scope of instructional communication research: Looking beyond classroom contexts. *Communication Studies, 66*, 417–432.

Sellnow, D. D., & Sellnow, T. L. (2019). The IDEA model of effective instructional risk and crisis communication by emergency managers and other key spokespersons. *Journal of Emergency Management, 17*(1), pp. 67–78. doi:10.5055/jem.2017.0000

Sellnow, T. L., Parker, J. S., Sellnow, D. D., Littlefield, R. R., Helsel, E. M., Getchell, M. C., ... Merrill, S. C. (2017). Improving biosecurity through instructional crisis communication: Lessons learned from the PEDv outbreak. *Journal of Applied Communications, 101*(4). Advanced online publication. doi:10.4148/1051-0834.1298

Sellnow, T. L., & Seeger, M. W. (2001). Exploring the boundaries of crisis communication: The case of the 1997 Red River Valley flood. *Communication Studies, 52*, 153–167.

Sellnow, T. L., & Sellnow, D. (2010). The instructional dynamic of risk and crisis communication: Distinguishing instructional messages from dialogue. *The Review of Communication, 10*(2), 112–126.

Sellnow-Richmond, D. D., George, A. M., & Sellnow, D. D. (2018). An IDEA model analysis of instructional risk communication in the time of Ebola. *Journal of International Crisis and Risk Communication Research, 1*, 135–157.

Sitkin, S. B. (1996). Learning through failure: The strategy of small losses. In M. D. Cohen & S. S. Sproull (Eds.), *Organizational learning* (pp. 541–575). Thousand Oaks, CA: SAGE.

Stohl, C., & Cheney, G. (2001). Participatory processes/paradoxical practices: Communication and the dilemmas of organizational democracy. *Management Communication Quarterly, 14*(3), 349–407.

Ulmer, R. R., Sellnow, T. L., & Seeger, M.W. (2018). *Effective crisis communication: Moving from crisis to opportunity* (4th ed.). SAGE, CA: SAGE.

Venette, S. J. (2006). Special section introduction: Best practices in risk and crisis communication. *Journal of Applied Communication Research, 34*(3), 229–231.

Weick, K. E. (1993). The collapse of sensemaking in organizations: The Mann disaster. *Administrative Science Quarterly, 38*(4), 628–652.

Wenger, E. (2008). *Communities of practice: Learning, meaning, and identity*. New York, NY: Cambridge University Press.

Wootson, C. R., Jr. (2018, November 26). The deadliest, most destructive wildfire in California's history has finally been contained. *The Washington Post.* Retrieved from https://www.washingtonpost.com/nation/2018/11/25/camp-fire-deadliest-wild-fire-californias-history-has-been-contained/?utm_term=.39986bd9008e

Zillman, D. (1996). Exemplification theory: Judging the whole by some of its parts. *Media Psychology, 1*, 69–94.

Chapter 7
Communication Is ... Constitutive

Deanna L. Fassett
San José State University

Benny LeMaster
Arizona State University

Communication is constitutive, but what does that even mean?

B AKING OFFERS US A USEFUL GLIMPSE into what constitution may mean as a metaphor for communication. Regardless of what you choose to bake, you will inevitably combine ingredients and subject them to heat. Take, for example, cupcakes. You would likely include flour, eggs, flavorings, and, if you're feeling festive, decorations, like sweet frosting and rainbow sprinkles. Yet, if you were to pour all the ingredients into a bowl and stir the mixture together, you wouldn't have a cupcake. At least not one that you'd want to eat. There are steps to follow to mix the batter; followed by more steps to bake the batter in the oven, shaping the batter into cupcakes or a sheet cake or brownies or some other treat; and making sure it's cooked throughout. These are followed by still more steps for decorating what you've made. You have combined the ingredients, but they have become something more.

Sure, we don't usually say that we are "constituting cupcakes," but that is what's happening. Although we know that they're made of all those different component parts, the process of baking transforms those components into more than themselves, into something that can no longer be reduced to those elements. You could try to dry out the batter or crumble the cooked cake, but you could not extract the egg, at least not in its original form, as something precious you cracked over the mixing bowl. But constitution is more than just the *how* something (a cupcake, a relationship, a meaning) forms, it emerges from, nurtures, and becomes context—our cultural connections with one another. While some of you may enjoy baking from scratch for the sheer joy of it, and some of you may add a little sass to box cake mix, there is usually a reason for our baking, whether procrastination, a birthday party or a special holiday, or a particular someone who enjoys yummy foods. The reasons for our baking, like the reasons for our communication, are often inextricable from others' expectations and others' own communication. Take, for example, our assumptions about a baby shower: What sort of cupcakes are best to serve? And with what color will we dye the frosting? According to whom? Who decides?

Many of us rely on an understanding of communication that is fundamentally misleading, one that is linear and takes communication to consist of sending and receiving messages. Even our language reinforces this, as when we think of having to "get our point across" or feeling as though it is important to "think before you speak," as though thinking and languaging are separate processes. In these moments, we practice communication as representation, as an additive layer that enhances or confuses something that is "actual" or "real." While communication does do this—certainly the word "cupcake" isn't the same thing as the cupcake in the bakery window, nor does the word "cupcake" evoke the same image for each of us—to believe that is all communication is and does is not only misleading, but it is dangerously irresponsible at best, and, at worst, violent. Yes, the word "cupcake" can represent or stand in for the sweet frosted creation you may hold in your hand, but what about words like "democracy" or "justice" or even "woman"?

Communication, in the form of our most mundane and unreflective language practices, gives rise to, follows from, and reinforces our reality. Lakoff and Johnson's (2003) work offers us a helpful and practical example of how language is metaphorical (how humans inevitably make sense of one concept in terms of another, linking the unfamiliar to the familiar) and therefore constitutive of our social reality (making sense of one concept in terms of X often makes it difficult to understand that same concept in terms of Y or Z). They note pervasive Western understandings of argument as war (e.g., "I really had to fight to make my point," "I lost that argument") and how these shape speakers' and listeners' attitudes, behaviors and understandings with respect to conflict. Were we to describe conflicts in terms of choreography—as dance—then we would illuminate (and obfuscate or hide) different aspects of the experience of disagreement (e.g., as less of a battle to win or avoid, and more of a necessary collaboration that may be creative and even enjoyable).

Our communication with one another constitutes our own identities, our relationships with each other, as well as with other cultural groups and organizations. As such, an awareness of and a willingness to act on communication as constitutive challenges us all to engage communication (and engage *in* communication) in ways that are critical, consensual, and compassionate. This demands that we communicate reflexively, in an effort to understand ourselves as constituting others and ourselves in and through that communication. This insight has the potential to guide us toward mutuality, self-care, and interpersonal justice. On this point, we turn to Schrag's (1986/2003) communication philosophy, which helps us to frame communication as constitutive in reflexive terms. But first, we return to the context for our cupcakes ...

Earlier, we baked—constituted—cupcakes. However, cupcakes serve a broader purpose. Said differently, the cupcake itself serves broader communicative ends and, as such, constitutes cultural meaning. And when baked in service of a gender reveal party, cupcakes serve the communicative purpose of constituting a projected gendered sense of self onto a fetus based on genital morphology. Gender reveal parties are a contemporary Western cultural phenomenon emerging in the earlier part of the 21st century. The ritual is predicated on a Western medicalized gaze that categorizes body parts based on a phallocentric model of reproductive potential that presumes a non-trans experience for the fetus. While the medical industrial complex has long interpreted and disclosed a phallocentric reading of fetus genital morphology linked to gendered scripts (e.g., phallus = "boy"; no phallus = "girl") to hopeful parents, the shift to public rituals is what distinguishes a difference in cultural performance. And hence, the cupcake plays a communicative role buttressing medicalized interpretations of body parts. Moreover, Lugones (2010) frames gender as a "colonial imposition" that distinguishes European (White) men from European (White) women (p. 748). Unlike European "men" and "women," non-Europeans (e.g., savage, tribal, foreign, exotic outsiders) were sexed based on a presumed model of sexual dimorphism that informed a racist sense of reproductive and concomitant labor potential under racial capitalism. This is to say that "gender" was used to distinguish White men and from White women while "sex" was used to categorize non-White men from non-White women in terms of reproductive potential. And to put a still finer point on it: White supremacy undergirds binary gender, and the gender binary's function is to construct a normative ideal that distinguishes "good" White manhood from "good" White womanhood (binaohan, 2014; Snorton, 2017). Thus, the question of cupcake "appropriateness" has broader implications that far exceed the ritualized nonconsensual disclosure of sexed genitalia through the use of pink or blue frosting, filling, or batter. Indeed, cupcakes in a gender reveal party context communicate and, in turn, constitute broader cultural meaning, including codes of racialized gender expectation and intelligibility.

More than the words we use to communicate, Schrag (1986/2003) theorizes communication as the basis of and for subjectivity. In other words, communication constitutes our sense of self and that of others. More precisely, subjectivity emerges through thought, discourse, and action. Taken together, thought, discourse, and action comprise what Schrag terms the "space of communicative praxis." In this space, communication is a performative act *about* (thought) something and that is accomplished *by* (discourse) someone and *for* (action) someone. In the context of gender reveal parties, the cupcake is understood as a performative act *about* something (collectively celebrating the naming of a fetus as either "boy" or "girl") and that is accomplished *by* someone (colonial discourses animated through a medicalized gaze taken as authority) and *for* someone (the parents/family/community members who seek to contain gender potentiality). Schrag writes: "The being of the subject is an implicate of communicative praxis—not a foundation for it" (p. 142). Thus, we are implicated in and through our communication and, as a result, come to know who we are in relation to other(s). In this regard, communicators are intersubjective co-emergents such that a distinction between an "I" and a "you" is blurry at best as both parties rely on one another for their sense of self to emerge. The cupcake then serves the concurrent function of naming and thus delimiting the gender potentiality in both the fetus and that of the party attendees whose sense of gender is interpreted and limited through the same colonial imposition. Party attendees are at once projecting gendered meaning onto a fetus while affirming their own understanding of gender as a "natural, normal, neutral, or necessary" cultural ritual (Langellier as cited in Gingrich-Philbrook, 2010, p. 455).

The implications here are significant. In light of this insight, we are no longer using language as a tool to clarify our thoughts and intentions; instead, communication *creates* us. We continuously become in tension with one another, forged together in language at an elemental level. We do so, according to Schrag, situated in temporality or time, multiplicity or possibility, and embodiment or space.

First, temporality. In communicative praxis, the subject is understood as an "event of temporalization" (p. 146). Schrag takes each communicative utterance as innovative and rife with temporal insight as subjects draw on—in Aristotle's words—*the available means of persuasion* so as to meet a moment. Regardless of intent, however, the intersubjective co-emergent subject is implicated in and through the effect of their communication with a desire to shift and transform communicative conventions. As an event of temporalization, the co-emergent subject is announced in the "*living* present, coming from a past and projecting into a future. As such it is the enabling of repetition and anticipation, preservation and creation, conservation and invention" (p. 146). Let's imagine we have baked our cupcakes, and we have frosted them to align with the medicalized interpretation of genital morphology as either blue or pink. The significance of the cupcake frosting and the party decorations is informed by histories of gendered meaning; so, too, are the concomitant gendered life trajectories projected onto the fetus. The significance granted to the medicalized and colonial gaze is made meaningful only over the course of history in which medicalized assessments and diagnoses informed by trajectories of gendered colonial violences are privileged over a subjective sense of self. The cupcake emerges as a communicative utterance perpetuating historically significant communicative forms. Considering temporality in communicative praxis reveals the potential we have in intervening in the performative sedimentation of cultural meaning-making. Serving green cupcakes at the gender reveal party certainly resists compulsory renderings of gender as being either blue or pink. At the same time, however, the green cupcake is still made meaningful only because of the exclusivity of blue/pink as synecdoche of gender meaning. As synecdoche, the exclusivity of pink/blue come to represent—and thus delimit—the greater whole of gender. Still, this invites transformative potential: How else can a gender reveal party look or feel? What of the cupcakes? Do we abandon the ritual? What do we risk in forgoing the revealing of gender at all? How much control do "we" have over the sexing/gendering of a fetus when we consider the institutionalization of racialized gender as a core mechanism ordering education, religion, or employment? Understanding communication as constitutive, as communicative praxis, means working to recognize the oppressive and problematic communicative means we may draw on (perpetuation of colonial and medicalized discourses in this example) while reflexively working to shift and transform those same communicative conventions.

Second, multiplicity. In communicative praxis, the co-emergent subject is understood as multiple. Specifically, subjects embody multiple, often contradictory, identities and lived experiences. As a result, communication is as complicated as our intersubjective sense of self. In addition, the living present highlights the importance of context and, in turn, the multiplicitous communicative means co-emergent subjects may draw on in a given moment. To theorize subjects as multiple necessarily requires complex theorizing of identity. Here we may take the cupcake to be a communicative means that forces a universe of gender diversity into two distinct and mutually independent categories. Indeed, cupcakes in the context of a gender reveal party construct a gender trajectory that disallow for gender transition later in life. The utterance of the gender projects a lifetime: My child will be a boy/girl scout and I will be a den leader; my child will play baseball/gymnastics and I will coach; my child will be a doctor/nurse and they will make me proud; my child will have a boy/girl and they will make me a grandparent. In turn, and from the vantage of a trans person, the trajectory equally projects: My child will always and exclusively be either a boy/male/man or a girl/female/woman, and I do not have to plan otherwise. In this framework, trans subjects are confronted not only with their own gender sense of self that chafes against medicalized interpolation but also the temporal life trajectories cultural structures (i.e., familial, education, religious, medical, etc.) project and expect across time and space. Developing Schrag's philosophies, Pensoneau-Conway and Toyosaki (2011) suggest we "aim for descriptions and interpretations of the praxis-oriented subject in the actual context of subject performances" as opposed to one-dimensional attempts to define, and thus limit, a subject and/or the communicative means a subject draws on in a given moment (p. 384). In this way, "gender revealing" cupcakes constitute a sense of gender for a fetus that affirms the reduction of gender diversity into two unstable categories against which we are all forced to toil. Multiplicity encourages the exploration of racialized gender in terms we may not yet have access. What we do know is this: The cupcake can never fully capture gender meaning whether in discursive or material terms.

Third, embodiment, which includes space. Gestures provide a useful way to understand this idea. Gestures are physical enactments of culturally sedimented conventions. How we gesture or use our bodies communicates cultural conventions and meaning. This is where Schrag locates the "lived" space of communicative praxis where, "The bodily presence of the subject is announced through the expressivity of this complex of gestures and bodily bearing, which are themselves events of hermeneutical disclosure" (p. 153). The cupcake communicates gender, which, in turn, projects expectations of embodiment and comportment. The blue cupcake enables the "boy" to boldly explore *his* world. His sense of curiosity is often encouraged. He is taught to move through the world taking up space: spreading out on public transportation, speaking loudly and over women, offering unsolicited advice (e.g., "mansplaining"), for instance. The pink cupcake passifies the "girl," encouraging her to embrace the private sphere. Her emotions are tied to her body. Her sense of curiosity is held with suspicion as her predetermined path is bounded by a compulsory sense that reproduction is her highest (or perhaps exclusive) calling. The cupcake serves as communicative gesture that programs a cultural trajectory of racialized gendered meaning that effectively informs and shapes and thus delimits the embodied means by which the fetus might move through the world otherwise.

Taken together, Schrag's three dimensions provides a more nuanced and less violent understanding of communication—one that is grounded in understandings of communication as more than representation of the real, but constitution of what's real. The space of communicative praxis is a dynamic and shifting space that challenges us all to engage communication (and to engage *in* communication) in ways that are critical, consensual, and compassionate. The cupcake becomes so much more than flour and sugar and sprinkles; it becomes the means by which we become ourselves. To say communication is constitutive means we have the responsibility to explore a far more epistemologically and ontologically vital set of questions than whether we have chosen the right word to describe something: What communicative function does the cupcake serve, and to what degree do we want to participate in the perpetuation and/or challenging of compulsory framings of gender as both racialized and as exclusionary to gender diversity for trans and non-trans subjects alike? In what ways might the blue cupcake curb a "boy's" capacity to express emotions? In what ways might the pink cupcake curb a "girl's" capacity to explore math and science? In what ways do gendered cupcakes constitute the broader communicative apparatus of racialized gendered intelligibility and to what degree do we want to participate in its unquestioned maintenance?

References

binaohan, b. (2014). *decolonizing trans/gender 101*. Toronto, Canada: biyuti publishing.

Gingrich-Philbrook, C. (2010). Removed, and making do. *Text and Performance Quarterly, 30*(4), 453–455.

Lakoff, G., & Johnson, M. (2003). *Metaphors we live by* (2nd ed.). Chicago, IL: University of Chicago Press.

Lugones, M. (2010). Toward a decolonial feminism. *Hypatia, 25*(4), 742–759.

Snorton, C. R. (2017). *Black on both sides: A racial history of trans identity*. Minneapolis, MN: University of Minnesota Press.

Chapter 8

Communication Is ... Digital

Ahmet Atay
College of Wooster

It was 7:30 a.m. I woke to the digital sounds of my smartphone. I picked it up, quickly swiped right, and punched in my passcode to snooze the phone's alarm clock function. Instead of getting out of my warm bed, though, I stayed under the covers and grabbed my glasses to see if I had received any text messages or notifications while I was asleep. I glanced over some text messages as well as the messages sent through the Facebook Messenger and the notifications from a geolocation-based hookup application that I had forgotten to delete. I placed the phone on the nightstand before finally getting out of bed.

Once in my favorite armchair with my coffee, I began to look at my computer screen, reading the news and listening to a song from my favorite Swedish singer. As he hit the high notes, my phone began vibrating, indicating that I was receiving emails from my university account. I switched tabs and began reading the emails. Like so many other days, I began my day through digital communication. As I finished reading my emails, I switched tabs again to play the next song while I read the news from the BBC website.

I AM NOT A MILLENNIAL NOR CONSIDERED a "digital native," but I am a functional multitasker, effortlessly moving from one digital platform to another, living in only one domain or simultaneously functioning within multiple social network sites. Since I live alone with my lovely cat Plum, most of the time, my morning communication is limited to digital means. In fact, most of my communication with my family members, partner, and friends dispersed throughout the United States and the globe take place on multiple digital platforms. They are "digitally" present in my life, despite being physically absent. Our relationships are thus digitalized, and the aspects of my identity are digital as these people encounter me day in and day out in this digital ecosystem. Hence, in this chapter, I argue that a significant portion of our communication and everyday practices are digital or influenced by the digitalization of our society. To illustrate these points, I will first define the idea of the convergence culture in relation to digital communication. Second, I will discuss the ways in which digital communication is constructing our everyday lives and identities and how these lives and identities are digitalized. Finally, I will use my own narratives to illuminate these interrelated issues, thereby suggesting that our communication is increasingly digital.

Convergence Culture and Digital Communication

In his influential work, *Convergence Culture: Where Old and New Media Collide,* Henry Jenkins (2006) theorizes the different dimensions of "convergence culture" and explains the ways in which the convergence of media has shifted our understanding of media texts and products, production processes, consumption, and audiences. Furthermore, this newly emerged convergence culture is influencing how we communicate, consume mediated texts, engage in online communities, and construct and perform our cultural identities. Hence, understanding the various aspects of convergence culture is crucial for millennials and the members of Generation Z, also known as "digital natives" (Palfrey & Gasser, 2013; Parment, 2012; Faruk Tanyel et al., 2013), as well as for the rest of us who are digital arrivals but still heavily situated in this digital ecosystem. As millennials and the members of Generation Z have been born into this convergence culture, their media practices and the ways they live their everyday lives are widely influenced by this very idea of convergence. However, those of us who were not born into this digital culture but rather, like immigrants, arrived at it later in life are not exempt from the convergence culture's wide-reaching influence. Like those of digital natives, our everyday lives are also shaped by the digital culture around us. We use digital means to communicate, connect, and exist within a community.

Regardless of our generational divisions and sense of belonging, we are surrounded by and immersed in a digital ecosystem composed of traditional (legacy) media forms, computer technologies, the Internet, smartphones, cyberspace forums, digital platforms, social network sites, geolocation-based applications, immersive cyberspace experiences, robots that make our lives easier, and more. We live in a media-based and visual culture-based society where most of our experiences, in one way or another, are shaped, influenced, or enabled by digital technologies. We live in a highly digitalized culture.

Most of us, especially millennials and Generation Z members, at least in the United States, own a laptop, smartphone, or tablet (often we own all of these technological devices), and therefore spend a significant portion of our lives looking at screens. Perhaps more so, the members of these three generations—Generation Y, Millennial, and Generation Z— spend most of their waking moments using technological devices, and if they are not using them, they are surrounded by them. Most likely, even members of the older generations, including the baby boomers, are now spending more time communicating by digital means. We text message. We use our smartphones for quick media applications such as Snapchat, Twitter, or geolocation-based hook-up applications. We use our computers to engage in online social communities and write papers, reports, journal articles, books, or blog entries. We shop online and play video games, and we use the same technologies to watch films and television shows, listen to music, or simply "hang out" in cyberspace.

Perhaps because millennials are the digital natives, they spend more time and heavily rely on platforms of cyberspace to communicate, and their communication is increasingly digitalized. According to Jiang's (2018) Pew Research Center article, "Millennials Stand Out for Their Technology Use but Older Generations Also Embrace Digital Life,"

> More than nine-in-ten Millennials (92%) own smartphones, compared with 85% of Gen Xers (those who turn ages 38 to 53 this year), 67% of Baby Boomers (ages 54 to 72) and 30% of the Silent

Generation (ages 73 to 90), according to a new analysis of Pew Research Center data. Similarly, the vast majority of Millennials (85%) say they use social media. For instance, significantly larger shares of Millennials have adopted relatively new platforms such as Instagram (52%) and Snapchat (47%) than older generations have.

I must add that, similar to millennials—perhaps even more so—the members of Generation Z own a significant number of technological devices and spend more time than the members of the previous generations in communicating digitally.

Digitalization

Our communication is digital. Our culture is a highly visual one, and as a society we heavily depend on digital means to communicate locally, nationally, and globally. The digitalization of everyday life has changed or drastically altered our everyday events, activities, and communication. The expansion of computer and new media technologies and the increased use of online platforms and quick media applications, as well as the automatization of work has turned our basic communicative acts and practices into digital texts that can be eternally stored or preserved. Moreover, the expansion of the machines that operate electronically or digitally in our everyday lives, such as those that package our goods at the factory, the mowers that cut our grass, or the automatic floor cleaners that scoot around our houses, have mechanized or digitalized our interactions with one another, nature, and the goods around us. The same technologies, while improving our communication with others in global contexts, have also brought new issues and anxieties, such as the politics of self-presentation, surveillance in these domains, and a complete dependency on these machines to help us experience the world around us. In the following paragraphs, I will further discuss these issues. First, I will examine how new media technologies, cyber platforms, and quick media applications construct digital communities where digital communication is the key. Second, I will reflect on the ways we create and recreate identities on online domains and platforms. Finally, I will discuss how our presence in digital spaces and platforms shapes and influences our everyday interactions.

Not completely separate or unrelated, this digitalization in our everyday lives works along two veins. One is the digitalization of our communication through computer technologies, smartphones, social networking sites, online and quick media applications, and other digitally based forms. In this vein, we use these tools, technologies, and platforms to communicate with others, understand and represent our identities, cultivate and belong to different communities, and conduct our everyday lives. In the second vein, digitalization works in our favor by making our lives faster, allowing us to perform activities, or simply making our lives easier without our attendance or full participation. Hence, technological devices, robots, or other digitally operating machines replace us and our involvement in acts, performances, or events in which we would be otherwise involved. They make our lives easier or replace our presence.

To describe our relationships with new media technologies, computers, and other machines, Sherry Turkle (1998) writes, "We come to see ourselves differently as we catch sight of our images in the mirror of the machine" (p. 5). Turkle's statement supports the argument that the Internet, along with new media technologies, helps us to understand our identities and make sense of who we are. Although computer technologies and new media platforms have evolved, Turkle captures the essence of the computer, the Internet, and the other technologies in our lives. She postulates:

> At one level, the computer is a tool. It helps us write, keep track of our accounts, and communicate with others. Beyond this, the computer offers us both new models of mind and a new medium on which to project our ideas and fantasies. Most recently, the computer has become even more than tool and mirror: We are able to step through the looking glass. We are learning to live in virtual worlds. (p. 5)

In the last 20 years, a great deal has changed within technological domains, and our lives have become more digitalized due to the development of new devices, platforms, and machines that enable us to create more fantasies about our lives and new ways of representing ourselves and the others around us.

Digital Communities

One of the direct outcomes of the Internet and other computer technologies has been to enable users to create online or cyber communities. According to Steven Jones (1998), "In the physical world, community members must live together" (p. 4). He argues that this is not a requirement of online or cyber communities. Moreover, he claims that the issue of geography is crucial to understanding computer-mediated communication (CMC) and "the increasingly complicated relationship between mass communication, individuals, and new media technologies" (p. 6). The development of new media technologies, cyberspaces, social media platforms, and quick media applications has altered our ideas of geography by allowing us to communicate with people from all parts of the world through images and texts, both aurally and digitally, without requiring us to be physically present in the same location. Now people are maintaining long-distance relationships or keeping up with family members afar through these media. Furthermore, the same technologies have also reshaped our understandings of community by eliminating the necessity of physical connection or geographic proximity. These technologies also allow us to belong to more than one community and communicate with multiple members simultaneously. Jones writes:

> CMC not only structures social relations, it is the space within which the relations occur and the tool individuals use to enter that space. Consequently it is more than the context with which social relations occur (though it is that, too) for it is commented on and imaginatively constructed by symbolic processes initiated and maintained by individuals and groups, via software and hardware designed and modified by numerous people. (p. 12)

Hence, based on Jones' argument, I suggest that the spaces and communities we create and belong to within online domains are digitally created through software and hardware and enabled through satellite technologies. Therefore, not only the communities we belong to but also our communication with the communities' members are digital.

Most of us belong to more than one cyber-based community. For example, millennials, Generation Z members, and others, such as the digital arrivals like me, have an online presence on Facebook, but we also use Twitter, Snapchat, Instagram, geolocation-based quick media applications, dating or hook-up applications, and a number of other blogs or digital communities that exist on the Internet or through smartphone applications. We belong to multiple communities simultaneously. We may or may not know the members of these platforms with whom we share our digital spaces. Regardless, we communicate with them in order to cultivate a community or achieve a goal. Our communication is indeed digital.

I, for example, have a community composed of people I know on Facebook. This is the most convenient way to keep in touch with my friends who are dispersed around the world. Regretfully, I do not know their phone numbers, home addresses, and in some cases their personal email addresses, but I can communicate with them digitally through Facebook. I am also part of several other digital communities. For instance, for my research on queer geolocation-based quick media applications, I use a number of digital communities and access them with my smartphone's capabilities. Even though I have never met most of the people on these sites or applications in person, I nonetheless communicate with them. We are a part of a digital community, communicating digitally with our digital selves and digital others in digital spaces.

Digital Identities

The development of the Internet, new media technologies, multiple cyberspaces, online gaming platforms, social network sites, quick media applications, and other forms of digital communication and technologies began to offer new ways of cultivating communities, understanding the self in relation to others (even though the others might be digital others), constructing and performing our identities, and finally, representing and performing our cultural identities within different digital domains, platforms, and spaces. Due to these technologies, we started to engage in the creation of the digitalized versions of our identities. Sometimes, the way we present ourselves on online domains might reflect who we are in our offline and physical realities, and other times, these technologies allow us to perform the marginalized or oppressed aspects of our identities to empower ourselves and make sense of the power dynamics and cultural structures that limit us. Cyberspace and identity scholars such as Gajjala (2002, 2004, 2006), Jenkins (2006), boyd (2014), Ong (2017), and queer scholars such as myself (2015, 2018, 2019) have examined and theorized digitalized transnational and/or queer cultural identities and the ways these identities are presented or performed in varying digital spaces.

In these digital spaces, such as Facebook, Twitter, Tinder, blogs, or digital communities, we digitally present and perform our identities. We communicate with others through digital means or webcams. We also construct and understand who we are in relation to those with whom we digitally communicate on these domains and platforms. Hence, nowadays, we are always a mixture of our actual physical selves and our online selves. We are always partly digital.

I came to the queer social network sites to make sense of my identity and belong to a community. It was the spring of 2002 when I discovered Gay. com. At that time, I was a graduate student earning my master's degree. I went online with great hesitation to become a member, and once I had created my profile, I chose not to upload a photo. Unlike most of the other members, I was faceless. The lack of a photo holds great importance on social network sites, dating sites, and hook-up applications. Before getting to know someone, people often want to see the person with whom they are communicating. In the absence of a photo, the information I provided became the only dimension of my identity available to other users. Before coming out to the people around me, I wanted to talk with others who knew a bit about queer culture and surviving as a gay man in the middle of Iowa. To my surprise, I met dozens of people online. Our conversations and friendships were limited to the chatroom, and I never met them in person.

Like so many others, I was trying to make sense of my queer identity. Others might go online to understand who they are for many reasons. Regardless of our intentions and goals, we all come to social network sites, blogs, or other online domains not only to cultivate a community and meet with others but also to make sense of our identities, especially when the offline communities we belong to might discriminate against us or silence our experiences and voices in so many ways. These platforms and domains become the vehicles with which we make sense of who we are. They also allow us to represent the aspects of our identities in various ways. They give us a voice and spaces to belong to even though they are indeed commercial and part of the larger capitalistic media landscape. On these domains, we are digitally present. Our photos, profile information, and anything we willingly upload to our profiles construct a particular version of our identities. Our identities are indeed digitalized, existing in digital spaces.

Besides social network sites, we might also belong to a number of other cyber domains and digital platforms. On each, we represent ourselves with specific idea of the person we want to portray in mind. Hence, we perform who we are differently as we try to cultivate a community or an image on dating or hook-up sites, academic or professional networks, blogs that share our experiences, or quick media applications, such as Snapchat and Instagram. We represent who we are through limited words and strategically taken and uploaded photos. We present our identities digitally, and we make sense of the myriad of digitalized identities as we communicate with others.

Digital Lives

We are situated in a highly digitalized culture that attributes so much meaning and power to the images, digital texts, and platforms around us. We use and also depend on new media technologies, cyber domains, and digital platforms because of their widespread reach and invasion into every corner of our lives. So many aspects of our lives are digitalized, from the ways we communicate with others to how we shop, date, or even make sense of who we are in the world. As Henry Jenkins (2006) argues, we live in a convergence culture. For Jenkins (2006), "Media convergence is more than simply a technological shift" (p. 15), and he argues that convergence is not only a new state of being but also a shift in perspective. Increasingly, we are spending more time looking at different screens—television sets, laptops, tablets, smartphones, smartwatches, and all the others that are part of our everyday lives. Subsequently, our experiences are digitalized.

On any given day, I receive more than a hundred emails and dozens of text messages, and I send and receive messages on Facebook Messenger. Some days I tweet, and other days I talk to random strangers on multiple queer geolocation-based quick media applications. I regularly attend discussion boards on soap operas. I shop online. I check the weather and keep track of my steps for fitness purposes. I talk with my parents through Skype and with others on different online meeting or hangout applications. I watch television shows and sometimes read novels on my tablet or laptop. And sometimes, I just hang out online. I experience the world through my screens, and I am sure I am not the only one. We live in a highly digitalized convergence culture that makes shutting our connectivity down rather difficult or simply impossible.

Other aspects of our lives are equally digitalized. We teach in or work at highly wired classrooms or offices. We use automated checkout services at grocery stores or gas stations. We swipe our credit cards to use our digitalized money to purchase goods and services. We press or switch or click on so many other machines, often digitally operated, to make something or move something or just do something. We live highly digitalized lives. We live and communicate digitally.

Conclusion

Our communication is digital because we spend so much of our time working with the machines around us. A significant portion of our communication with others is through digital means. For example, I live alone, and if I do not leave my apartment, most of my communication with those either around me or in different geographic locations takes place through smartphones, emails, or online domains. Moreover, we belong to multiple online communities, represent ourselves on social network sites and other digital platforms, and make sense of who we are and where we belong through these cyber domains and digital platforms.

References

Atay, A. (2015). *Globalization's impact on cultural identity formation: Queer diasporic males on cyberspace.* Lanham, MD: Lexington Books.

Atay, A. (2018). Digital life writing: The failure of a diasporic, queer, blue Tinker Bell. *Interactions: Studies in Communication & Culture, 2*(1), 183–193.

Atay, A. (2019). Examination of transnational geolocation-based online dating and hook up application. In A. Atay & M. D'Silva (Eds.), *Mediated intercultural communication in a digital age.* New York, NY: Routledge.

boyd, d. (2014). *It is complicated: The social lives of networked teens.* New Haven: CT: Yale University Press.

Gajjala, R. (2002). An interrupted postcolonial/feminist cyberethnography: Complicity and resistance in the "cyberfield." *Feminist Media Studies, 2*(2), 177–193.

Gajjala, R. (2004). Negotiating cyberspace/negotiating RI. In A. Gonzales, M. Houston, & V. Chen (Eds.), *Our voices: Essays in culture, ethnicity, and communication* (pp. 82–91). Los Angeles, CA: Roxbury.

Gajjala, R. (2006). Cyberethnography: Reading South Asian digital diaspora. In K. Landzelius (Ed.), *Native on the net: Indigenous and diasporic peoples in the virtual age* (pp. 272–291). London, UK: Routledge.

Jiang, J. J. (2018, May 2). Millennials stand out for their technology use, but older generations also embrace digital life. Pew Research Center. Retrieved from http://www.pewresearch.org/fact-tank/2018/05/02/millennials-stand-out-for-their-technology-use-but-older-generations-also-embrace-digital-life/

Jones, S. G. (1998). Information, Internet, and community: Notes toward an understanding of community in the information age. In S. G. Jones (Ed.), *Cybersociety 2.0: Revisiting computer-mediated communication and community* (pp. 1–34). Thousand Oaks, CA: SAGE.

Ong, J. C. (2017). Queer cosmopolitanism in the disaster zone: 'My Grindr became the United Nations.' *International Communication Gazette, 79*(6–7), 656–673.

Palfrey, J., & Gasser, U. (2013). Born digital: Understanding the first generation of digital natives. In D. Hauge & S. Musser (Eds.), *The millennial generation* (pp. 35–42). Detroit, MI: Greenhaven Press.

Parment, A. (2012). *Generation Y in consumer and labor markets.* New York, NY: Routledge.

Tanyel, F., Stuart E. W., & Griffin, J. (2013). Have 'millennials' embraced digital advertising as they have embraced digital media? *Journal of Promotion Management, 19*, 652–673.

Turkle, S. (1998). Identity in the age of the Internet: Living in the MUD. In R. Holeton, *Composing cyberspace: Identity, community and knowledge in the electronic age* (pp. 5–11). Boston, MA: McGraw-Hill.

Chapter 9
Communication Is ... Media

Quaquilla Rhea Walker
Northern Arizona University

C OMMUNICATION IS "A FEW THINGS" ACCORDING to Peters (2006), and is constantly changing, especially with regards to developing technology (Dearing, 2006). Hence, communication is not only complicated, but also must have changed drastically since Aristotle's definition of communication as action. But this is not necessarily the case. Communication is still action. How different is a YouTube video from oral communication as defined in the first era of communication (Campbell, Martin, & Fabos, 2019)? Or, how different is texting on a smartphone from printing in the print era? Is the development of Facebook really any different in its impact on cultures than the development of the telegraph in the electronic era? Texting and Facebook are the types of media that are considered part of the digital era, and the "stuff" of this discussion explicating what is meant by "communication is media."

Campbell et al. (2019) define the four eras of communication as oral, print, electronic, and digital. Although overlapping McLuhan's five ages of media (as cited in Griffin, Ledbetter, & Sparks, 2019)—tribal, literate, print, electronic, and not quite digital—Campbell et al.'s eras more accurately express the influence of technology on communication. Further, McLuhan doesn't consider communication to be in the digital age based on his more symbolic definition of technology based on human history. Campbell et al.'s oral era is the spoken word of 1000 BCE, encompassing poets, teachers, and tribal storytellers. Emerging in the 15th century, the print era encompasses books, newspapers, and magazines. Starting about

1840, the electronic era includes communication by telegraph, radio, film, movies, and television. (The telegraph was discontinued in 2006.) Lastly, the current era, the digital era, starting about 1940, is made up of images, texts, and sounds converted into electronic signals of binary language and decoded back to original images for communication exchange. These eras frame the following discussion of the meaning of "communication is media" by using the humanness of communication in the oral era being pervasive throughout all of the other eras as technology is developed to communicate, and finally, redefining oral communication as its own form of technology.

I discuss how "communication is media" by dipping into Aristotle's action aspect of communication, or "techné" as Sterne (2006) argues, because it is applicable today, and then leaping into 1964 to McLuhan's salient quote: "the medium is the message." Much of the study of communication initiates with McLuhan's famous quote, which influences my discussion and has driven much research claiming that the technology or the medium controls the message exchange. But, in being true to my education and practice in math, science, and the social science of communication, I must argue for the continued salience of human influence on media. Humans not only create the media that they use to communicate, but also modify it as they use it to meet their needs in communicating. Ever-changing technology is the result of human ingenuity, and not a stagnant philosophical statement limited to a robotic use of technology to communicate. With the technology of Internet's Web now being in a 5.0 stage of development—read, write, execute, concurrent, symbiotic (Kambil, 2008)—media becomes more of a "sensory emotive space" expressing the human message rather than a medium that is exclusively controlling message exchange. I will develop my argument starting with Aristotle's techné moving on to the impact of McLuhan and media ecology on communication before looking at notable communication theories with an example of the not-so-future of "communication is media." Communication is media because the human influence in communicating with media is arguable, recognizable, and established in practice and theory.

Aristotle's Techné

Techné was defined by Aristotle as "practical art and practical knowledge" (Sterne, 2006, p. 21). Stern goes on to explain it as follows:

> First, techné is embodied knowledge, not formal or logical knowledge. Techné is meant to be distinguished from abstract knowledge ... the ability to play a song that rocks or to perform a masterful interpretation of Bach's cello etudes is a form of techné, because it demonstrates the unfolding of a sensibility. ... Thus, techné bridges the chasm between possibility and actuality ... Techné has, in our time, given way to two terms that designate some of the most important aspects of communication: technique and technology. (pp. 91–92)

Both terms, technique and technology, are further argued by Sterne to embody the uniqueness that humans bring to communication. He defines Aristotle's technique as a learned skill that implies communication as art in "subtle gestures of casual conversation ... hundreds of different techniques of empathy and avoidance, closeness and distance." He then defines Aristotle's technology historically as, "nothing more and nothing less than collectivized, amalgamated, and routinized techniques of communication," but currently having new social significance "associated with habits and practices ... structured by human practices so that they may, in turn, structure human practices" (pp. 93–95).

Techné includes the human element beyond just the physical technology by acknowledging that the artist who interprets Bach is also creating art. Or in other words, it allows for human action or intervention of choice in communication using technology beyond the demands of the technology itself. For example, as texting has become the choice of 18- to 22-year-old college students, they have changed their world culture to include it excluding other communication "technology," such as phone and email; and they often need to be educated on how to write effective email messages to professors or prompted by parents to call their grandparents. Professors may use all of the available technologies, changing their culture to encompass existing and newer technologies of communication. Both the students and professors have defined their own interaction with sending messages using technology much like Aristotle defined with techné, which is opposed to the limiting interpretation of the statement, "the medium is the message" (McLuhan, 1964, p. 6). Therefore, the statement "communication is media" can be understood through Aristotle's techné to include human influence in communicating as it is recognizable and arguable.

McLuhan and Media Ecology

Jumping ahead through the development of technologies in the print and electronic eras to the digital era and the computer, McLuhan initially stated that "the medium is the message," ignoring the human element so eloquently explained by Aristotle's techné (Sterne, 2006). McLuhan's insight is often the accepted perspective in the study of media and communication. Through McLuhan's broad sense of "medium," he explains that the light bulb is a demonstration of his concept because it has a social effect on how people create nighttime spaces, but without any content. "A light bulb creates an environment by its mere presence." (McLuhan, 1964, p. 8). Hence, people focus on the obvious, which is using the light bulb to have light at night, rather than the cultural implications of having extended light. What is McLuhan stating beyond this with his famous insight? First, it is a statement much like the historical term of technology in techné, which states, "nothing more and nothing less than collectivized, amalgamated, and routinized techniques of communication" (Sterne, 2006, p. 92). But then, it may also be an inquiry for further study of communication and media as he offers an explanation of this in his comment that "fish being entirely unaware of water" might need to understand water as well as themselves (Strate, 2017, p. 245). Lastly, it is not a final statement on the relationship between communication and media, but is more of a challenge to further explore the environment in which we communicate. Even McLuhan moves to a discussion of how older and newer media are intertwined.

Media ecology and other deterministic theories of communication are built upon McLuhan's insight, with the "medium" defined as communication media and the "message" defined as the communicative exchange. However, this discussion of "communication is media" begs for more than just a deterministic view of technological developments. Consider, further, a more constructivist perspective to understand communication and media, where humans use technology for a variety of personal and social ends and that they construct technology to achieve them. While technology comes in many forms and can influence many aspects of the message, it is chosen to be used by humans for effectiveness and efficiency (Walther, 2011). First proposed in social construction theory by Berger and Luckman (1966), Walther (2011) later posited how technology and humans interact in theories such as media richness theories and the information communication technology (ICT) succession theory. But before exploring these perspectives further, an understanding of media ecology is necessary.

Media ecology posits that communicative technologies shape not only our social relationships but also the history of our world in cultural behavior and thinking (Humphreys, 2016). Further, Humphreys argues that media ecology has developed to mean:

1. The medium can shape the message.
2. The older and newer media can affect new and different media.
    a. Newly invented media cast light onto older forms of media.
    b. Different media are interrelated in a social context.

When comparing this definition of media ecology to McLuhan's ideology, note the further softening of the deterministic perspective with the use of words and phrases such as: "can," "cast a light on," and "interrelated in a social context." In support of this softening, Strate (2017) introduces the concept of "technological evolution" as an important concept when discussing communication and media, introducing "evolutionary" concepts of humanness in understanding both. Nystrom and Postman further redefine media ecology as the study of communication media as systems of human perception, understanding, feeling, thought, value, and behavior with a focus on human survival. Again, they introduce the salience of the human in communication and media. Using the nascent state of media ecology as a field of thought about media and communication and the changes in evolution from McLuhan's famous insight, media's effect on communication is more accurately discussed using social construction theory, which holds that people play a critical role in shaping technology and adapting its uses and meaning to suit their own ends (Humphreys, 2016). The developing understanding, then, is that communication is intertwined with media, and humans assigning, at minimum, equal roles to communication and media in society and between humans. An associate of McLuhan's, John Culkin, proposed a corollary as early as 1967 to the statement "medium is the message" that is: "we shape our tools and thereafter they shape us"; or in other words, media are a major influence over the content that is communicated, but it is not necessarily the content (Strate, 2017). Therefore, the statement "communication is media" is understood to be influenced by humans beyond the control of technology because the human influence in communicating with media is arguable and related to theories.

Theory and Practice

As communication media was initially studied through the technologies of email and desktop computers in the digital era (Campbell et al., 2019), interpersonal theories of communication did not initially predict the impact of media richness or multiple uses of media in messaging (Walther, 2011). The initial interpersonal theories of computer-mediated communication predicted that the media would drive the message, much like McLuhan argued. Rooted in linear communication models, media effects theories, and cultural frameworks much like McLuhan's concept of the medium-and-message relationship, researchers posited that communication with technology was solely at the mercy of the technology and that it limited message exchange between humans, particularly with a decrease in nonverbal communication cues. However, over time and with usage of email and the subsequent explosion of social networking tools on smartphones, researchers found these original theories failing or at the very least needing to be enhanced and revised. Media richness and ICT succession theories are great examples of current theories applied by researchers to explain the practice of "communication is media."

For example, media richness theories (including social influence and channel expansion) posit that when a task is matched to the best media—based on the richness of the media—a more efficient message exchange transpires, and that as perceptions and experiences of the users change relative to the media even more effective communication occurs. Note the heavy influence of the human in this statement. Richness in communication media is defined based on the number of communication cues, the immediacy of communication interaction, the personalization of message, and the formality of the conversational language. These theories would identify face-to-face communication as the richest form of communication, because all verbal and nonverbal cues are present and it is immediate with a personalized conversational exchange. Email would be considered less rich because it is text based and missing nonverbal cues and immediacy, with a less personalized conversational message exchange. Matching a task, as the theory posits, requires a human being to want to communicate and to make a determination of the best media to use for the communication and then to use it. However, this choice may not always be the "richest" choice of media because another "less rich" choice may be better. For example, when a professor is limited by teaching a blended class—in/out classroom teaching mixed with online course management assignments—they might choose to communicate with students through an email blast rather than waiting to announce a course change in the next class meeting. Thus, the human being is choosing the media that is most effective and efficient for the message. In this example, the professor could choose to wait and orally announce the course change in the next class meeting, but that would cause a delay that might negatively affect student's planning coursework. The media is not choosing them, but only has an influence on their choices. Further, a person's perceptions about the media from social influences might change their decision on what media to use, and the person's experience of using the media might also change their decisions on what media they use. None of these actions are under the demands of the media to determine the communication of the message but are under the choice and supervision of the human as the user of the media. Obviously, the media has been created for certain types of messages and does shape those messages (including constraints of the tool), but only when chosen to be used by a human being. Media richness theories incorporate Aristotle's techné as well as the future direction expressed in McLuhan's ideology.

Next, the ICT succession theory states that multiple channels of communication (media) enhance message delivery and comprehension of the message. Again, this is a human choice about how to communicate driving the choices of media, although, media does have predetermined purposes and uses that may lead users to choose it. Whereas media richness theories focus on how rich, efficient, and effective the communication is with the choice of media, ICT succession theory suggests that more than one channel of communication need always be used for the most effective understanding of the message; again suggesting that humans make that choice. For example, a professor when lecturing might choose to also use PowerPoint/slides to provide a second form of communication beyond just their voice to enhance the understanding of the message by the students. This choice-making of human beings confuses and introduces a complexity to the original assumptions of McLuhan's famous statement capturing the intent of Aristotle's everlasting techné that society is a human product and communication is a human experience using media to communicate.

Co-creation is an excellent example of these two theories in practice, and further shows the practice of "communication is media." Co-creation is a current popular extension of social media that involves humans as active users; it is defined by Humphreys (2016) as "the audience [users] become[ing] especially active and begin[ing] to produce things of value (either to themselves or others)" in a participatory culture without remuneration (p. 64). It is the process through which consumers work with each other and/or with a company to produce something that has value for themselves or another. Co-creation is an example that shows the current human influence on messaging and technology. In this example, media richness theories come into play through use of the app Threadless, which is a socially acceptable app for buying T-shirts and known to the experienced user, Janie. ICT succession theory impacts Janie as she chooses to communicate with more than just Threadless for her T-shirt buying and design by running her decisions by the discussion board. Consider the following example from Humphreys (p. 63):

> Janie loves going to Threadless when she needs a basic, but cool
> T-shirt. After a few months on the site, she tries her hand at a

few designs. ... She posts a few early ones to a discussion board on the site to get some early feedback. There are a few duds, but there is one she particularly likes. After making a couple tweaks suggested by the community, she submits it to Threadless's ... grand prize competition alongside other t-shirt designs ... for a community vote. Overnight, there are 105 votes! For her! Elated, she eagerly agrees to have Threadless produce her shirt [despite not winning the competition]. ... After waiting a few weeks, Janie finally receives her shirt in the mail. It looks just as great as she imagines, ... and Threadless sells several hundreds more [of her] T-shirts. Janie reflects on the many hours she put into this design. Shouldn't she be getting paid for this?

Could you imagine such a co-creation of a piece of clothing in Aristotle's or even McLuhan's time? Aristotle probably had homespun clothing. McLuhan most likely went to a brick-and-mortar store to buy clothing. This is a valuable example of how human beings modify media to meet their intended message. Rather than a T-shirt on Threadless being modified by human users of technology, it can be a Wikipedia article, travel using Expedia, Facebook post, Instagram, participation in online communities, lead user interaction, user-generated content and funding, seeding on blogs, eWOM (Electronic Word Of Mouth), and/or user technical support (Humphreys, 2016). Users may produce content alone, with each other, or collaboratively with a company to produce social media. Co-creation is a strong example of the practice of humans changing technologies, and supports my argument that the medium is more than the message: humans shape media. This example of practice in co-creation and these two theories have not only led to an obvious redefining of communication media to include oral communication again, but also is an example of "communication is media" because the human influence on communicating with media is arguable, recognizable, and established in theory and practice.

Having discussed the eras of human communication tied to technology through Aristotle's techné, McLuhan's ideology, media ecology, interpersonal theories such as media richness and ICT succession, and current practice through an example of co-creation, "communication is media" arguably includes human influence on communicating through media. Because of the explosion of use of the Internet in 1990s, humans are well past early versions of the Web (Web 2.0) used in the first social media explosion in early 2000s into Web 5.0 development where we are able to move the Web from an emotionally flat environment to a space of rich interactions where the focus is the communication exchange void of concern about human or media origination of the message to focus on just the communication itself. Throughout all of the eras of new developments in the technology, the importance of the human being shaping the technology is present, further revolutionizing the original insight of McLuhan's "the medium is the message." Despite the limiting attempts of McLuhan, Media Ecologists, and early interpersonal scholars to understand developing technology and communication, and the humans using it, "communication is media" still acknowledges Aristotle's use of techné to identify human ingenuity and drive to go beyond the technology demands to create relevant, useful, and significant communication. Communication is media because the human influence in communicating with media is arguable, recognizable, and established in practice and theory.

Notably, the inclusion of oral communication in the current definition of technology-based communication is only further evidence that the human being is ever present in communication by any media.

References

Berger, C., & Luckmann, T. (1966). *The social construction of reality*. New York: NY: Doubleday.

Campbell, R., Martin, C., & Fabos, B. (2019). *Media and culture: An introduction to mass communication*. New York: NY: Bedford/St. Martin's.

Culkin, J. (1967). Each culture develops its own sense ratio to meet the demands of its environment. In G. Stern (Ed.), *McLuhan: Hot and cold* (pp. 49–57). New York, NY: New American Library.

Dearing, J. (2006) Diffusion. In G. Shepard, J. St. John, & T. Striphas (Eds.), *Communication as ...: Perspectives on theory* (pp. 174–179). Thousand Oaks, CA: SAGE.

Griffin, E., Ledbetter, A. M., & Sparks, G. (2019). *A first look at communication theory* (10th ed.). New York: NY: McGraw-Hill.

Humphreys, A. (2016). *Social media*. New York, NY: Oxford University Press.

Kambil, A. (2008). "What is your Web 5.0 strategy?" *Journal of Business Strategy*, *29*(6), 56–58.

McLuhan, M. (1964). *Understanding media*. New York, NY: McGraw-Hill.

Peters, J. (2006). Dissemination. In G. Shepard, J. St. John, & U. T. Striphas (Eds.), *Communication as ...: Perspectives on theory* (pp. 211–222). Thousand Oaks, CA: SAGE.

Postman, N. (2006). Media ecology education. *Explorations in Media Ecology*, *5*(1), 5–14.

Sterne, J. (2006). Techné. In G. Shepard, J. St. John, & T. Striphas (Eds.), *Communication as ...: Perspectives on theory* (pp. 91–98). Thousand Oaks, CA: SAGE.

Strate, L. (2017). Understanding the message of understanding media. *Atlantic Journal of Communication*, *24*(4), 244–254.

Walther, J. B. (2011). Theories of computer-mediated communication and interpersonal relations. In M. L. Knapp & J. A. Daly (Eds.), *The handbook of interpersonal communication* (4th ed., pp. 443–479). Thousand Oaks, CA: SAGE.

Chapter 10
Communication Is ... Production

Anji L. Phillips
Bradley University

Tony E. Adams
Bradley University

A S A VERB, "PRODUCTION" CAN REFER to processes of making, constructing, and creating; as a noun, it can refer to a performance, presentation, or a creative work. Production also can be understood in stages of "preproduction"—planning the details and execution of a production—and "postproduction"—a time for reflection, understanding, and altering a production for an audience. In this chapter, we discuss the concept and components of production in two communication contexts: interpersonal communication and media. Both contexts invoke novel ideas about what communication is, how communication happens, and why communication matters.

Communication Is Production: An Interpersonal Perspective

A mundane interaction between coworkers Jorge and Sara. When Jorge, a veteran employee, met Sara, a new employee, he assumed that she was a cisgender woman. In their first interaction, in a hallway on Sara's first day of work, Jorge greets Sara. "Hey," he says. "Welcome to the company!"

Jorge and Sara proceed to have a long conversation about the weather, previous employment, and her skills and desire to work for the company. Based on this initial conversation, Jorge perceived Sara as approachable and friendly, and he decided to inquire about her relationship status.

"Do you have a boyfriend?" Jorge asks.

"No," Sara replies.

A sufficient answer—Jorge trusted Sara and believed that she does not have a boyfriend. The conversation ends and he asks her to lunch the following week.

That evening Jorge logs on to Facebook, finds Sara's profile, and sends her a "friend request," which she quickly approves. Jorge reads her profile information—age, hometown, where she attended school, preferences for music and movies. In the relationship section, Jorge notices that Sara is in a relationship with (he assumes) a cisgender woman. Jorge feels frustrated: He assumed he asked Sara about her relationship status and she did not disclose her girlfriend/partner. He feels deceived by her withholding information about her relationship status and her sexuality.

At lunch the following week, Jorge mentions his frustration: "On Facebook, I noticed you're in a relationship with a (cisgender) woman. Why didn't you tell me about your girlfriend when I asked about your relationship?"

"You didn't ask about my relationship," Sara responds. "You asked if I had a 'boyfriend.' I don't have a boyfriend, so I said 'no.'"

Although Jorge did ask about a boyfriend specifically, he felt as though he was asking, generally, if Sara was in an intimate and meaningful relationship.

"Had you asked if I was 'in a relationship,'" Sara continues, "I would have mentioned my girlfriend. I also felt uncomfortable disclosing my relationship during my first week at work. Disclosing same-sex attraction is an act fraught with anxiety and fear, and I didn't know if you, or others, would judge me."

Jorge appreciated Sara's honesty, understood why she may not have easily offered information about her relationship, and recognized that she never told a lie; he had asked about a boyfriend, and she did not have one.

Preproduction in Interpersonal Communication

The "preproduction" characteristics of interaction include the presumptions, prior knowledge, tacit rules, and preconceived ideas a person has about a situation, as well as the planning and preparation that occurs before an interpersonal encounter. A person may consider what to (not) ask, what to (not) wear, past experiences, and future goals that inform the present encounter (e.g., maintaining cordial relationships). Further, the preproduction characteristics of interaction depend on how an interaction is punctuated—that is, where the interaction is perceived to begin and end (Watzlawick, Beavin, & Jackson, 1967).

The Jorge–Sara situation exhibits several preproduction characteristics. Jorge may have assumptions about workplace greetings, meeting new employees, about people being approachable and friendly, questions he can/should ask a new employee, and when it is appropriate to "friend request" someone on Facebook. There are gendered assumptions as well, with Jorge assuming that Sara is "cisgender" and "female," and the corresponding heterosexist assumption that cisgender females are attracted mostly to cisgender men, hence the "Do you have a boyfriend" question. As a new employee, Sara might assume she should try to make a good first impression and establish collegial workplace interactions. This assumption might involve having conversations with, and responding to questions from, other employees. Further, Sara may fear disclosing her sexuality and relationship too early in the workplace, as there could be consequences for disclosing same-sex attraction (Adams, 2011; McKenna-Buchanan, 2017).

Preproduction consists of the prior knowledge required for an interaction, and this knowledge can also be observed by considering "breaches" of everyday "decorum" (Garfinkel, 1967). For example, what if Jorge or Sara did not greet each other on their first encounter? What if Sara refused to respond to Jorge's greeting? What would Jorge ask, or how would Sara respond, if Sara was a cisgender man or a transgender woman? How did Jorge know the "safe" topics to discuss—why didn't Jorge first ask Sara about her medical history, finances, or political and religious beliefs? Prior knowledge can even be observed with language use and fluency. Why did Jorge use the phrase "Do you have a boyfriend?" instead of "Boyfriend have a you do?"

Preproduction in interaction can exist in other interpersonal encounters as well. We might call a friend to ask for a favor and strategize about how to best make the request. We might see a text or call from a parent and consider if and how to respond, as well as think about what response, from the other, we might desire.

Production in Interpersonal Communication

The "production" characteristics of interpersonal communication happen in contact itself; the face-to-face interaction, the letter received, the email exchanged, the Instagram post seen and (not) liked. In this stage, perspectives—"realities"—are made together, in contact and interaction. Talk produces realities; speech acts (see Butler, 1997). With the phrase, "I sentence you," the judge produces the reality for the criminal; the marriage becomes official when the reverend says, "I pronounce you spouses for life"; and when the doctor says, "You are pregnant" or "You have cancer," the diagnosis becomes real. Phatic communication—those everyday greetings, small talk, and chit-chat—can produce "an atmosphere of sociability and personal communion between people" (Žegarac & Clark, 1999, p. 328). We give reports of bad situations to the police in an attempt to produce ideas about what happened; we frown or cry to produce concern or worry in others; we may use a fancy dress or pleasing cologne in an attempt to produce esteemed feelings in others; and we seek to practice affirmative consent with sexual relations. We use words in this chapter to produce the idea that communication is production.[1]

Jorge used phatic communication to acknowledge Sara. Doing so can contribute to a collegial work environment, as well as build trust and respect. If Jorge did not acknowledge Sara, or if Sara did not respond to Jorge's initial greeting, their silences might "speak volumes" and produce a negative response. Imagine moving through a day refusing to great people, refusing to say "hello," refusing to make eye contact, refusing to address others when they address us. What might happen? What realities—productions—would occur? As Hyde (2005) writes, "positive acknowledgment"—making time and space for others—is a "moral thing to do" (p. 96).

With talk, Sara also produced the reality of not having a boyfriend and, for Jorge, suggested that she was not in a relationship. The relationship status on Sara's Facebook profile produced a different, contradictory

---

1   The premise that words and nonverbal acts create impressions for others and produce ideas about society is a core premise of key communication theories, including the social construction of reality (Berger & Luckmann, 1966), family systems theory (Yerby, 1995), and the coordinated management of meaning (Pearce, 2005).

reality for Jorge, and, at lunch, through talk, Jorge and Sara clarified misperceptions and produced new realities about the assumptions and limitations of Jorge's questions and Sara's relationship. Note we do not suggest that realities are correct or incorrect, but rather that should divergent, incorrect realities exist, we might want to engage in talk and action to remedy misperceptions and produce shared realities. As (present) interactions become the past, they may be referred to as productions (noun). Examples might include a parent telling a misbehaved child, "you sure put on a production," or we might describe an interaction (production) as a life-changing epiphany, a moment when, in an instance, life changes quickly, for example, being diagnosed with a disease, learning of a pregnancy, living through a car accident, sexual assault, or unexpected death.

Postproduction in Interpersonal Communication

The "postproduction" characteristics of interpersonal communication occur after an interaction (or after a particular moment in an interaction), after the face-to-face encounter, email exchange, or Instagram post that is seen and (not) liked. Such postproduction consists of various acts: reflection, reframing, and sense-making; attempting to understand why the other said and acted as they did; wondering, maybe regretting, why you did not say or act otherwise.

In the Jorge–Sara situation, postproduction can be noted in the following ways. After the first interaction, Jorge sent the coworker a Facebook friend request, an act that probably would not have happened if the initial interaction did not happen or if Jorge did not perceive Sara as friendly and collegial (impressions produced from the interaction). In hindsight, an aspect of postproduction, Jorge adheres to an assumption of trust, particularly when he believes Sara's response about not having a boyfriend.

After the lunch meeting (production), Jorge and Sara may have further reflected (postproduction) on their actions in their previous interaction (productions). For instance, if Jorge believed Sara's explanation about why she did not mention her partner, then he may recognize the gendered and heterosexist assumptions of such a question, assumptions he took into the initial meeting. He may learn that instead of asking "Do you have a boyfriend" (or "girlfriend"), he should have asked, "Are you dating anyone?" or "Are you partnered?" Jorge also might recognize that disclosing same-sex attraction could be an act fraught with anxiety and fear, something he did not consider when he first met Sara. Sara, too, might reflect on her role in the initial interaction. She might continue to reflect on when she should disclose her same-sex attraction and relationship. She may even understand how Jorge's question about a "boyfriend" was a general question about relationship status, and consequently how her "no" response to the question and then learning about her (same-sex) relationship could have been perceived as a lie.

If Jorge and Sara did not clarify her relationship status at the lunch meeting, Sara may not have realized Jorge's concern, or may have perceived Jorge as homophobic for assuming her heterosexuality. The next time someone, maybe another new coworker, asks about a "boyfriend," she also might recall this encounter with Jorge and call out another's problematic assumptions about gender and sexuality or respond that she has a partner. Conversely, if the lunch meeting did not happen, Jorge may have perceived Sara as secretive and manipulative for lying to him, which might affect his future interactions with her. Now, instead, Jorge may try to improve their relationship by trying to curb assessments of homophobia, heterosexism, and maybe even inappropriate romantic advances in the workplace. Further, if Jorge and Sara leave the lunch interaction satisfied, they may never mention the misunderstanding again. But if Jorge or Sara leave the interaction unsure, they may conjure additional questions and when to have the next meeting (preproduction).

Although we describe an interpersonal encounter in terms of preproduction, production, and postproduction, these "stages" are interrelated, fluid, and not fully distinct. In practice, all three can coexist in an interaction *as it happens*. If Jorge asks a question and Sara responds, Jorge might reflect on his question and her response (postproduction) and prepare for the next question or his response to her response (preproduction). What each person says and does, or chooses to not say or do (silence is action), can create (produce) new ideas about the situation and the relationship; there is always the present encounter (production), reflection on the past (postproduction), and preparation for what might happen next (preproduction).[2] Postproduction can be simultaneously preproduction, especially if a production, the interpersonal encounter, motivated new ways of thinking and behaving. Yet, separating these stages can allow us to understand the myriad factors that contribute to an interpersonal encounter.

Communication Is Production: A Media Perspective

A third interaction between coworkers Jorge and Sara. Jorge, embarrassed by his behavior, is thinking about how to try a fresh start with his new coworker. Similar to their first interaction, in a hallway on Sara's first day of work, Jorge greets Sara. "Hey," he says. "Welcome to the company!"

Sara looks at Jorge cautiously, trying to determine what he means.

"Have you ever played Six Degrees of Kevin Bacon[3]?" Jorge asks.

"Yes," Sara replies skeptically.

"Great! Would you want to play?" Jorge asks. "Honestly, I'm really embarrassed by my behavior, and I would like to start over if you're willing."

Sara thinks about how she would like to respond.

"Sarah Michelle Gellar," says Sara with a very serious face.

Jorge smiles.

Sara smiles back.

Think about a film you may have watched or know about: *Jaws* (1975), *Star Wars: The Empire Strikes Back* (1980), *Clerks* (1994), *Titanic* (1997), *Little Miss Sunshine* (2006), *Avatar* (2009), *Winter's Bone* (2010), *Black Panther* (2018). Do you think about where you were in your life at the time? Not

---

2   This circular and ongoing perspective of communication resembles the transactional model of communication, where feedback is constant and there are no definitive beginnings or endings to an encounter (Barnlund, 1970). However, the transaction model doesn't understand communication in terms of preparation (preproduction), making and creating (production), and reflecting and reframing (postproduction).

3   Six Degrees of Kevin Bacon (SDKB) is a trivia game based on the theory of six degrees of separation that posits that all people are connected within six social connections (degrees) to each other (Backstrom, Boldi, Rosa, Ugander, & Vigna, 2012). SDKB suggests that any actor can be connected to a movie starring Kevin Bacon within six degrees (Porter, 2017). The lower the "Bacon Number" the closer the connection (The Oracle of Bacon, n.d.). Bacon also created a charity called SixDegrees.org to support grassroots nonprofits due to the popularity of the game.

alive? School, work, relationships? Or, do you think about how these films made you feel? Happy, sad, scared, empathetic, sympathetic, or proud? Now, think about what narratives you may or may not have liked from a film; that is, are you #TeamEdward, #TeamJacob, or #TeamNoBitLit? What about films you have watched more than once, or may have only heard about, but have never watched? Maybe you shared films you like with someone to get to know them better.

Movies, music, books, and art have the ability to transport us through space and time. This time travel can provide historical context into the past, and possibilities into the future. We also have the ability to share experiences with our best friend, family members, a first date, someone whom we have never met, or even a coworker. We acquire these shared experiences through text, aural, and visual communication of love, loss, pride, and sorrow through the "lens" of media. This shared experience happens through storytelling (e.g., Burgess, 2007; Phillips, 2013). Communicating the story of life: the beginning, middle, and end is how, at a very basic level, we produce stories.

Preproduction in Media

Preproduction is not reserved for interpersonal communication or face-to-face interaction. When thinking about approaching an interaction, or creating a text, ideas are developed, assumptions are noted and shared, and our histories and experiences with content and technique inform how we approach and appreciate a project/production. Preproduction, in a media context, is the plan content creators follow to create a "product" to distribute to audiences. We create (preproduce, oftentimes in animation and special effects) media narratives from the bricolage of life, meaning we very literally cull and create stories (i.e., treatments, scripts, storyboards) from a wide range of lived or imagined experiences that we craft (produce/postproduce, oftentimes in live-action and digital effects) into stories that we hope our intended audience will want to consume (Rüling & Duymedjian, 2014; Wells, 2011). The challenges we face as creators are the many variables that constrain our desired outcome, which is to communicate (produce) a story that may resonate with an audience, or one where they find the production aesthetically pleasing, or a story where an audience member can relate, or maybe even use as a form of escapism from their everyday lives.[4] The meaning for each consumer of said media follows postproduction, and is polysemic in nature, meaning we cannot plan, during preproduction, for every possible interpretation of our "text" by the audience (Rockler, 2001; Tracy, 2001).

However, there are several factors associated with preproduction in media we can plan. Consider budget. Do we have enough money to make a feature film, or will we tell a story using independent film money? Consider audience. How will our intended/unintended audience access our content? Consider screen size and distribution. Are we planning a film, television, online web series, podcast? Will the screen size or distribution affect how we choose to tell our story from an aural or visual perspective? For example, a closer shot is better viewed on smaller screens, and panoramas are viewed better on larger screens (Barnwell, 2008; Zettl, 2017). All of these choices during preproduction can inform how future audiences interpret the production.

Also consider the communicative response from the audience through social media. As producers of media, we are no longer broadcasting, we are "nichecasting," which becomes interactional in itself, but not necessarily face to face. Broadcasting transitioned to narrowcasting, which was conceived early on as a comparison to "the electronic versions of selective mailings and subscription-only magazines" (Cushman & Cahn, 1985, p. 151). This transition was seen as a way to communicate "interpersonally" through technology. Gone was the traditional broadcast model of one to many. We now plan for multiplatform, multiscreen, audience demographics, and psychographics that impact the life of a project in an ever-faster studio-to-consumer model (Gunter, 2018). Preproduction is determining how to best communicate a living and dynamic process, which impacts how a story will be told. We account for script iterations, storyboarding, casting talent, and, of course, the budget (Barnwell, 2008; Cartwright, 2012). Preproduction is, therefore, communication of a multihuman plan working together to create the foundation for a story through production.

---

4   The idea that we use media for a variety of reasons, including escapism, is the basis of early media effects research, particularly uses and gratifications theory (McQuail, 2005; see also Ruggiero, 2009).

Production in Media

We can then view production as a noun, used in reference to the creation of a story. We read from books, we view art, we listen to stories, and we watch theatre and film productions. We also may experience a production, and we may either agree or disagree with the experience. The message we receive as an audience member may challenge our beliefs, provide a different account of experience, entertain us, allow us to escape, or make us angry. Think about films that challenged your ideas about religion, sexuality, love, families, or war. Regardless of your personal beliefs, you will most likely experience a reaction to a production. From this perspective, there is making, doing, arranging symbols to produce (communicate) an effect. Production, then, is the execution of the preproduction communication plan, which includes capturing/recording, at minimum, text, audio, and/or video using an aural and/or visual "grammar" that is known by the practitioner, and "known" by the audience through consistent employment of this grammar in storytelling (Meyrowitz, 1998).

Aural or visual grammar is an idea or way of producing a story that draws from traditional methods of media aesthetics that is inherently understood by audiences who consume the media; it is a way for storytellers to create and communicate meaning. Aural or visual grammar gives both the practitioner and the public the foundation that we put into words, a description, position, or critique of media content we create and consume. From a media practitioner perspective, we have a way of telling or presenting a story using established "rules" or "grammar" for the purpose of enhancing aural and/or visual appeal born from language we use in criticism of our work (Metallinos, 2009). From a consumer perspective, we decide certain content may appeal to us because we like the content (or not), because of (or regardless of) the aural or visual grammar used by the professional. Media aesthetics thus comprise the mutual agreement of the aural and visual grammar practitioners use to tell stories, and how audience members consume and make sense of these stories.[5] Further, refining the intended meaning becomes possible with postproduction.

---

5   Zettl (2017) offers a good primer on aesthetic theory as it relates to the fundamental understanding of how aspects such as lighting, color temperature, and audio contribute to film and television aesthetics in productions.

Postproduction in Media

The end. At least an attempt to provide closure to stories we tell. From a traditional media perspective, postproduction means finalizing the production. This might include editing text, audio, and/or video. Postproduction also includes packaging the media for distribution (Spohr, Clark, Higginbotham, & Bakhru, 2019). However, most filmmakers will tell you that they are never truly finished with a project. Filmmakers are just finished working on a project at one moment in time, or the story would never be "finished" for an audience. The open-ended nature of communicating a story aligns with life. A story we communicate is never finished; it just ends at that moment in time for those interacting with particular content. Similar to the difference between a "goodbye" and "so long": Goodbye may mean we never see that person again; so long (for now) provides the possibility of continuing the conversation at another time. The possibility of continuing the conversation about "finished" content, however, is easier than ever with the use of social media by both the content creator and the content consumer. Think about how a film has an open ending, without closure. Does this communicate a sequel, or just the continuation of the story at another time? Could this also mean that we as an audience get to imagine how we would like the story to end? Do we have interpersonal communication with our friends about "shared" meaning? Interactive fictions (productions) like a "choose your own adventure," gameplay like Dungeons and Dragons, certain graphic novels, or even written, aural, or visual fan fiction "texts" can offer multiple endings from which to choose (Cova & Garcia, 2015; Parrish, 2010). The audience then, becomes a "member" of the preproduction/production/postproduction team. The integration of the audience in the creation of the storyline in written, aural, and/or visual text blurs the line of content creator when each aspect of a traditional production ends.

Postproduction gives us the choice. The choice as an editor to craft the story, or to communicate particular meanings. The choice as an audience member to critique the choices of the director, or how we want to interpret a story (or even create our own story). We communicate by delivering our production to the world for the interpretation by others to question our choices, and we share our creation to soar, live, and fly, or falter, wither, and die. The dissection of our creative works is a sacrifice of our creativity. Postproduction becomes the postmortem of the story from the perspective of the audience. The end is then the determination by the audience whether our imbued meaning resonated or is reviled. Do two people who have never met have a shared communicative experience through the aural and visual grammar of production? Do they both feel? The same way? Was this feeling the intended communication from the director for the audience? These are primary questions (not always answered) of postproduction in media contexts.

Interpersonal/Media Communication Is Production

Interpersonal communication is production means preparing, making, and reflecting on the interconnectedness of interactions; thinking about how we prejudge or have preconceived ideas of a person or situation; recognizing beginnings, middles, and endings; and aiming to curtail or create particular meanings. As such, this perspective allows us to notice the ways we create realities together and how our re/actions contribute to others' re/actions. We might then take more responsibility for our communicative acts and have a different understanding for others' responses, thus motivating more productive and empathetic relations.

Media communication is production means exploring how art imitates life and life imitates art. The practical implications of thinking about communication in this way allows us to explore how creating and consuming mediated texts enables us to share and understand humanity through the gaze of someone else (i.e., the loss of a child, first kiss, winning a gold medal, experiences with racism). Having the ability to consume media that is either un/like us gives us the opportunity to learn to develop a shared understanding by experiencing, connecting, and communicating across, or in spite of, difference.

Collectively, communication is production because we use and engage pre/pro/postproductions. Producing communication is at the heart of how we tell/share stories regardless of whether the purpose is to have a conversation with a loved *one* (interpersonal) or to entertain *many* (media).

"Sarah Michelle Gellar, huh?" says Jorge.

"Yup." replies Sara.

"OK, Gellar starred with Bacon in *The Air I Breathe* (2007), for a Bacon number of one!" says Jorge.

"Well played, Jorge. It's nice to meet you." replies Sara.

Fin.

References

Adams, T. E. (2011). *Narrating the closet: An autoethnography of same-sex attraction.* New York, NY: Routledge.

Backstrom, L., Boldi, P., Rosa, M., Ugander, J., & Vigna, S. (2012). Four degrees of separation. *Proceedings of the 3rd Annual ACM Web Science Conference.* Evanston, IL: ACM. Retrieved from http://web.stanford.edu/~jugander/papers/websci12-fourdegrees.pdf

Bar-Anan, Y., Wilson, T. D., & Gilbert, D. T. (2009). The feeling of uncertainty intensifies affective reactions. *Emotion, 9*(1), 123–127. doi:10.1037/a0014607

Barnlund, D. C. (1970). A transactional model of communication. In K. K. Sereno and C. D. Mortensen (Eds.), *Foundations of communication theory* (pp. 83–92). New York, NY: Harper and Row.

Barnwell, J. (2008). *The fundamentals of filmmaking.* New York, NY: AVA Publishing.

Berger, P. L., & Luckmann, T. (1966). *The social construction of reality: A treatise in the sociology of knowledge.* New York, NY: Penguin.

Burgess, J. (2007). Hearing ordinary voices: Cultural studies, vernacular creativity and digital storytelling. *Continuum: Journal of Media and Cultural Studies, 20,* 201–214. doi:10.1080/10304310600641737

Butler, J. (2013). *Excitable speech: A politics of the performative.* New York, NY: Routledge.

Cartwright, S. (1996). *Pre-production planning for video, film, and multimedia.* Newton, MA: Focal Press.

Cova, F., & Garcia, A. (2015). The puzzle of multiple endings. *The Journal of Aesthetics and Art Criticism, 73,* 105–114. doi:10.1111/jaac.12163

Cushman, D. P., & Cahn, D. D., Jr. (1985). Telecommunication and interpersonal relationships. In D. P. Cushman & D. D. Cahn, Jr. (Eds.), *Communication in interpersonal relationships* (pp. 147–164). New York, NY: State University of New York Press.

Garfinkel, H. (1967). *Studies in ethnomethodology.* Englewood Cliffs, NJ: Prentice Hall.

Gunter, B. (2018). *Predicting movie success at the box office* [e-book]. New York, NY: Palgrave Macmillan. doi:10.1007/978-3-319-71803-3

Hyde, M. J. (2005). *The life-giving gift of acknowledgment.* Lafayette, IN: Purdue University Press.

McKenna-Buchanan, T. (2017). It's not all "one" story: A narrative exploration of heteronormativity at work. *Departures in Critical Qualitative Research, 6,* 11–29. doi:10.1525/dcqr.2017.6.1.11

McQuail, D. (2005). *McQuail's mass communication theory* (5th ed.). Thousand Oaks, CA: SAGE.

Metallinos, N. (2009). *Television aesthetics: Perceptual, cognitive, and compositional bases.* New Mahwah, NJ: Lawrence Erlbaum.

Meyrowitz, J. (1998). Multiple media literacies. *Journal of Communication, 48,* 96–108. doi:10.1111/j.1460-2466.1998.tb02740.x

Parrish, J. (2010). Back to the woods: Narrative revisions in New Moon fan fiction at Twilighted. In M. A. Click, J. S. Aubrey, & E. Behm-Morawitz (Eds.), *Bitten by Twilight: Youth culture, media, and the vampire franchise* (pp. 173–188). New York, NY: Peter Lang.

Pearce, W. B. (2005). The coordinated management of meaning (CMM). Theorizing about intercultural communication. In W. B. Gudykunst (Ed.), *Theorizing about intercultural communication* (pp. 35–54). Thousand Oaks, CA: SAGE.

Pettigrew, T. F., & Tropp, L. R. (2006). A meta-analytic test of intergroup contact theory. *Journal of Personality and Social Psychology, 90,* 751–783. doi:10.1037/0022-3514.90.5.751

Phillips, L. (2013). Storytelling as pedagogy. *Learning Literacy: The Middle Years, 21*(2), ii–iv. Retrieved from https://search.informit.com.au/documentSummary;dn=355892307046496;res=IELHSS

Porter, M. (2017, January 25). Mr. Kevin Bacon plays six degrees of Kevin Bacon. *YouTube.* Retrieved from https://youtu.be/Rmn-amJ9UA4

Rockler, N. R. (2001). A wall on the lesbian continuum: Polysemy and *Fried Green Tomatoes. Women's Studies in Communication, 24,* 90–106. doi:10.1080/07491409.2001.10162428

Ruggiero, T. E. (2009). Uses and gratifications theory in the 21st century. *Mass Communication and Society, 3,* 3–37. doi:10.1207/ S15327825MCS0301_02

Rüling, C. C., & Duymedjian, R. (2014). Digital bricolage: Resources and coordination in the production of digital visual effects. *Technological Forecasting and Social Change, 83,* 98–110. doi:10.1016/j.techfore.2013.05.003

SixDegrees.org. (n.d.). *What we do.* [About]. Retrieved from https://www.sixdegrees.org/about

Spohr, S. J., Clark, B., Higginbotham, D., & Bakhru, K. (2019). *The guide to managing post-production for film, TV and digital distribution* (3rd ed.). New York, NY: Routledge.

The Oracle of Bacon. (n.d.). *Sarah Michelle Gellar.* [Bacon Number]. Retrieved from https://oracleofbacon.org/movielinks.php?a=Kevin+Bacon&b=Sarah+Michelle+Gellar&use_role_types=1&rto=on

Tracy, J. F. (2001). Revisiting a polysemic text: The African American press's reception of *Gone With the Wind. Mass Communication and Society, 4,* 419–436. doi:10.1207/S15327825MCS0404_6

Watzlawick, P., Beavin Bavelas, J., & Jackson, D. D. (1967). *Pragmatics of human communication: A study of interactional patterns, pathologies and paradoxes*. New York, NY: W.W. Norton.

Wells, P. (2011). Boards, beats, binaries and bricolage: Approaches to the animation script. In J. Nelmes (Ed.), *Analysing the screenplay* (pp. 89–105). New York, NY: Routledge.

Yerby, J. (1995). Family systems theory reconsidered: Integrating social construction theory and dialectical process. *Communication Theory, 5*, 339–365. doi:10.1111/j.1468-2885.1995.tb00114.x

Žegarac, V., & Clark, B. (1999). Phatic interpretations and phatic communication. *Journal of Linguistics, 35*, 321–346. doi:10.1017/S0022226799007628

Zettl, H. (2017). *Sight, sound, motion: Applied media aesthetics* (8th ed.). Boston, MA: Cengage Learning.

Section 3

Appreciating

Chapter 11

Communication Is ... Consequential

Christina S. Beck
Ohio University

Communication as Consequential

My husband and I sat in small chairs near the teacher's desk, listening as she described our daughter's progress. A short distance away, our young elementary school student looked quietly at books in the room. Near the end of our discussion, I asked the teacher for ways that we could improve our daughter's reading comprehension, and the teacher responded with a comment that we possibly won't ever forget. "Well," she observed, "You shouldn't expect her to necessarily be as smart as her sisters."

I'm not sure how, but I managed to control my temper while affirming my daughter's intelligence and potential in a hushed voice before leaving the conference a short time later. Although I was shaken by the interaction, we weren't prepared for just how jarring that the teacher's statement had been for our little girl who, unfortunately, overheard it. She started referring to herself as "stupid," stopped trying to finish tests, and found any excuse to avoid books, puzzles, educational games, etc. After now years of intentional interventions and success in nontraditional and traditional learning environments, finally her confidence in academics has returned, to some extent. Sadly, even though it wasn't obviously meant for her ears, that one statement shattered how our daughter perceived her abilities, and, even though we've been doing whatever we can to pick up the pieces, it might well haunt her for the rest of her time in school—and beyond.

That moment during an otherwise ordinary and uneventful parent–teacher conference can truly be labeled as "consequential"; yet, in this chapter, I argue that communication is implicitly consequential, even when "ordinary" and "uneventful." Stuart Sigman titled his 1995 book, *The Consequentiality of Communication*, so the notion of communication as consequential is certainly not new. However, for reasons that I outline in this chapter, understanding communication as consequential has become increasingly important and complicated, not only for communication scholars but also beyond the academy.

I begin by revisiting classic communication texts that provide useful theoretical foundations for conceptualizing communication in this way, and I then explore the challenges of this perspective in light of contemporary communication in the postmodern era. I conclude by considering the usefulness of envisioning communication as consequential for serious societal problems such as bullying.

Conceptualizing Communication as Consequential

As the introductory example illustrates, three key principles underscore the consequentiality of communication. First, extending from arguments advanced by Watzlawick, Beavin, and Jackson (1967) more than 50 years ago, actions (and nonactions) that are available to others in any form are implicitly communicative, whether intended or not. Second, as Watzlawick et al. as well as Goffman (1959) and Burke (1967) affirmed, those observed actions (or nonactions) convey multiple concurrent messages. Third, as Sigman (1995) insightfully noted, those messages matter.

Communicative Nature of Actions/Nonactions

To borrow from *When Harry Met Sally* (a popular movie in the late 1980s), once performed (or not), actions (or nonactions) are "out there" and accessible to others for interpretation. As Watzlawick et al. (1967, p. 49) observed, "one cannot *not* communicate." Watzlawick et al. emphasized that "[a]ctivity or inactivity, words or silence all have message value: they influence others and those others, in turn, cannot *not* respond to these communications and are thus themselves communicating" (p. 49).

Returning to the introductory example, the teacher's statement was, obviously, communicative, even though not directly responsive to our query about strategies for improving reading comprehension. Moreover, even though she aimed the message for us, it also communicated something to the nonintended recipient. As Watzlawick et al. (1967, p. 49) clarified, "[n]either can we say that 'communication' only takes place when it is intentional, conscious, or successful, that is, when mutual understanding occurs." Indeed, we only realized that our daughter had heard and interpreted the teacher's statement nearly a month later as we sought to understand her subsequent comments and behaviors.

Importantly, we treated not only our daughter's "under-the-breath" negative comments but also her emergent passive and dismissive approaches to academic work as communicative, even if she might not have designed them as cries for help. Embracing this axiom of communication, as articulated by Watzlawick et al. (1967), expands our awareness of communication beyond the purposeful, overt, and direct to encompass the unspoken, indirect, and unintended. As I will describe later, this perspective permits us to understand the potential for communication to hurt as well as to help in social interactions.

Concurrent Messages

One of our family's favorite Christmas movies is *Christmas with the Kranks* (starring Tim Allen and Jamie Lee Curtis), chronicling the fictional story of a couple who decides to "skip Christmas" when their only daughter, Blair, joins the Peace Corps and doesn't plan to be home for the holidays. To the consternation of their disapproving neighbors and friends, the couple opts not to decorate, buy gifts, or host their traditional Christmas Eve party, instead spending their money on a cruise that leaves at noon on Christmas. Near the end of the movie, the unsuspecting daughter surprisingly decides to come home for Christmas, bringing her new fiancé. Not wanting to disappoint Blair, the couple scrambles to prepare their home and host the annual Christmas Eve party, with the help of their disgruntled neighbors and friends who decide not to "make the daughter suffer for the sins of the father," to quote one. At the festive gathering, the fiancé toasts his future in-laws. The guests look at Mr. Krank (still bitter over now having to miss the cruise due to Blair's unexpected visit), who remains silent. After an awkward pause, his wife offers a grateful toast to their guests and welcomes their new family member.

Certainly, individuals can choose not to celebrate a holiday or even give a toast, but, as noted in the previous section, we can't choose not to communicate. By announcing their decision to take a cruise instead of spending money on gifts and parties, the Kranks communicated. By opting to not decorate their home, the Kranks communicated, and, by refusing to respond to the fiancé's toast, Mr. Krank communicated in his silence.

Notably, actions and nonactions hold multiple potential concurrent messages more than simply the assertion of a decision or choice. As Watzlawick et al. (1967, p. 51) explained, "any communication implies a commitment and thereby defines the relationship." Thus, the "simple" act of the Kranks deciding to go on a cruise would likely have not been as problematic for the neighbors, friends, and coworkers as the unstated but implied relational message that also got sent simultaneously—"we care about us, not you." As Watzlawick et al. noted, "All such relationship statements are about one or several of the following assertions: 'This is how I see myself ... this is how I see you ... this is how I see you seeing me ...' and so forth in theoretically infinite regress" (p. 52).

By not decorating their home (as usual), the Kranks impacted the neighborhood's entry in the annual city decorating contest and reflexively implied a lack of commitment to their neighbors (who all decorated their homes, per tradition). By not hosting the party (as usual), the Kranks suggested different relational priorities than in the past. By not toasting the new fiancé (per societal expectations), Mr. Krank snubbed his future son-in-law in front of all of their guests, sending a direct relational message to him as well as presenting himself in a negative, insular, selfish light to the rest of the party attendees.

In addition to content and relational messages, as scholars who do work in ethnomethodology and conversation analysis have extensively articulated, our actions and nonactions also signify awareness of and reflexively reify interactional and social structures (see, for example, Boden & Zimmerman, 1991; Garfinkel, 1967). Garfinkel argued that "[n]ot only do members ... take that reflexivity for granted, but they recognize, demonstrate, and make observable for each other the rational character of their actual, and that means their occasional, practices while respecting that reflexivity as an unalterable and unavoidable condition of their inquiries" (p. 8). Moreover, Garfinkel noted that "by his accounting practices the member makes familiar, commonplace activities of everyday life recognizable *as* familiar, commonplace activities" (p. 9).

As we go through everyday life, we act as if our behaviors fit with "how things work here" in terms of conversational structures and, indeed, more macro features such as communities. As Boden and Zimmerman (1991) contended, "[s]tructure ... is accomplished in and through the moment-to-moment turn-taking procedures of everyday talk in both mundane and momentous settings of human discourse" (p. 17).

Although we take these practices for granted, when disrupted, others express surprise, confusion, frustration, etc. When Mr. Krank handed letters to his coworkers that outlined his choice to "skip Christmas," their mouths dropped, and his secretary bemoaned the fact that she would now "have to buy her own cheap perfume this Christmas." A neighbor responded to Mr. Krank's decision by recounting all of the time-honored community traditions, closing with "we do it for the kids." A group of carolers tried to make sense of the unlit Krank house, asking a neighbor, "Are they Jewish or something?" Upon hearing that the Kranks were going on a cruise instead of celebrating Christmas, the carolers expressed their dismay. When the fiancé offered his toast and Mr. Krank did not respond, others in the room treated the silence as an evident social shortcoming. Some guests looked down; others stared at him, and Mrs. Krank, realizing that her husband was not going to reply in kind and observing that a response was, most definitely, expected by the guests, returned the toast instead. Notably, in each of these cases, others treated the actions (or non-actions) as communicative and also as problematic—both relationally and structurally. Thus, utterances, silence, actions, and inaction implicitly become available to others for interpretation on multiple levels, holding the potential to inform, inspire, stifle, anger, and a host of other possible responses (which then also become available as messages to be interpreted).

The Impactful Nature of Communication

Thus far in this chapter I've articulated two examples—one personal and one fictional—but exemplars of communication impacting us individually, socially, relationally, and structurally emerge every day and, arguably, multiple times daily. In his book, *The Consequentiality of Communication*, Sigman (1995) asserted:

Communication is consequential both in the sense that it is the primary process engendering and constituting sociocultural reality, and, in the sense that, as it transpires, constraints on and affordances to people's behavior momentarily emerge. In this view, communication is not a neutral vehicle by which an external reality is communicated about, and by which factors of psychology, social structure, cultural norms, and the like are transmitted and are influential. The communication process: (a) exerts a role in the personal identities and self-concepts experiences by persons; (b) shapes the range of permissible and impermissible relationships between persons, and so produces a social structure; and (c) represents the process through which cultural values, beliefs, goals, and the like are formulated and lived. (p. 2)

Sigman (1995) began his book with the claim that "[c]ommunication matters" (p. 1), and it does so in a host of multifaceted, intertwined, and often conflicting ways. For example, Erving Goffman (1959, 1963a, 1963b, 1967, 1974, 1981) wrote about the implications of micro-level behaviors for presenting ourselves and interacting with others in varied social settings, underscoring that our choices and even unintentional blunders make a difference in how others perceive and treat us (and, likewise, how we position ourselves in relation to others).

Expanding the scope beyond interpersonal encounters, the ways in which stakeholders communicate about any number of important topics absolutely matters. Health communicators face the challenge of designing messages in ways that can enable individuals to understand and equip them to make informed decisions consistent with their values and traditions (see, for example, Hsieh, 2016; O'Hair, 2018; Singhal & Rogers, 1999, 2003; Thompson, Parrott, & Nussbaum, 2011). Community leaders navigate interactional, philosophical, and political obstacles in leading public conversations and striving to build community (see, for example, Black & Wiederhold, 2014; Shumow, 2015; Sprain & Black, 2018; Wolf, Black, Munz, & Okamoto, 2017). As individuals, communities, and, indeed, nations strive to live peacefully, productively, and proactively on this one planet (or not), we cannot underestimate the impact of communication or its consequentiality, especially as we reflect on this perspective of communication in the post-modern era (see Gergen, 1991, 1994).

Adding Another Layer of Complexity

In the opening pages of his book, *The Saturated Self*, Gergen (1991) described a bygone era:

> Recently I spoke with a neighbor who had just celebrated her hundredth birthday. She talked about her childhood, and the joys of a life based on a limited and unchanging set of relationships. As a child she knew virtually everyone she saw each day. Most relationships were carried out face to face, with visits to friends made on foot or by carriage. Calling cards were essential to signal one's intention for connection. She remembered her thrill when her father announced to the family that an apparatus called the telephone would soon be installed—now they would be able to talk to neighbors three blocks away without leaving the house. (p. 3)

As I've noted throughout this chapter, even "simple" face-to-face exchanges between individuals reflexively function rhetorically and relationally (see related arguments by Garfinkel, 1967; Goffman, 1959, 1963b, 1981; Watzlawick et al., 1967), regardless of an individual's intentions. However, as Gergen (1991) asserted, the blur of contemporary life contrasts sharply with the relative simplicity of a more modernist era. The Internet connects us to communities far beyond our local neighborhoods, forever complicating how we envision ourselves, relationships, work, "community," and, indeed, communication. Contemporary communication platforms bombard us daily as our phones "ding," alerting us to texts, emails, Snapchat messages, Instagram posts, tweets, Facebook posts, etc.

Amid the onslaught of messages and frenzy of contemporary life, we struggle to navigate multiple, varied, and perhaps competing online and face-to-face relationships and identities. Moreover, unlike Gergen's elderly neighbor, we might not stay in one physical location long enough to know others who live around us, let alone invest time in developing relationships (see also Putnam, 2000). As Gergen (1991, p. 182) explained, "social saturation and self-population throw traditions into disarray; committed forms of relationship become antiquated, and a multiplicity of partial relationships is favored."

In her book, *It's Complicated: The Social Lives of Networked Teens*, boyd (2014) quoted one of her teen participants:

> I can't really go see people in person. I can barely hang out with my friends on the weekend, let alone people I don't talk to as often. I'm so busy. I've got lots of homework, I'm busy with track, I've got a job ... If they go to a different school it's really hard and I don't exactly know where everyone lives ... so Facebook makes it a lot easier for me. (p. 20)

boyd noted that "[o]ver the past decade, social media has evolved from being an esoteric jumble of technologies to a set of sites and services that are at the heart of contemporary culture" (p. 6). Further, she explained that "[w]hat the drive-in was to teens in the 1950s and the mall in the 1980s, Facebook, texting, Twitter, instant messaging, and other social media are to teens now" (p. 20). As boyd articulated throughout this insightful volume, teens actively seek to be part of an increasingly "networked" world, and, in so doing, employ communication to present themselves and connect with others.

Although I'm obviously no longer a teen, I can kind of relate to boyd's young participant. Typical days involve fulfilling work commitments, transporting children to activities, ensuring that our girls do what they need to do with school, trying to keep the house clean enough, and putting food on the table (or in hands as we fly out of the door to one more commitment). We interact briefly with other adults at work, church, and our daughter's softball games before dashing to the next event on our calendar. In the evening, after everyone goes to bed, I allow myself a few minutes on Facebook, enabling me to connect with friends and get a taste of the "outside world," even if in cyberspace.

However, the massive and jumbled nature of that "outside world" can clutter, confuse, and confound quests to understand. When each message matters, and we get contradictory ones at an accelerating pace daily, how can we best respond? Myriad outlets compete for our attention, launching competing, often contradicting, messages into the onslaught of efforts to attract our attention. One scene from *Ralph Breaks the Internet: Wreck-It Ralph 2* depicts the plague of pesky (yet potentially profitable) "pop-ups" as Ralph and Vanellope (characters from a video game who are trying to earn some money on the Internet) learn about the pervasiveness (and persuasiveness) of links that pop up on our computers, striving to lure us to yet another place online. Each click, whether prompted by a tempting pop-up or our own curiosity, constitutes another consequential distraction.

The swirl of messages includes meta-communicative public labeling of still other messages (such as dubbing a report as "fake news" or "fact") by those who talk on television or radio or who post on social media. Such utterances work to monitor, silence, alert, empower, etc., depending on interpretations by diverse listeners and readers, especially as we juggle multiple competing social commitments (and diverse interpretations and concurrent relational consequences) when "simply" responding to a post or tweet.

Even if someone claims that "I didn't mean X as Y" (whether or not that claim holds true or false), the characterization of "X as Y" on Twitter, Facebook, Instagram, Snapchat, etc. plants "X" "out there" to be construed (see Ronson, 2015). Notably, the mediated storm brings multiple (and often divergent) interactional, relational, organizational, and/or political consequences as varied camps of vocal voices launch subsequent defenses of "X" and "Y" and spark reflections and reactions (even if not expressed publicly) by those impacted by "X" or "Y." The multiplicity of platforms for communicating and the rapid rate at which posts, tweets, texts, etc. get propelled into the public sphere foster re-tweeting, re-posting, and often re-framing, amending, commending, or critiquing.

Ronson (2015) told the following story in his book, *So You've Been Publicly Shamed*:

> A black woman had been trying to get her passport ... in Tel Aviv. She later reported on her Facebook page that a female official had refused to allow her to use a special fast lane for people with babies ... So she complained to the office manager, Ariel Runis, who rudely brushed her off ... Her Facebook post was shared seven thousand times. (p. 303)

In response, Ariel Runis wrote his own Facebook post. "Up until two days ago my life looked rosy," he wrote. "But each [Facebook share] is a sharpened arrow driven into my flesh. All my life's work has at once vanished, with the thrust of a word, disappeared. For years I have worked to make a name for myself, a name now synonymous with the vilest of terms—racism. This will be my fate from now on." He posted his message. Then he put a gun to his head. His body was found a few hours later. (p. 304)

Ronson (2015) concluded his book, underscoring the inherently consequential nature of communication in our networked world. He noted that

[w]e can lead good, ethical lives, but some bad phraseology in a tweet can overwhelm it all—even though we know that's not how we should define our fellow humans ... The great thing about social media was how it gave a voice to voiceless people. Let's not turn it into a world where the smartest way to survive is to go back to being voiceless. (p. 310)

Notably, even the social construction of someone as "voiceless" constitutes (and implicitly entails) communication (whether through online platforms or face-to-face interactions) with serious consequential implications.

The Consequentiality of Communication: Reflections on Bullying

Envisioning communication as consequential can be especially useful in understanding serious societal issues, such as bullying. Bullying behaviors (and responses to those behaviors by a host of stakeholders, including the target) clearly constitute communication (see West & Beck, 2019), and bullying behaviors as well as responses to bullying incidents could not be more consequential for all involved.

Whether on a playground, in a classroom or an office, or during a neighborhood or family gathering, derogatory utterances and actions hold the potential to hurt, with potentially tragic results (see, for example, Cowan

& Bochantin, 2019; Danielson & Youngvorst, 2019; Keashley, 2019; Myers, Kennedy-Lightsey, Anzur, Baker, & Pitts, 2019; Razzante, Tracy, & Orbe, 2019; Socha & Sadler, 2019; Tye-Williams, 2019). Opportunities to send messages exploded amid the emergence of the Internet and cell phone usage, and, with the ease and often anonymity of those platforms (such as Facebook, Twitter, Snapchat, Instagram), cyberbullying has escalated (see Dillon & Rhodes, 2019; Jones & Savage, 2019; Sumner, Brody, & Ramirez, Jr., 2019).

In 2014, as then Second Vice-President of the National Communication Association, I established the NCA Anti-Bullying Project, with the goals of bringing scholars together for research and advocacy (see https://www.natcom.org/advocacy-public-engagement/nca-anti-bullying-resource-bank). Notably, these scholars seek to understand communicative practices by the various participants in bullying incidents (such as those who have been targets, bullies, bystanders, advocates, educators, etc.).

Although tragic ramifications of bullying incidents absolutely merit attention, underscoring the consequentiality of communication by all involved, directly or indirectly, in bullying incidents and prevention efforts can be key to answering important questions. How can we best equip bystanders to most effectively intervene in bullying incidents and/or to provide social support to those who have been targeted (see related work by Jones & Savage, 2019)? What interactional resources can we provide to those who have been targeted that might best equip them for responding to bullying behaviors? How can we raise awareness about the consequentiality of what and how we post online? What else can we do to educate individuals about the power of their words and concurrent relational, moral, and ethical implications?

As scholars in the communication discipline continue to study these and other related aspects of bullying (as well as to develop and implement interventions and advocacy efforts), I'd like to close by emphasizing the importance of individuals and individual actions to inspire and enact social change. Just as one shove in a hallway can discourage someone, a smile can comfort. Just as one negative post can crush a recipient, a positive one can encourage. Just as one person can ignore another, someone else can reach out.

The officers of the National FFA referenced this potential when they chose the 2018 FFA National Convention theme—"Just One":

> Just One. One moment, one encounter, one opportunity is all it takes to radically change the course of our lives ... We hope to encourage members to take Just One risk. Just One step. Just One moment of courage. We are capable of shaping the future of agriculture, our homes, communities and the United States of America, when we believe in the power of Just One! (https:// convention.ffa.org/just-one/)

As part of his keynote address during the 2018 FFA Opening Session, Kyle Scheele linked the theme of "Just One" to bullying, stressing that "just one" can make a difference in someone else's life. Because all communication is consequential (including utterances that uplift and utterances that tear down), what we say empowers us to impact others with each and every one of our actions as well as each and every time that we choose to remain silent.

Conclusion

As I was finishing up this chapter, a friend shared an article on Facebook, "Virginia Study Finds Increased School Bullying in Areas That Voted for Trump." The article noted:

> Their findings could lend credence to the anecdotal reports from teachers around the country after the election, says Dorothy Espelage, a psychology professor at the University of Florida who researches bullying and school safety in middle and high schools. "Anybody that's in the schools is picking up on this," she says. "You don't have to be a psychologist or a sociologist to understand that if these conversations are happening on the TV and at the dinner table, that these kids will take this perspective and they're going to play out in the schools." (https://woub. org/2019/01/09/virginia-study-finds-increased-school-bullying-in-areas-that-voted-for-trump/?fbclid=IwAR25xRSKTEXJU7OZe8f_7cCNpPWQuYdJezNzMtByyj5z29UZGSOqgjofHYg)

Thinking that the article could be useful as I worked on this chapter, I shared it on my Facebook page, planning to return to it later. Within a few minutes, one of my Facebook friends commented, defending President Trump and critiquing the researchers' findings. Moments later, another friend responded, noting some of the president's actions and agreeing with the article. Even in posting an article on Facebook, inadvertently, I communicated something about my own beliefs, with potential implications for my relationships with friends with their own deeply held (and sometimes divergent) convictions.

Perhaps more than ever before, communication can be messy and controversial, but it is always consequential. Messages that we see on television, especially from influential figures, matter. Messages that we read on social media, especially from our friends and loved ones, matter. Messages that we hear in the workplace, classroom, living room, communities, etc. matter.

I began this chapter by recounting a difficult moment for one of my daughters. A teacher said something without ever intending it to impact her, but it did. Each day, we interact with others—checking out at the supermarket, giving feedback on a report, correcting our children, posting online, etc. Understanding communication as consequential enables us to realize the power of those moments for not only sharing information but also speaking volumes about who we are, who we want to be, and who we are in relation to others in our world.

References

Black, L. W., & Wiederhold, A. (2014). Discursive strategies of civil disagreement in public dialogue groups. *Journal of Applied Communication Research, 42*, 285–306.

Boden, D., & Zimmerman, D. (Eds.). (1991). *Talk and social structure: Studies in ethnomethodology and conversation analysis.* Berkeley, CA: University of California Press.

boyd, d. (2014). *It's complicated: The social lives of networked teens.* New Haven, CT: Yale University Press.

Cowan, R., & Bochantin, J. (2019). Understanding workplace bullying from two perspective: The case of the Persian Gulf and the United States. In R. West & C. S. Beck (Eds.), *The Routledge handbook of communication and bullying* (pp. 93–103). New York, NY: Routledge.

Danielson, C. M., & Youngvorst, L. J. (2019). To tell or not to tell: Bullied students' coping and supportive communicative processes. In R. West & C. S. Beck (Eds.), *The Routledge handbook of communication and bullying* (pp. 145–154). New York, NY: Routledge.

Dillon, K. P., & Rhodes, N. (2019). Defining cyberbullying: Analyzing audience reactions to anti-bullying public service announcements. In R. West & C. S. Beck (Eds.), *The Routledge handbook of communication and bullying* (pp. 221–229). New York, NY: Routledge.

Garfinkel, H. (1967). *Studies in ethnomethodology*. Englewood Cliffs, NJ: Prentice Hall.

Gergen, K. (1991). *The saturated self: Dilemmas of identity in contemporary life*. New York, NY: Basic Books.

Gergen, K. (1994). *Realities and relationships: Soundings in social construction*. Cambridge, MA: Harvard University Press.

Goffman, E. (1959). *The presentation of self in everyday life*. New York, NY: Anchor Books.

Goffman, E. (1963a). *Behavior in public places: Notes on the social organization of gathering*. New York, NY: Free Press of Glencoe.

Goffman, E. (1963b). *Stigma: Notes on the management of spoiled identity*. Englewood Cliffs, NJ: Prentice Hall.

Goffman, E. (1967). *Interaction ritual: Essays on face-to-face behavior*. New York, NY: Pantheon Books.

Goffman, E. (1974). *Frame analysis: An essay on the organization of experience*. Cambridge, MA: Harvard University Press.

Goffman, E. (1981). *Forms of talk*. Philadelphia, PA: University of Pennsylvania Press.

Hsieh, E. (2016). *Bilingual health communication: Working with interpreters in cross-cultural care*. New York, NY: Routledge.

Jones, S. E., & Savage, M. W. (2019). Examining cyberbullying: Bystander behavior. In R. West & C. S. Beck (Eds.), *The Routledge handbook of communication and bullying* (pp. 230–240). New York, NY: Routledge.

Keashley, L. (2019). Bullying in seniors' communities: What's identity got to do with it? In R. West & C. S. Beck (Eds.), *The Routledge handbook of communication and bullying* (pp. 210–218). New York, NY: Routledge.

Myers, S. A., Kennedy-Lightsey, C. D., Anzur, C., Baker, J. P., & Pitts, S. (2019). Verbal aggressiveness as bullying in the emerging adult sibling relationship. In R. West & C. S. Beck (Eds.), *The Routledge handbook of communication and bullying* (pp. 198–209). New York, NY: Routledge.

O'Hair, D. (Ed.). (2018). *Risk and health communication in an evolving media environment*. New York, NY: Routledge.

Putnam, R. (2000). *Bowling alone: The collapse and revival of American community*. New York, NY: Simon & Schuster.

Razzante, R. J., Tracy, S. J., & Orbe, M. P. (2019). How dominant group members can transform workplace bullying. In R. West & C. S. Beck (Eds.), *The Routledge handbook of communication and bullying* (pp. 46–56). New York, NY: Routledge.

Ronson, J. (2015). *So you've been publicly shamed*. New York, NY: Riverhead Books.

Shumow, M. (Ed.) (2015). *Mediated communities: Civic voices, empowerment, and media literacy in the digital era*. New York, NY: Peter Lang.

Sigman, S. (Ed.) (1995). *The consequentiality of communication*. Hillsdale, NJ: Lawrence Erlbaum.

Singhal, A., & Rogers, E. (1999). *Entertainment-education: A communication strategy for social change*. Mahwah, NJ: Lawrence Erlbaum.

Singhal, A., & Rogers, E. (2003). *Combatting AIDS: Communication strategies in action*. Thousand Oaks, CA: SAGE.

Socha, T. J., & Sadler, R. (2019). A look at bullying communication in early childhood: Towards a lifespan development model. In R. West & C. S. Beck (Eds.), *The Routledge handbook of communication and bullying* (pp. 188–197). New York, NY: Routledge.

Sprain, L., & Black, L. W. (2018). Deliberative moments: Understanding deliberation as interactional accomplishment. *Western Journal of Communication, 82*, 336–355. doi: 10.1080/10570314.2017.1347275

Sumner, E. M., Brody, N., & Ramirez, A., Jr. (2019). Textual harassment as a form of bullying, drama, and obsessive relational intrusion. In R. West & C. S. Beck (Eds.), *The Routledge handbook of communication and bullying* (pp. 241–252). New York, NY: Routledge.

Thompson, T., Parrott, R., & Nussbaum, J. (Eds.). (2011). *Routledge handbook of health communication* (2nd ed.). New York, NY: Routledge.

Tye-Williams, S. (2019). Disciplining the office: The past, present, and future of communication research on bullying. In R. West & C. S. Beck (Eds.), *The Routledge handbook of communication and bullying* (pp. 73–80). New York, NY: Routledge.

Watzlawick, P., Beavin, J. H., & Jackson, D. D. (1967). *Pragmatics of human communication: A study of interactional patterns, pathologies, and paradoxes*. New York, NY: W. W. Norton.

West, R., & Beck, C. S. (Eds.). (2019). *The Routledge handbook of communication and bullying*. New York, NY: Routledge.

Wolfe, A., Black, L. W., Munz, S., & Okamoto, K. (2017). (Dis)Engagement and everyday democracy in stigmatized places: Addressing brain drain in the rural United States. *Western Journal of Communication, 81*, 168–187. doi:10.1080/10570314.2016.1236980

Chapter 12
Communication Is ... A Gift

Stephanie L. Young
University of Southern Indiana

*You offer a very clever, original, and insightful model here. It really
helps you explicate and integrate various aspects of communication.
You write well—clearly and cogently. And, it's clear that you have a
good understanding of class readings. Very well done!*

I REREAD THESE WORDS SCRAWLED ACROSS MY paper, in a professor's almost
indecipherable handwriting. Fifteen years ago. An eight-page essay.
On the surface, it sounded like a simple assignment—to create a general
model of communication. But as an undergraduate, this was a daunting
task. How does one go about explaining the nature of human communication and how communication works?

I remember now. How after much contemplation, I decided to write
about communication utilizing a gift-exchange metaphor. "I highly rec-
ommend you don't use metaphors for this paper," my professor scolded me,
with his deep, booming voice, in front of my peers. I remember now. How
his terse response made me feel belittled, disappointed, and embarrassed.

Clever, original, and insightful. I reread his comments scribbled across
that paper. What if I hadn't been stubborn? What if I hadn't believed in
myself? I shake my head in wonderment. Fifteen years later. And now
I am a professor who often scribbles illegibly on students' papers. And
I have learned how our words matter. How we communicate with one
another matters. And how sometimes those who challenge us, teach us.

Dr. Burleson gave me an opportunity, a gift, to be resolute. And I have never forgotten that class.

As Jeffrey St. John (2006) once wrote, communication is about failure. Failure, as he points out, is "a lived communicative experience, one both raw and unpredictable in its interpersonal effects" (p. 250). He discusses the huge chasm between our ideals for communication and the reality that the communicative process is an imperfect one. And he notes how examining our failed attempts at communication can provide us with a better understanding of communication.

While I agree with St. John, particularly with the key role of imagination in relation to failure and how imagination "plays in transforming our unreal encounters with unreal failure into rhetorical resources serviceable for our real grapplings with real failure" (p. 255), I am more of an optimist. In a world that seems to value greed, power, and hate, we must find ways for communication to cultivate empathy, kindness, and human dignity. We must consider communication as a creative, constructive entity that has the potential for connecting and *communing* with others.

Our ability to communicate is a gift. It is a fundamental essence of who we are as human beings. We coexist in symbolic systems of meaning. We are born into our families and cultures and societies, learning how to speak and language ourselves into being. And while our words, experiences, and knowledge enrich us, they also can be our "terministic screens," as Kenneth Burke argues, limiting how we see and understand the world around us. This is why we interpret messages differently, how our perceptions can be so vastly different from one another. And this is why often there is miscommunication between and among individuals—misspoken words and misinterpretations, misgivings and missed opportunities.

Yet, even in the struggle to connect with one another, there is hope. Even in failed, faltered, miscommunication, there is an opportunity, a gift if you will, for learning, for understanding, for communing, for change. Therefore, I view communication as an act of gift giving. Communication is a gift, and theorizing it as such reminds us about the *possibilities* of communication and its altruistic capacities.

What does conceptualizing communication as a gift look like? How can a gift metaphor as a theoretical framework help us to better understand communication? Let's start with this idea of gift giving. Much anthropological and sociological research has explored gift giving within social relations (Levi-Strauss, 1949/1969; Mauss, 1923/1989), the symbolic meaning of gifts (Ekeh, 1974; Zhang & Epley, 2012), and a social exchange model of gifting (Nye, 1978). There are norms of reciprocity that guide the mutual exchange within relationships (Gouldner, 1973). According to Mauss, gift-exchange economies view gifts as obligatory—there is an obligation for the give receiver to repay the gift. For example, Aktipis, Cronk, and de Aguiar (2011) examine the gift-giving rules of the Maasai, Joy (2001) explores the implications of gift giving among Hong Kong Chinese, and Lawler, Yoon, Baker, and Large (1994) look at the relationship between mutual dependence and gift giving. As Komter and Vollebergh (1997) note, "gift giving is the cement of social relationships" (p. 747).

Philosophers, too, have critically examined giving—from Nietzsche's (1999/1911) gift-giving virtue (see also White, 2016) to Derrida's (1992) paradox of the gift (see also Johnstone, 2004; Neil, 2010). According to Richard White, a central theme to Frederick Nietzsche's (1999/1911) *Thus Spoke Zarathustra* is the gift-giving virtue, a "generosity of spirit" (p. 357), that "involves giving oneself rather than money or things" (p. 356). It is a virtue because "whatever is given is given freely and without the expectation of any kind of return" (p. 356).

Furthermore, Derrida (1992) questions if it is possible to give without entering into an exchange model of repayment and debt. Is giving truly possible? As Neil (2010) explains, crucial to Derridean analysis of gift giving is "the notion of *purity of intention* [emphasis added]" for "a gift to be truly genuine it must reside beyond any mere self-interest or calculative reasoning and outside of the oppositional demands of giving and taking" (p. 230). Derrida, ultimately, argues that there are no genuine gifts for gifting as gifts always exist within the cycle of giving and taking.

Indeed, there is a dark side to gift giving that involves power, money, obligation, and coercion. For example, Hyun, Park, and Park (2016) critically examined the gift-giving motivations of individuals in romantic relationships, noting that individuals who are more narcissistic use gift giving as a tool for relationship maintenance and power. And Garber (2014) argues that the term "gifting" evokes a commercialization of the act of gift giving, for "it takes one of the purest expressions of generosity humans have—the gift—and turns it into something transactional." Gifting is "associated with obligatory transactionalism."

But *ideally*, a gift is a thing given willingly without payment. As Schulze (2017) argues, gift giving is about,

> engendering gratefulness even when they are not exactly what we wanted. We tend to be thankful enough to accept a gift because of the generosity of the giver. We don't just study the gift. We don't question the motive of the giver—at least not usually. Instead we celebrate the gift and, if appropriate, use it well in order to recip-rocate by honoring the giver.

Giving a gift means thinking about the other person, attempting to understand them in a way to bring them joy. And receiving a gift means accepting the other's offering. Oftentimes, gifts are exchanged during particular holidays, to celebrate, to commemorate, to honor. We have gifts for all occasions—from birthdays to funerals to graduations. To be a competent gift giver (communicator), one must know what type of gift to give to the receiving party. What gift is appropriate for the situation? One would not give a bottle of wine to a pregnant mother at a baby shower. Situational appropriateness is necessary. Even the ancient Greeks recognized the concept of *kairos* and the rhetorical situation—saying the right thing at the right time. Therefore, "person-centered messages take into account and adapt to the subjective, emotional, and relational aspects of communicative contexts" (Burleson, 2007, p. 113).

So, to be communicatively competent—the ability to communicate effectively—we must continuously strive to craft our communication, our message "gift," to the needs of the other. And this requires a "socio-linguistic competence" or "knowing how to use and interpret expressions in socially correct and appropriate ways" (Burleson, 2007, p. 107). We are each "gift givers" and "gift receivers" who construct and interpret messages within sociocultural contexts in an attempt to connect with others.

However, we need to go beyond this simplistic giver–receiver model and view communication as gift as a starting point for exploring ways in which we cultivate relationships. Rather than viewing giving within a framework of gift economies, as a type cultural ritual, or as a philosophical conundrum,

Weiner (1992) develops the idea of the "spirit of the gift" in terms of "the paradox of keeping-while-giving" (p. x). She argues that for the symbolic nature of gifting, "there are possessions that are imbued with the intrinsic and ineffable identities of their owners which are not easy to give away" (p. 6).

Communication scholars need to consider how this "spirit of the gift" can be an uplifting approach toward understanding communication and communication theory. Specifically, how does communication as gifting involve the reciprocity of self and other, not as an exchange, but, rather, within a logic of charity? This logic of charity can be found in Gregory Shepherd's (2006) idea of communication as transcendence, a relational ontology in which "communication is the mutual giving of selves," a "being-together" (p. 25). For example, Shepherd explains how communication involves interdependence and the gift of self, for

> Without your gift of self, others will miss the opportunity to expand their senses of self. Without your gift of self, the potential sense of community that lies waiting to be accomplished will always be limited. Without your gift of self, we will all be smaller, less than we could have been. (p. 27)

Communication, then, is a gift that includes reciprocity of communing with one another. Drawing upon the lyrics for the famous rock band U2's song "With or Without You," Rawlins (2014) further emphasizes this "willingness to gift oneself and enter into relation with others" (p. 80). Communication as gift means risk, an opportunity to be truly vulnerable with another soul. It means communing with others—being with, identifying with, empathizing with—and becoming something more. It means creating a world in which we give ourselves away.

However, communication is a co-constructive phenomenon of relationality, one with the inherent risk of rejection. If it is a gift that can be given, it may not always be returned with generosity. Sometimes, we may have good intentions, but our communicative gesture is dismissed, misinterpreted, or ignored. Sometimes, we are denied the opportunity to be with and commune with others. And sometimes, communication is not always of good will—humans can manipulate, intimidate, threaten, coerce, and torment each other. Our words can cut each other like knives.

And sometimes words are not enough. Communication is not a panacea, and miscommunication is ever pervasive. While we must recognize these limitations of communication, we must also continue to strive for a generosity of spirit with our communicative acts.

Sometimes, life presents us with a possibility for connection. Once, on a flight to El Paso, Texas, I sat next to a couple who were traveling to Sydney, Australia. I asked the gentleman, in his early 60s, if they were traveling to the land down-under for work or pleasure. Little did I know that this seemingly innocuous question would lead to a 6-hour conversation. While his wife slept, he disclosed to me how they were going to visit his brother who suffered from severe depression. They were trying to convince his brother that he should return to the United States for shock therapy. He disclosed with me his fears of losing another family member—his mother had committed suicide when he was boy, his sister had committed suicide 12 years later. As he shared his story, he began to cry. This was a desperate man who longed to help his brother live. At the end of the conversation, he apologized for burdening me, a total stranger, with so much personal information. I paused for a moment and smiled. "Thank you," I said. "For allowing me to listen to you."

Every day, we humans are given endless possibilities to connect with both loved ones and strangers. Each greeting and meeting has the potential to be an act of communion. In fact, "every moment of our lives holds potential for change—for noticing or becoming something new" (Rawlins, 2014, p. 77). As Rawlins continues,

> We come to understand "the present" as a jointly lived span of time, our ongoing experience of *now*. Yet we also regard this shared opening as a *gift*—an opportunity for us to convert our potentials into actualities and to enhance the potentials of our current realities. (p. 85)

In the present, is a present (gift). Each moment reveals itself. Each interaction that we have with one another is filled with possibilities, potential gifts for connection and communication, to experience the divine in each other. Indeed, communication can be a "mysterious gift," (Schulze, 2017). There is sacredness in not only the words that we speak and the symbolic meanings that we co-construct, but also in the act of communication. Communication is a mystical gift. At the root of communication is communing—to share and come together. Commune and communion connote a spiritual, transcendent dimension. In the *Encomium of Helen,* Gorgias argues that "speech is a powerful lord." There is transcendence to be touched by the words—our hearts stir and our minds move. As Harter and Buzzanell (2007) explain, spirituality exists in community (another word that shares commune), in and between persons and their organized collective efforts. The sacred gift of a meaningful life is realized *with* others.

Summer 2008. Riding on a Greyhound bus from Columbus, Ohio, to Greenville, South Carolina. I sit next to a woman in her 70s, and we start chatting. She tells me that she is on her way to Florida for her nephew's wedding. She explains how she works as a tour guide at Monticello, Thomas Jefferson's home. She is a widow. She enjoys bus rides, and she hates flying. Plus, riding a bus allows her endless time to read for pleasure. She talks about her three sons. She tells me about how she married a man who worked for General Electric. They moved around a lot. When they lived on the East Coast, surrounded by neighbors with old money, it was her sons who were the only ones with summer jobs.

But what I remember the most about our conversation was the way she talked about her husband and their 37 years of marriage. She shares with me about how they met in college, both competing on the forensics team. And how, when he proposed, she asked him for some time to think. She went to see her parents and asked them about love. Her father, a practical man, told her to type up two columns—pros and cons—on a sheet of paper. And given the 37 years of marriage, I guess he had more pros than cons. She shares with me her advice about love—try to marry someone who is similar to you. And then, she tells me about the day her husband died—a heart attack while she was driving. He grabbed his forehead, tilted it back, and slumped over. Tears filled her eyes as she recalled the memory. The hospital was too far away.

> You
> May have been conceived in the womb
> But you were born in this world and languaged into being
> Into a system of signs

Of chicken scratch marks
Of a cacophony of sounds
That when strung together allow us
To think, to speak, to be

You ask
Is there no original thought?
Yes and no.
Because we do not exist in binaries like a computer spinning
    ones and zeros.
Because isn't life just a sequence of qualifiers
of maybes and sometimes and I-supposes and I-dunnos and
    perhaps?
Because in the beginning there was the word
And the word was the utterance
Bounded by silence
The already-always
That defines us as human
That allows us to commune
(Commune from the Latin *communis* that means universal)

And yet ...
What I say is only half of my own and half someone else's
And for every speech-act that brings us together, there is one that
    drives us apart.

And yet ...
Each day we reach out, longing for an answer
Giving our selves away.

There is always uncertainty when it comes to communication. When
one reaches out, speaks up, and shares with, there is the risk of rejection
and of being turned away by the listener or completely ignored. For us
humans, we keep trying. In hopes of being heard, acknowledged, and
known by the other. Because there are consequences for what we do or do
not say in our relationships, in our classrooms, and in our communities.

Because to be seen, to speak, to share, is an act of vulnerability. As Audre Lorde (1984) stated, "I have come to believe over and over again that what is most important to me must be spoken, made verbal and shared, even at the risk of having it bruised and misunderstood" (p. 40). How do we cultivate empathy? How do we engage in true encountering? How do we promote human dignity? It is in these conversations, in these small vignettes, and in these tiny passing moments that we share ourselves with one another and build relationships. As Martin Buber (1937) once wrote, "All actual life is encounter." Through communicative relationality, we create spaces and presents for identification with, for encounter. These moments are like precious gifts waiting to be unwrapped, invitations to commune, and embodied with a spirit of charity. We must search for the sacred in the everyday, in every moment of life. We must grant one another the gift of communing with one another. And we must continue to find ways to celebrate this gift of communication in developing a more compassionate world.

References

Aktipis, A., Cronk, L., & de Aguiar, R. (2011). Risk-pooling and herd survival: An agent-based model of a Maasai gift-giving system. *Human Ecology, 39*(2), 131–140.

Buber, M. (1937). *I and thou*. R. G. Smith (Trans.). Edinburgh, UK: Clark.

Burke, K. (1966). *Language as symbolic action: Essays on life, literature, and method*. Berkeley, CA: University of California Press.

Burleson, B. R. (2007). Constructivism: A general theory of communication skill. In B. B. Whaley & W. Samter (Eds.), *Explaining communication: Contemporary theories and exemplars* (pp. 105–128). Mahwah, NJ: Lawrence Erlbaum.

Derrida, J. (1992). *Given time: 1. Counterfeit money*. (P. Kamuf, Trans.). Chicago, IL: University of Chicago.

Ekeh, P. (1974). *Social exchange theory*. London, UK: Heinemann.

Garber, M. (2014, December 12). "Gift" is not a verb. *The Atlantic*. Retrieved from https://www.theatlantic.com/entertainment/archive/2014/12/gifting-is-not-a-verb/383676/

Harter, L. M., & Buzzanell, P. M. (2007). (Re)storying organizational communication theory and practice: Continuing the conversation about spirituality and work. *Communication Studies, 58*(3), 223–226. doi:10.1080/10510970701518322

Hyun, N. K., Park, Y., & Park, S. W. (2016). Narcissism and gift giving: Not every gift is for others. *Personality and Individual Differences, 96*, 47–51. http://dx.doi.org/10.1016/j.paid.2016.02.057

Johnstone, B. (2004). The ethics of the gift: According to Aquinas, Derrida, and Marion. *Australian Journal of Theology, 3*, 1–16.

Joy, A. (2001). Gift giving in Hong Kong and the continuum of social ties. *Journal of Consumer Research, 28*, 239–256.

Kearney, R. (1999). On the gift: A discussion between Jacques Derrida and Jean-Luc Marion. In J. D. Caputo & M. J. Scanlon (Eds.), *God, the gift, and postmodernism* (pp. 54–78). Bloomington, IN: Indiana University Press.

Komter, A., & Vollebergh, W. (1997). Gift giving and the emotional significance of family and friends. *Journal of Marriage and Family, 59*, 747–757.

Lawler, E. J., Yoon, J., Baker, M. R., & Large, M. D. (1994). Mutual dependence and gift giving in exchange relations. In B. Markovsky, K. Heimer, & J. O'Brien (Eds.), *Advances in group processes: Volume 12* (pp. 271–298). Greenwich, CT: JAI Press.

Levi-Strass, C. (1969). *The elementary structures of kinship.* Boston, MA: Beacon Press. (Original work published in 1949).

Lorde, A. (1984). *Sister/outsider: Essays and speeches.* New York, NY: Random House.

Mauss, M. (1989). *The gift: The form and reason for exchange in archaic societies.* London, UK: Routledge. (Original work published in 1923).

Nietzsche, F. (1999). *Thus spoke Zarathustra.* (T. Common, Trans.). Mineola, NY: Dover Publications. (Originally published in 1911).

Neil, B. (2010). Models of gift giving in the preaching of Leo the Great. *Journal of Early Christian Studies, 18*(2), 225–259.

Nye, I. (1978). Is choice and exchange theory the key? *Journal of Marriage and Family, 40*(2), 219–232.

Rawlins, W. K. (2014). Brimming moments: Rhythm, will, readiness, and grace. *Departures in Critical Qualitative Research, 3*(1), 76–88.

Shepherd, G. J. (2006). Transcendence. In G. J. Shepherd, J. St. John, & T. Striphas (Eds.), *Communication as …: Perspectives on theory* (pp. 22–30). Thousand Oaks, CA: SAGE.

Schulze, Q. (2017). Human communication as gift. Retrieved from http://quentinschultze.com/communication-as-gift/

St. John, J. (2006). Failure. In G. J. Shepard, J. St. John, & T. Striphas (Eds.), *Communication as …: Perspectives on theory* (pp. 249–256). Thousand Oaks, CA: SAGE.

Weiner, A. (1992). *Inalienable possessions: The paradox of keeping-while-giving.* Berkeley, CA: University of California Press.

White, R. (2016). Nietzsche on generosity and the gift-giving virtue. *British Journal for the History of Philosophy, 24*(2), 348–364.

Zhang, Y., & Epley, N. (2012). Exaggerated, mispredicted, and misplaced: When "It's the thought that counts" in gift exchanges. *Journal of Experimental Psychology, 141*(4), 667–681. doi:10.1037/a0029223

Chapter 13
Communication Is ... Poetic

Lynn M. Harter
Ohio University

William K. Rawlins
Ohio University

*"Our lives and our histories are constantly in the making. Though
the materials of experience are established, we are poetic in our
rearrangement of them."*

—Kenneth Burke,
Permanence and Change (1954/1984, p. 218)

C OMMUNICATION IS POETIC, A MEANING-MAKING PROCESS imbued with
transformative potential. The poetic performance of everyday life
involves "everyday making," an ongoing process of "making-up (mental
imagining) and making-real (material realization)" undertaken with
others (Scarry, 1985, p. 220). An aesthetic mindset emphasizing narrative
allows contemplators to consider what storytelling *does* for participants
(see calls by Frank, 2010). Stories can reinvent selves in the midst of life
disruption, create empathy and identification across social locations, and
set the stage for collective action. We adopt a poetic framework to explore
communication as storytelling and its *worlding of possibilities*. As we argued
in an earlier essay, "The aesthetic worlding of possibilities is the first step
in acting on a belief that conditions can be changed" (Harter & Rawlins,
2011, p. 287). What are we making together? How can we make better
social worlds? These questions motivate our work as teacher-scholars.

In this chapter, we draw on our own experiences as artists and as ethnog-
raphers to illustrate how communication is poetic. Among other activities,

Harter has coproduced and directed four PBS documentaries, films that function as subtle, surreptitious, and multidimensional forms of protest. She approaches documentary filmmaking as embodied and engaged scholarship, storytelling that connects academics with broader publics (Harter, 2013b; Harter, Pangborn, Ivancic, & Quinlan, 2017). Rawlins' recent work has taken seriously the "symphonic quality" Burke (1954/1984) would celebrate in human arrangements "whereby the notes of coexistent melodies can at the same time both proclaim their individual identity and function as parts in a whole" (p. 249). Rawlins (in press) is exploring the stories fashioned through making music together that welcome us across diverse backgrounds to belong communicatively with others while affirming our singular qualities as individuals. With Burke's writings as a backdrop, we contemplate bodies, sensations, affect, movement, rhythm, and sound, all of which inform meaning-making and the worlding of possibilities.

To begin, we engage the early work of Burke to explore the poetic nature of storied forms and connect it with contemporary narrative theory and practice. We illustrate the efficacy of this position by bringing into focus a multiyear project led by Harter that resulted in a nationally syndicated documentary, *A Beautiful Remedy* (Harter & Shaw, 2014), distributed by PBS affiliates across the United States and digitally available through Amazon. The documentary profiles the Arts in Medicine (AIM) program at the University of Texas MD Anderson Cancer Center. Directed by Ian Cion, AIM provides art programming to pediatric and adolescent patients and their families. We weave film excerpts throughout the chapter, illustrating how communication is poetic insofar as it (1) offers opportunities for *sensemaking* and *self-expression*; (2) fosters moments of *solidarity* with others; and, (3) *worlds possibilities* through counternarratives.

Burke's Poetic Perspective

I started the Arts in Medicine Program in collaboration with Dr. Martha Askins about 5 years ago. I was really trying to do two things. I was working with patients to create artwork around what was meaningful for them in their own lives and then the other thing that I was really interested in focusing on was community projects and connecting people. And how community art projects could impact patients, their families, and the larger culture of the institution.

—Ian Cion, Director, Arts in Medicine,
from *A Beautiful Remedy*

Ian and AIM realize in action what Burke argued: Artful experience, if answerable to the ongoing events of living, can enrich relational life and fashion previously unimagined possibilities. Burke's writings remain influential in scholarly conversations about how humans engage in storytelling to express their socialized points of view and bring order and meaning to their lives. Yet, when Burke's ideas materialize in communication theory, they typically appear in connection with his dramatistic pentad (see critiques by Blakesley, 2002; Hawhee, 2008; Quinlan & Harter, 2010). Burke's (1931/1968) early fascination with poetic processes and the rhetorical capacity of artistic expression is minimized in narrative theorizing. We pick up threads of his work on *form* as *incipient action* and communication, directing critics' attention to sociohistorical realms from which narratives arise and actions ensue.

Burke advanced what he termed a "new poetics" that moved beyond understanding art as mere self-expression to acknowledging its communicative potential to connect individuals. "I was trying to work out of an esthetic theory that viewed art as self-expression, into an emphasis upon the communicative aspect of art," reflected Burke as he reminisced about his early work (1976, p. 62). As communicators, we are all poets, storytellers who act, account, and recount through symbolic acts completed with others. Focusing attention on experience and interpreting it to achieve responses in others culminates in *form* (e.g., writing, imagery, musical scores). For Burke (1931/1968), though, form includes "a communicative relationship between writers and audience, with both parties actively participating" (p. 329).

Artists draw upon past experiences and prepare contemplators for settings and events, or in Burke's words, art functions as *equipment for living*. "Art forms like 'tragedy' or 'comedy' or 'satire' [can] be treated as equipments for living, that size up situations in various ways and in keeping with corresponding various attitudes" (1941/1973, p. 304). From a Burkean perspective, aesthetic encounters reflect and contribute to the cultural values shaping citizens' actions. "[A] great work, dealing with some hypothetical event remote in history and 'immediacy,' may leave us with a desire for justice," suggested Burke (1931/1968, p. 189), and "Art negotiates the conditions under which 'life' or 'aesthetic' value can be understood within a culture. In other words, art filters life through the pieties of human perspectives" (p. 314).

Poetic impact occurs when communicators use form to engage others, involve and move them toward future action. Storytelling is a process ripe with poetic potential. Drawing inspiration from Burke, Fisher (1984) positioned humans as *homo narrans* who rely on narratives to comprehend the world around us by organizing characters and experiences in time and space. Narratives connect past events with present states and imagined futures (Ricoeur, 1984). In boardrooms and news reports, around kitchen tables and on front porches, at public rallies and in classrooms, storytelling constructs beliefs and legitimizes actions. Narrators strive to create conditions in which contemplators identify with characters and storylines. Storytelling, like other artful communication, is poetic insofar as it allows individuals to size up circumstances and imagine new normals (Harter, 2013a). Storytelling matters. A well-wrought story can inform and unsettle social interactions.

As communication scholars, we focus on how stories animate individuals and groups. Meanwhile, we rely on narrative logics and practices in our scholarship and creative activity. In the remainder of this chapter, we articulate the poetic potential of storytelling to foster sensemaking and self-expression, relational connections, and progressive change.

Storytelling, Sensemaking, and Self-Expression

You're stripped down to beyond normal. You're stripped down to a medical record number and a gown and your stuff is taken from you. A lot of things, like your hair, things that are defining of who we are, are pulled back away from you. So in some ways it's a very Zen experience, in some ways that can be incredibly liberating. But in other ways it's frightening, devastating.

—Ian Cion, Director, Arts in Medicine,
from *A Beautiful Remedy*

Disruptions are defining features of narratives, what Burke (1969) termed "Troubles" with a capital T. There are few disruptions as life-altering as cancer. A diagnosis shifts one's sense of self even as treatment disrupts routines and strains relationships. A pediatric oncology unit is a world beyond most people's ability to perceive. There is simply no dress rehearsal for the events that accompany treatment and its aftermath. While their peers are mastering the alphabet and arithmetic, kids with cancer and their families are learning about triple-drug chemotherapy and its upsetting effects. As noted by pediatric oncologist Dr. Anderson and physician assistant Laura Kaye (2009), "It [cancer] is characterized by defining moments that humble patients, families, and health-care professionals" (p. 775). The capacity to reimagine is especially important in such moments. Consider Ian's testimony:

> From my point of view, it's a very interesting time to connect with a person when all of a sudden what they thought was real is not anymore, and there's this kind of openness there. And so creativity in that moment is essential because you are then starting to build from scratch. It's like you're playing Jenga and all of a sudden the whole thing collapses ... So that's when I want to step in, when the tower has just collapsed, and say, "Let's play again. Let's become something new."

Well-wrought stories transform "Trouble" with a capital T into narrative plight and possibility (Bruner, 2002). The process of emplotment is central to the meaning-making capacity of storytelling (Ricouer, 1984). "It is appropriate to speak of a plot, to call attention to the ordering peculiar to narrative," argued Burrell and Hauerwas (1977), "It is that ordering, that capacity to unfold or develop character, and thus offer insight into the human condition, which recommends narrative as a form of rationality" (p. 130). Narratives, then, endow experience with significance by temporally ordering events, and humanly figure causality by meaningfully connecting otherwise disjointed activities. Familiar elements of narratives include characters with differing motives and capacities to act, scenes in which events take place, and life lessons that offer both narrators and contemplators a sense of what to believe and how to act (Riessman, 2008).

Oncologists, surgeons, and physical therapists develop corporeal knowledge of patients' bodies as they *face illness*. Artists like Ian help patients *face life*. During cancer treatment and its aftermath, both bodies and selves are at stake, and patients need attention to their medical needs and embodied personhood (Ellingson, 2017; Ellingson & Borofka, 2018; Harter, 2013a, 2017). The creative process fosters healing through self-discovery, expression, and refashioning. In this way, artists perform *narrative care*, a process Kenyon, Randal, and Bohlmeijer (2011) characterized by, "acknowledging and respecting a person's lifestory" (p. xv). Ian invites participants to give meaningful form to their experiences, tapping what Burke (1968) described as "the element of self-expression in all human activities" (p. 52). Ian makes the expressive experience possible by organizing materials, engaging in conversation around patients' interests and the artistic mediums available, and demonstrating techniques. When he visits kids in their hospital rooms, he brings art materials and an invitation to create. Art making can open up sensory experiences and sensemaking that otherwise might remain dormant.

The arts include a range of modalities for patients to experience their ever-shifting body-selves in relation to other bodies and corporeal and material circumstances (Harter, 2013b). Artists can communicate through sound, including the rhythm and tempo of music and singing to invite shared attunement and emotional responses to unfolding melodies. The visual arts in turn can bring order and clarity to experiences that may be difficult or too painful to put into words and simultaneously imagine alternatives for embodied selves (Ellingson, 2017; Ellingson & Borofka, 2018). Visual narratives render experience seeable, if not always sayable (Reissman, 2008). Meanwhile, choreography and movement can embody characters' plights and advance storylines (Quinlan & Harter, 2010).

Consider the story shared by Gabby in describing a cherry blossom tree she painted as part of her self-portrait (see Figure 13.1):

> It's [art] kind of like a gateway to showing who I truly am. It opens myself up and shows the deeper, the truer me. I mean, I probably won't say it, but if I draw the artwork, you could kind of see what I'm feeling ... My emblem for me personally is a cherry blossom because the tree itself is a strong rooted tree, it's very strong and

powerful but yet the blossoms are very gentle and beautiful. Kind of like my personality.

Gabby's body bears stark visible reminders of cancer and its treatment. To cover the loss of her hair, she wears a wig with pink hues—a mix of colors that resemble the cherry blossoms. Her left leg is disfigured from numerous surgeries and she walks with a visible limp. On occasion, she relies on crutches and wheelchairs for mobility. Even so, her vivid self-portrait resists the marginal position that too often accompanies living in a body marked as disabled. Her body-self is reimagined as both rooted and dynamic, capable of changing through her artful efforts across dormant and active seasons of treatment.

FIGURE 13.1   Gabby's cherry blossom tree.

Childhood cancer represents a corporeal and social threat to patients' previously imagined futures. Ian helps patients grapple with new life circumstances. Importantly, he does so by "leading with art" in an effort to create "new narrative cycles." To provide a nuanced interpretation of his philosophy, we share extended testimony by Ian from *A Beautiful Remedy*, offered onsite between actual moments of creating art with children undergoing treatment:

I start with art, and use that to encourage storytelling. When doctors are in a patient's room, they have a certain authority that is like life or death, and the patients have a visceral physical response to that presence that is connected to fear ... But when I walk in as an artist, they see my cart and all this stuff and they are curious. I look different. There is a certain immediate response to my presence that is different. It is relaxing. I have the benefit of that from the start. Then deeper interactions can come into play naturally without being forced or coerced or extracted. They can come out in their own way and in their own time, in whatever way is comfortable for the patient. But that requires a time commitment. That is why when I go to patients I will sit with them for as long as it takes. ... And I won't be idle while they are making something. I am going to sit with them, right along with them, and I'm going to make stuff. If your hands are moving alongside theirs, the physical dynamic between you is equal and that is when they don't feel like they're under a microscope, and I think that is when it is easier to talk and create new narrative cycles that aren't medically based.

Ian actively pursues an inviting co-presence with these young patients, luring them into moving and creating things with him as a duo. Resembling the shared rhythms of a musical jam session (Rawlins, in press), Ian fosters their self-expression during the welcoming moments they are together. Matching rhythms, movements, and creative materials, they play off of each other in expressing anything they want during this involving co-presence. Focusing on whatever "stuff" they choose to make works to level many of the palpable differences between the participants, while encouraging and valuing their self-expression. The result of one of these duets for Gabby is "kind of like a gateway to showing who I truly am."

Artists draw on different toolkits than oncologists, surgeons, and nurses when attending to and joining with someone who suffers. Art creates meaning out of otherwise formless materials and, as such, is a powerful vehicle for sensemaking and self-expression. Irrespective of one's physical condition, struggle characterizes the aesthetic process. Exercising one's imagination requires courage (Andrews, 2014). "Creativity requires a certain bravery, a willingness to face a blank page, to face the unknown, and proceed," noted Ian, remarking, "The fundamental purpose of our endeavor is to ignite and help sustain this sense of bravery." Ian founded AIM with the belief that the courage required in art-making could help participants face extreme physical illness and invasive treatment. Dr. Kleinerman, an oncologist at MD Anderson Cancer Center, concurred, "When you create that kind of experience, that can very easily translate to a greater sense of capacity in facing the obstacles that they're facing in any kind of serious treatments."

AIM initiatives offer opportunities for storytelling, bringing clarity to difficult and painful experiences for many of its participants. The poetic impact of artful storytelling specifically and communication generally takes on heightened importance when individuals are facing profound vulnerability. Yet, *A Beautiful Remedy* reveals a deeper truth understood by narrative scholars: Storytelling is not an isolated event but is inherently relational. We tell stories with, for, and to others that simultaneously expand and define ourselves and our shared world. We live, we grieve, and we story with others as we narrate births and deaths and significant moments in between.

Storytelling and Social Solidarity

Sometimes it's not enough to be alone with your own courage. That's where encouragement comes in. We need to encourage, and that's the thing that in a hospital setting we have a tremendous opportunity to do. When somebody's down, when the chips are down and things are looking very dire, we have an opportunity to connect and encourage them.

—Ian Cion, Director, Arts in Medicine Program,
from *A Beautiful Remedy*

Health crises are occasions for communion. Even so, illness and its treatment can be isolating. Ailing children often are separated physically and geographically from their primary social networks. Meanwhile, stigmas that accompany medical conditions can contribute to relational avoidance (Smith, 2011). AIM offers opportunities for individuals to connect with other body-selves and opens up conversations that might otherwise remain dormant. Shelby Robins, a pediatric oncology nurse and a survivor of childhood cancer, shared the following:

> Seeing the community that they develop and the fellowship they have with one another is amazing. They're fast friends and they're all going through the same thing. Providing that sense of, "you're not alone," and giving them that sense of normalcy. They're not the only bald one in the room, they're not the only one with an IV pull.

In its finest moments, AIM brings together similarly situated individuals and fosters social solidarity. Patients make sense of their own shifting bodies and the instruments of treatment—from medications to machines—in creative activities pursued with others.

Ian strives to build relational connections, what Putnam (2000) might term "social capital." He is emphatic about his primary mission, "I want to build relationships with and between patients and families. So it goes beyond art appreciation. It goes into the realm of shared experience." By design, artful encounters are generative processes, fostering new and enriching potentials through human connection. Art is a way to engage with others and spur moments of dialogue between patients, hospital staff, family members, and fellow artists.

Consider the testimony of Kate, a childhood cancer survivor and participant of AIM:

> Meeting other patients that have had similar experiences or maybe helping others or other people helping you, that's great. Malcom and I have had the same kind of cancer so we can relate and he's a really creative person. And then on top of that another girl came in one time and she'd had the same thing as I had so I actually felt that I was able to help her, you know, being an older version of her, with some of the things that she might be dealing with. I got to share some of my experiences with her, some of what I have been through. Because what I've gotten from all this is what bigger purpose is there than to help others? And so that's what I like to do.

Telling stories and pursuing dialogue remain at the heart of communicating friendship (Rawlins, 2009), processes that shape our identities, convictions, and possibilities. As stressed by Rawlins, "They [friends] help us identify who we are through helping us locate where, with whom, and how we belong" (p. 50).

Among other initiatives, *A Beautiful Remedy* chronicles the evolution of The Dragon Project, including the creation of a sculpture that stands approximately 100 feet long and 12 feet high. The base of the dragon was constructed of repurposed materials, including cardboard and popsicle sticks. Over a 5-month period, the scales for the dragon were decorated by over 1,300 patients, family members, and staff (Figure 13.2). Ian's reflections reveal the relational motivations behind the project:

> The dragon was unique because it was totally community-wide. In the past I've been working exclusively with pediatric and young adult patients, but for the dragon project we wanted to see what it would be like if we opened it up and just set up an art table in a very public location. ... We just built the sculpture, I kind of like roped it off and then started collecting the artwork to add to it. And we did that for 5 months. ... And, to me, that says something. That in the midst of a life-altering crisis, 1,300 people find it important enough to sit and hang out and draw and talk with other people.

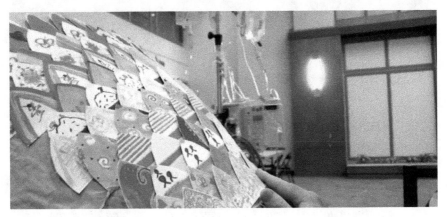

FIGURE 13.2   Dragon scales.

The creative process remained nimble enough for individuals to offer unique contributions. Orchestrated by Ian throughout its communal creation and unveiling, the dragon has enlivened the social space of the hospital like a symphony. As a "musical concert," it has actively involved and included an inspiring range of participants and audience members in the unfolding processes of its composition, improvised parts, and resulting performance. During its realization, the dragon project required each artist to attend to, acknowledge, and complement the work of others in creating the emerging piece. In doing so, everyone—from patients to parents—had the chance to be recognized as individuals and to be collectively affirmed in tangible solidarity with the other contributors (Rawlins, in press). The dragon sculpture itself endures as an art installation, initially exhibited at the hospital but now traveling offsite in venues including the Museum of Fine Arts in Houston (Figure 13.3).

FIGURE 13.3   Dragon sculpture.

Counternarratives and the Worlding of Possibilities

This is more than traditional medicine, and that's something very special. It's not just, "okay we have to give chemotherapy and they have to get the radiation therapy. Or we have to get this test and look at the tumor size." It's actually watching a child and a family evolve because of all these creative programs that we have. And getting to know a different aspect of our patients. That is unique.

—Dr. Kleinerman, Oncologist, MD Anderson Cancer Center,
from *A Beautiful Remedy*

MD Anderson Cancer Center is a clinical mecca with staff generally wedded to scientific logics that legitimize technological interventions for acute and chronic health conditions. The "technology as progress" master narrative is encapsulated in the metaphor of "body as machine," in which illness is approached as malfunction of a part(s), and care involves restoration of the parts to working order (Lupton, 2012). Master narratives articulate possibilities and preferences that social actors invoke (Mumby, 1987). A case in point: Too often the personal experience of illness is overtaken by technical expertise leveraged by specialists who use language that is opaque to common sense, a process described by Frank (2013) as narrative surrender. Even so, professional cultures are contested terrains—dynamic, situated, and indeterminate webs of sensemaking (Peterson & Garner, 2018). A case in point: as suggested by Dr. Kleinerman, AIM complicates and reworks the traditional narrative of medicine to acknowledge and respond to patients' broader life-worlds.

Contemporary uptakes of Burke's "new poetics" inform our understanding of master narratives as contested terrain. Burke (1941/1973) used the metaphor of a "parlor" we enter into upon birth to illustrate the socially conditioned nature of meaning-making. The stories we encounter in the parlor offer cultural idioms, including archetypal characters (e.g., doctors as change agents), plots (e.g., healing involves restoration of health through medical intervention), and settings (e.g., clinical spaces). Despite the power of cultural plots, we do not simply subscribe to and follow them over time. We poetically *compose* lives in the present that adapt to and sometimes reach beyond master narratives. By recognizing the rhetorical elements of art forms, Burke described how politicized worldviews lead to trained incapacities. In explaining "The Poetry of Action" Burke (1954/1984) observed, "Life itself is a poem in the sense that, in the course of living, we gradually erect a structure of relationships about us in conformity with our interests" (p. 254). In his view, creative communicative activity is aesthetically engaged and ethically answerable. Consequently, he remarked, "Relevant inventions may follow, until eventually the point of view finds embodiment in our institutions and our ways of living" (p. 258). Alternative viewpoints linked together through storytelling can compose new worldviews and living arrangements.

Burke's work has inspired scholars to explore the emancipatory potential of "counternarratives"—clusters of histories, anecdotes, and other fragments woven together to disrupt stories of domination (e.g., Goodall, 2010; Lindemann-Nelson, 2001). Counternarratives can reconfigure people's relationships with each other and enable the pursuit of social justice, and as such hold particular significance for individuals living in vulnerable bodies (e.g., Fixmer & Wood, 2005; Harter, Scott, Novak, Leeman, & Morris, 2005). Although counternarratives resist and challenge oppressive patterns, we do not position counternarratives in a binary relationship with master narratives (see critiques by Peterson & Garner, 2018). Inspired by Burke, we pay attention to the *shape-shifting* (Frank, 2010) of master narratives as counternarratives unsettle stagnant scripts and challenge normative practices.

Key questions for narrative scholars interested in progressive change include: Who has the narrative resources to trouble dominant narratives? Under what conditions can counternarratives gain traction? *A Beautiful Remedy* implicitly wrestles with these questions. Socially located within mainstream medicine, AIM catalytically functions to unsettle rigid biomedical practices and to offer alternative bases for relating in a hospital setting. Consider the following reflection by Dr. Eduardo Bruera, an oncologist at MD Anderson Cancer Center:

> The Arts in Medicine program speaks to how important it is to have not only your armamentarium of medical technology and medicines, different types of drugs that we use, but also remembering that these strategies are incomplete if you don't integrate other complementary therapies.

AIM challenges the authority of a biomedical model that too often fosters narrative surrender on the part of patients (Frank, 2010). In doing so, its poetic projects productively contest institutionalized power relations.

AIM appropriates and confronts the canonical storyline by inserting patients as creative protagonists, individuals who would typically fulfill subordinate roles in the dominant story of healing. Patients, of course, remain benefactors of modern medicine. Yet, AIM provides them with opportunities to serve others, in part by beautifying and transforming spaces of care. Ian maintains that patients become healers in their own right:

> Creating public art with patients gives them an opportunity. Especially in the context of the hospital, gives them an opportunity to act as a healer. And fulfill that kind of urge to help others feel better. And I've talked about that at times with our patients when they know they're doing something that's public. A lot of times, they express pride and happiness at creating something that was going to make other people's day better.

Treatments require patients to exist in environments that, by design, are sterile. Patients are hooked up to machines while heart monitors in the background provide auditory reminders of their status. Outpatients settings and public lobbies, too, can be sources of great distress to patients and visitors. Participants of AIM transform such sociospatial dynamics through collaborative art projects that are publicly displayed.

The language and practices of science and technology will continue to inform clinical contexts. Such tools of the trade are equipped to address some aspects of suffering. Even so, artful communication addresses vulnerability in a different way, offering what Ian dubbed as "a beautiful remedy." AIM's capacity to envision otherwise, then, is less an exercise of free will to call an entirely different world into being and more a movement that finds footing in prior practice. The gaps and oversights in dominant narratives can be exploited by those who seek to unsettle and reenvision normative expectations and practices. In this way, AIM serves as a potent check on otherwise unbridled faith in science and technology through the creative efforts and alternative stories of affected persons.

The interactive practices of art-making relationships emerge from and engage with complex, lived rhythmic configurations of patient, staff, and family life in a medical institution. Just as making music together unfolds over time through coordinating rhythms, playing certain notes, and then experiencing their effects on performers and audiences, as AIM participants cocreate artworks they are changed and change others around them in the process. In doing so, they simultaneously refashion themselves, other persons, and the proximate world in which they dwell. These communicative activities poetically extend the potentials for how children undergoing treatment, family members, and medical staff think about and go about life in a healthcare facility. Instead of merely waiting for visits from staff or passively experiencing physically trying treatments and regimens—young patients are given colorful materials, art-making tools, and involving opportunities to express themselves and actively transform moments and places they occupy in the facility with other persons sharing their plight. In doing so, they accomplish a worlding of possibilities, that is, a collective alternative arrangement of actions and outlooks that compose edifying spaces for the human spirit. This shapeshifting of hospital life from within the system encourages collaborative works of art, the self-expanding stories they embody, and the social relationships through which they are created to alter the meanings and expected activities of medical settings.

Conclusion

To work in the arts in healthcare contexts is a unique point of view on how to help patients. And the thing that grants us such a unique perspective is that we have an opportunity to connect with the patients around what's meaningful to them and not around their immediate medical needs. It's funny, because a lot of times people think the artist is not the pragmatist, the artist is not the realist, the artist is the visionary, the dreamer. They are thinking in a way that is more abstract or more non-practical, right? But in this sense, I think the artist is the practical one. We're all gonna end up there [sick], you know.

—Ian Cion, Director, Arts in Medicine Program,
from *A Beautiful Remedy*

The realities of children undergoing treatment for cancer remind us that human life is finite and vulnerable. Yet witnessing their brave creative efforts to narrate and depict their worrisome circumstances with heartening meanings and expanded possibilities also poignantly asserts that communication itself is poetic. Communication is a capacity we all have to exercise our imaginations to transform the meanings, relationships, stories, and to varying degrees the shared conditions of our lives.

We have drawn support from Kenneth Burke's notion of the poetry of action, as well as his and others' conceptions of crafting narratives as one of the primary ways we structure time, express our identities, strive to belong with others, and give shape and meaning to our lived experiences. Accordingly, we have argued that communication is poetic in the ways it: (1) offers opportunities for storytelling, sensemaking and self-expression; (2) encourages moments of solidarity and belonging with others; and, (3) accomplishes a worlding of possibilities through advancing counternarratives. We illustrated our view of communication using excerpts from the documentary *A Beautiful Remedy*, which presents persons and creative activities associated with the Arts in Medicine Program at the MD Anderson Cancer Center.

We have explored storytelling as inherently relational and achieved with affirming others. We learned about young persons with altered and vulnerable body-selves creating art that involves them in experiencing their possibilities differently—including the ordeals of their own treatments. Encouraged by a resourceful facilitator, Ian Cion, we saw children playing a meaningful role in expressing, shaping, and defining their own well-being, and making art with others that fostered a shared sense of belonging. These children are given aesthetic agency, poetic license to reshape the dominant medical narrative from within its confines. In turn, they cultivate their communicative capacity to build out possible ways of living with illness and radical treatment on their own narrative terms and images.

We consider communication to be embodied, ethical, poetic *making* (though sometimes unethical unmaking) of selves and others. Beyond the healthcare context, we wonder how our artful communicative activities work to create the kind of worlds we want to live in and share with others. Where and how can we find the courage to create and narrate enhanced possibilities for our own and others' everyday lives? Aesthetic, ethical, and humane action often requires courage. How can we encourage each other to be better people? We view communication as involving poetic activities that body forth and story possible worlds, a meaning-making process imbued with transformative potential.

References

Anderson, P., & Kaye, L. (2009). The therapeutic alliance: Adapting to the unthinkable with better information. *Health Communication, 24,* 775–778.

Blakesley, D. (2002). *The elements of dramatism.* New York, NY: Longman.

Bruner, J. (2002). *Making stories: Law, literature, life.* New York, NY: Farrar, Strauss, Giroux.

Burke, K. (1931/1968). *Counter-statement.* Berkeley, CA: University of California Press.

Burke, K. (1941/1973). *The philosophy of literary form.* Berkeley, CA: University of California Press.

Burke, K. (1954/1984). *Permanence and change. An anatomy of purpose* (3rd ed.). Berkeley, CA: University of California Press.

Burke, K. (1969). *A grammar of motives.* Berkeley, CA: University of California Press.

Burke, K. (1976). The party line. *Quarterly Journal of Speech, 62,* 62–68.

Ellingson, L. E. (2017). Realistically ever after: Disrupting dominant narratives of long-term cancer survivorship. *Management Communication Quarterly, 3,* 321–327.

Ellingson, L. E., & Borofka, K. G. E. (2018). Long-term cancer survivors' everyday embodiment. *Health Communication.* Advance online publication.

Fixmer, N., & Wood, J. T. (2005). The personal is still political: Embodied politics in third wave feminism. *Women's Studies in Communication, 28,* 235–257.

Frank, A. (2010). *Letting stories breathe. A socio-narratology.* Chicago, IL: University of Chicago Press.

Frank, A. (2013). *The wounded storyteller. Body, illness, and ethics.* (2nd ed.). Chicago, IL: University of Chicago Press.

Goodall, H. L., Jr. (2010). *Counter-narrative. How progressive academics can challenge extremists and promote social justice.* Walnut Creek, CA: Left Coast Press.

Harter, L. M. (2013a). The poetics and politics of storytelling in health contexts. In L. M. Harter (Ed.), *Imagining new normals: A narrative framework for health communication* (pp. 3–27). Dubuque, IA: Kendall Hunt.

Harter, L. M. (2013b). The work of art. *Qualitative Communication Research, 2,* 326–336.

Harter, L.M. (2017). Engaging narrative theory to disrupt and reimagine organizing processes. *Management Communication Quarterly, 31,* 297–299.

Harter, L. M., Pangborn, S. M., Ivancic, S., & Quinlan, M. M. (2017). Storytelling and social activism in health organizing. *Management Communication Quarterly, 31*, 314–320.

Harter, L. M., & Rawlins, W. K. (2011). The worlding of possibilities in a collaborative art studio: Organizing embodied differences with aesthetic and dialogic sensibilities. In D. K. Mumby (Ed.), *Reframing difference in organizational communication studies: Research, pedagogy, practice* (pp. 267–289). Thousand Oaks, CA: SAGE.

Harter, L. M., Scott, J., Novak, D., Leeman, M., & Morris, J. (2006). Freedom through flight: Performing a counter-narrative of disability. *Journal of Applied Communication Research, 34*, 3–29.

Harter, L.M., & Shaw, E. (2014). *A beautiful remedy*. Athens, OH: WOUB Public Media Center.

Hawhee, D. (2008). *Moving bodies: Kenneth Burke at the edges of language*. Columbia, SC: University of South Carolina Press.

Kenyon, G., Randall, W. L., & Bohlmeijer, E. (2011). Preface. In G. Kenyon, E. Bohlmeijer, & W. L. Randall (Eds.), *Storying later life. Issues, investigations, and interventions in narrative gerontology* (pp. xiii–xviii). Oxford, UK: Oxford University Press.

Lindemann-Nelson, H. (2001). *Damaged identities, narrative repair*. Ithaca, NY: Cornell University Press.

Lupton, D. (2012). *Medicine as culture. Illness, disease and the body*. Los Angeles, CA: SAGE.

Mumby, D. K. (1987). The political function of narrative in organizations. *Communication Monographs, 54*, 113–127.

Peterson, B. L., & Garner, J. T. (2018). Tensions of narrative ownership: Exploring the rise of (counter) narratives during the fall of Mars Hill Church. *Western Journal of Communication*. Advance online publication.

Putnam, R. (2000). *Bowling alone: The collapse and revival of American community*. New York, NY: Simon & Schuster.

Quinlan, M. M., & Harter, L. M. (2010). Meaning in motion: The embodied poetics and politics of Dancing Wheels. *Text and Performance Quarterly, 30*, 374–395.

Rawlins, W. K. (2009). *The compass of friendship. Narratives, identities, and dialogues*. Thousand Oaks, CA: SAGE.

Rawlins, W. K. (in press). Approaching ethnographic research about human interaction as making music together. *Advances in Intelligent Systems and Computing*. New York, NY: Springer.

Riessman, C. K. (2008). *Narrative methods for the human sciences*. Thousand Oaks, CA: SAGE.

Ricouer, P. (1984). Narrative time. *Critical Inquiry, 7*, 169–190.

Scarry, E. (1985). *The body in pain: The making and unmaking of the world*. New York, NY: Oxford University Press.

Smith, R. (2011). Stigma, communication, and health. In T. L. Thompson, R. Parrott, & J. F. Nussbaum (Eds.), *Handbook of health communication* (2nd ed., pp. 455–468). New York, NY: Routledge.

Swartz, O. (1996). Kenneth Burke's theory of form: Rhetoric, art, and cultural analysis. *Southern Communication Journal, 61*, 312–321.

Figure Credits

Chapter 14
Communication Is ... Privilege

Danielle M. Stern

Christopher Newport University

"What is privilege?" I ask my Communicating Gender, Race, and Class students on the first day of fall semester 2018.

Silence.

For a while.

Like 30 seconds of silence. In a room of about 20 students. A room without windows.

"An advantage?" a student near the front of the classroom offers with a level of insecurity.

"That's a great start," I reply. "To that, may we add unearned advantages? It's something an individual has without effort and that often comes at the expense of someone else who does not have access to those advantages—or privileges." I assigned them to read the "Check your Privilege" chapter from Oluo's (2018) accessible yet quietly profound work, So You Want to Talk about Race, *and borrowed from her for the day's discussion.*

"Each of us in this room has different backgrounds and privileges, but we share one privilege in common across any of our differences. What might that be?" No one wanted to speak. No one. "What about education privilege?"

Some head nods, but mostly averted eyes.

"It's likely true that there are different school systems and different socioeconomic backgrounds represented, but we are all privileged to be here at a liberal arts institution with access to library databases, Internet, and other information technologies to enhance our learning and postgraduate opportunities."

More head nods.

"And it's also likely true that some of you are working multiple jobs, taking out loans, or doing without health insurance or other necessities to make ends meet."

Stronger head nods.

"And it's equally true that some of you do not have to worry about the things I just mentioned because you have support from your parents, scholarships, grants, or other privileges, correct?"

Other heads nod.

"What type of privilege would this be, then?"

"Class privilege?" a different student replies, with a closing inflection indicating her uncertainty.

"Yes!" I affirm enthusiastically. "We might also refer to it as socioeconomic privilege throughout the semester. Even though you will all graduate with a liberal arts degree in communication, the privileges you brought with you to university influence how you navigate the policies and practices of higher education, which therefore correlate with your graduate and career opportunities after you earn your degree. Our textbook chapter authors will offer us evidence for this argument. Let's get to it!"

P LEASE NOTE THAT I'M DOING MOST of the speaking in the interaction just described, an incredible privilege of being an educator that is not lost on me. Surprising no one, when I asked students to shift the discussion from class privilege to White privilege, crickets chirped. The course enrollment, like the rest of campus, was predominantly White. That's how it went for much of the first few weeks of the class. However, two units inflected some much needed life in the class: (1) Privilege Monopoly (Griffin & Jackson, 2011), where I modified the game to include nonbinary identity expression; and (2) mass incarceration (Alexander, 2010), where we read an excerpt of Alexander's (2010) book, watched brief videos about rates of mass incarceration, and discussed our privileges to communicate freely about these injustices. It was during these class experiences that the material for this chapter began to take shape. If privilege is a system of unearned advantages, and communication is a process of making shared meaning, then how do unearned advantages factor into meaning making? Privilege embodies power and access to knowledge that cocreate and structure meaning. Communication *is* privilege. This declaration recognizes the centering of issues of power at the core of our interdisciplinary approaches to rhetoric, relationships, culture, and pedagogy.

Power, privilege, and access to knowledge and communication are inextricably linked in the American university model, a model that students from underrepresented populations, including immigrants, undocumented persons, and international students are navigating during a time of immense political and social resistance to "the other." According to Calafell and Chuang (2017):

> Though racism and xenophobia have long been entrenched in universities, as Swartz and Ware McGuffey (2017) suggest, we are at a crucial moment. The challenges faced by undocumented students, including Dreamers, who are fighting for the right to stay in the U.S. and have access to affordable education, are at the forefront in higher education. (p. 110)

We must advocate for our vulnerable populations by striving for conversations about diversity, equity, difference, and privilege. We must "move beyond individualized location, expanding accountability from self, to others and self" in order to practice "coalitional activism" for possible social change (Jones, 2010, p. 122). Through social justice–inspired, everyday pedagogical activism, we need to find ways to productively intervene in this privileged space. Griffin (2012) offers one intervention of "bearing witness to struggle, reaching out to nurture, marking the presence of privilege, and advocating for humanization" (p. 216). In this chapter, I build upon and offer examples of what Griffin's call to action looks like in order to illuminate the cultural, political, and economic domain of communication. I originally set out to decenter privilege from communication, but in the reflexive process of writing I realized the misdirection of this goal—how privileged this intention was. Instead, I discuss the productive possibilities when considering that communication is privilege.

Excavating Privilege

Last week marked the end of the semester in which I taught two sections of Communicating Gender, Race, and Class for the first time. My department had offered the course for more than 10 years prior as Gender Communication. We have courses on Intercultural Communication and Social Movements, with units on class, ethnicity, and race splashed throughout the curriculum. However, prior to implementing this course, none of our curriculum was specific to issues of race and class, let alone privilege. The communication faculty in our department represent varied sexual orientations and socioeconomic class backgrounds, but unsurprisingly our department is incredibly White, as is the faculty and our students across our predominantly White institution. In the aftermath of the 2016 general election, our department spoke frankly about what we could do to help our students make sense of the incivility and bigotry that for many of them felt unexpected and new. We knew we had to do more to discuss racism and White privilege in our curriculum, but not all of us were in the position to do so—nor had the training. So we did something about it.

Martin and Nakayama (2006) challenged communication scholars to "embrace a more socially inclusive and responsible mission of our profession" (p. 81), which is what my department set out to do. I was grateful for the privilege to have the support of my department and institution for my sabbatical in spring 2017. My main project, which had been in motion prior to fall 2016, was to interview communication professors about how they integrate gender, sexuality, and feminism into their courses. During data collection, my participants continued to discuss topics of intersectionality and race as integral to their gender pedagogy. I had read some of the foundational works on intersectionality (Collins, 1990; Crenshaw, 1989), but had not taken the time to stay current in the field. I spent the second half of my sabbatical reading as much as I could on intersectionality, Black feminism, and critical race theory. This process led to a radical re-conceptualization of the existing Gender Communication course around the concepts of intersectionality and privilege.

Subject positions tied to socioeconomic class, education, and other identity markers that afford access to the means of communication limit the availability of shared meaning and ritual—which are the most basic of our discipline's definition of communication (Carey, 1989; Rothenbuhler, 2006). Communication should *not* be limited to the privileged classes, and it is our task as communication theorists, educators, students, and practitioners to acknowledge our own privileges in order to encourage our peers to do the same. Yep (2017) argued that all communication "occurs within a cultural domain where social differences are created, negotiated, and contested" in order to focus "on the nuances and complexities of communication rather than reifying certain normativities" (p. 238). The norm at stake here is a business model of education that does not readily align with the goals of compassionate, equitable communication. As Rudick and Dannels (2018) articulated, "[H]igher education in general, and communication studies in particular, draws its culture from the Enlightenment principles of knowledge production and dissemination" (p. 266). These values conflict with capitalism, a political economic system that has resulted in ever-increasing tuition and education costs. Allen and Wolniak (2018) found that tuition increases at U.S. public 2- and 4-year institutions are "negatively and significantly associated with the racial/ethnic diversity of enrolled students," (para 1). Although this chapter is not focused solely on communication education, it is within the context of learning and teaching that we develop communicative capacities and norms.

Communicating Privilege

Rothenbuhler (2006) described the social consequences of the ritual aspects of communication as a moral effort: "Because we live in realities created by our communication, we must think about what ought and ought not to be done by communication" (p. 19). We *ought* to be defining and recognizing privilege inherent in unequal access to and outcomes of communicative processes. We *ought not* to abuse those privileges. We *ought* to see communication as privilege so that we ought not stay bound by that privilege. Although my argument still exists within a normative frame, a critical approach to communication always centers issues of power—whether within pedagogical, interpersonal, rhetorical, or media/cultural areas of the discipline. Embodied power is another important communication concept within a frame of privilege. Marvin (2006) theorized communication as embodiment to distinguish the ways we communicatively rank the "textual class" of academics and other skilled elites above a body class who lack "textual credentials," need disciplining, and who are disposable (p. 70). Connecting communication and privilege helps us recognize which bodies lack the credentials to participate freely, equally, and productively in social, political, and economic life. Critical theories of feminism, queer studies, intersectionality, and political economy provide frameworks to link communication and privilege around bodily markers of gender, sexuality, race, class, ability, size, labor, and others. Although these various markers are unique and important in any communication theory building, the emergence of White privilege in the popular lexicon—and its salience within the discipline and practice of communication—compels me to spend a significant portion of this chapter on the concept.

Alexander (2010), DiAngelo (2018), Harris (1993), Lipsitz (2006), and McIntosh (1989), intentionally identified White privilege as the root of power imbalance and unequal access to social life in postcolonial United States. The communication field, which is already interdisciplinary, must continue to build from sociology, law, critical race studies, and gender studies, to interrogate how our discipline's embodiment of White privilege limits our very understanding and practice of shared, symbolic meaning. Martin and Nakayama (2006) detailed the raced foundations of the communication discipline that led to privileging the voices and philosophies of those in power, White men with economic means, a systemic issue that persists:

> Our point is not simply that communication has many more white students than its general demographics would indicate, but to question *the ways in which the study of communication continues to*

> *empower white people, while at the same time unwittingly remaining unresponsive to the needs of the rest of society.* (Martin & Nakayama, 2006, p. 78)

Encouraging my White students, colleagues, friends, and family, especially those of us who emerged from or are still firmly entrenched in a socioeconomic underclass, to question how our socially constructed race empowers us and affords us communicative privilege is no small task.

A challenge of framing the course I described earlier around privilege meant *consciously, intentionally, publicly* teaching to multiple student populations at once. Sure, we do this all the time—not just as educators, but as the symbol-using animal (Burke, 1966). However, those of us with White privilege are usually taught to ignore the differences, especially in the context of race, what Bonilla-Silva (2010) has discussed as colorblind racism. My task was to verbally call attention to the differences in the room. I had to "hail" (Charland, 1987) my fellow White students to use and embrace terms they had been taught to sweep under the rug. I had not been more nervous prior to teaching a class since the first time I set foot in the classroom as a graduate student instructor of record 17 years ago. The course is an elective, so I told myself that students were choosing to be there, which meant they were choosing to be in a space to have conversations about potentially divisive and disruptive—yet also constructive and productive—topics.

In a previous essay (Stern, 2018), I built from the evidence of more than 20 qualitative interviews with communication instructors to develop a theory of "privileged vulnerability" (p. 47) that explains how the privileged space of the communication classroom can lead us to question our subject positions of dominance and power, while at the same time recognizing our institutional vulnerabilities. I specifically called on communication instructors to practice vulnerability by recognizing and naming our privileges if we expect our students to do the same. Privileged vulnerability does not have to be limited to instructors. Communication practitioners occupy intersectional identity markers along axes of privilege and vulnerability in the various institutions in which we communicate. Communication is privilege because many of us have the unearned advantage of participating in the rituals of shared meaning that in turn provides access to improving our communication skills via informal and formal education. Communication is vulnerable when we do not have equity in the social, political, and economic access routes to shared meaning. Communication is privilege when we are able recognize the space that these advantages and vulnerabilities *share* in our everyday communication interactions in the classroom, workplace, home, and other public and private spaces.

Privileging Communication

Thus far, I have been discussing that communication is privilege. However, in order to use privilege productively in our communication interactions, it is important to discuss briefly how *privilege is communication*. If communication is privilege via the inequitable power structures that limit access to the ritual of shared meaning-making, then privilege is communication via the shared meaning-making process that grants us advantages in everyday rituals. Conversation, email exchanges, phatic rituals of "Hello, how is your day?" while the other person nods and smiles politely, nonverbal glances of empathy and understanding, and so on, define a mundane, yet privileged existence. Privilege is the opportunity to participate in communication.

But what of ability—experiences of mobility, sight, sound, speech, neurodiversity, and illness that might limit participation in some of these privileged everyday communication rituals? If we turn back to the metaphor that communication is privilege, disability studies is absolutely imperative to the communication discipline. Again, if communication is the process of producing shared meaning, all communicators possess varying degrees of privilege. People with disabilities participate in shared meaning on the daily, although it might not always be in the spoken and written means which our society privileges. It is those of us who identify as able-bodied or mentally/physically capable who, for various reasons, might have not taken the time to learn other shared meaning practices, such as American Sign Language. Or perhaps we do not practice the patience or mindfulness of communicating in alternative ways to match the needs and abilities of other coparticipants in a communication exchange. As Kafer (2013) eloquently posited, "How might we imagine futures that hold space and possibility for those who communicate in ways we do not yet recognize as communication, let alone understand?" (p. 67).

Communication is privilege when we *recognize* the myriad possibilities of producing shared meaning. Communication is privilege when we not only recognize, but also *accept* our unearned advantages to produce shared meaning. Communication is privilege when we not only accept, but also *act on* these advantages in ways that benefit our other cocommunicators. Communication is the privilege to be vulnerable, knowing that we are risking our individual and institutional advantages when we call on others to name their privilege. Communication is the privilege to produce meaning, to share meaning, and to transform meaning (Carey, 1989) when the process is exclusive and inequitable to vulnerable populations. Moreover, communication is the privilege to work within, and perhaps around, power structures that shape those interactions of culture, pedagogy, rhetoric, and relationships.

> *"We've spent 15 weeks discussing individual AND institutional privileges of gender, race, class, sexuality, and immigration status in communication," I say to my students on the last day of the semester before finals. "What is the point of spending so much time analyzing privilege?"*
>
> *Only a brief pause before a student in the back of the class replies, "If we don't recognize our privilege, we can't recognize how communication and media get it wrong sometimes."*
>
> *"What do you mean by, 'Get it wrong?'"*
>
> *"Well, so much of our media stories are framed around a privileged experience—of Whiteness, of wealth, and so on, that other things are left out, or looked down on. Like when we talked about how politicians and journalists refer to people as 'illegal aliens.' It dehumanizes them."*
>
> *"Yes, exactly," I say appreciatively. "And because it is so difficult already to talk about these topics with our family and friends, we often rely on media narratives to fill in the gaps so to speak. If our primary mode of speaking about undocumented immigrants is as 'illegals,' then we contribute to the problem rather than intervening in it."*
>
> *"Another wrap-up question: what should we do with our privileges once we are aware of them?" I ask.*

"We should use our privilege to find better, more humane ways to communicate about difference, ways that make others feel valued and worthy," a student offers.

I want to burst into tears of joy that they wrote this down from earlier in the semester, but instead I restrain and say, "What might this look like in practice?"

"Well," the student continues, "if we hear a friend say a joke about trans people, we should speak up."

"Yes, and what about in the case of the dreaded, wanted-to-be-avoided-at-all-costs topic of White privilege?" I say, "What might that look like?"

Ah, the silence returns. But only momentarily.

"Well, for starters, more of us need to use the phrase," another student replies.

"Of course," I offer. "I know it has been uncomfortable for many of us in the room to come to terms with the phrase, as well as accept White privilege. But as we've talked about previously, our discomfort is not as important as the humanity of others whom our privilege has, intentionally or unintentionally, devalued. Just as one of our authors [Witherspoon, 2017] argued that Black joy needs to be reclaimed in popular culture, we also need to acknowledge and not look away from the lived pain of being Black in America if we are to improve our communication about race. I want to thank you again for showing up and making space for discussions of privilege. For communicating with respect. For doing the work. And remember, the work isn't done. This is just the beginning."

References

Alexander, M. (2010). *The new Jim Crow: Mass incarceration in the age of colorblindness.* New York, NY: The New Press.

Allen, D., & Wolniak, G. C. (2018). Exploring the effects of tuition increases on racial/ethnic diversity at public colleges and universities. *Research in Higher Education, 59,* 1–26. Retrieved from https://doi.org/10.1007/s11162-018-9502-6

Bonilla-Silva, E. (2010). *Racism without racists: Color-blind racism and the persistence of racial inequality in the United States* (3rd ed.). Lanham, MD: Rowman & Littlefield.

Burke, K. (1966). *Language as symbolic action*. Berkeley, CA: University of California Press.

Calafell, B., & Chuang, A. K. (2017). From me to we: Embracing coperformative witnessing and critical love in the classroom. *Communication Education, 67*(1), 109–114. doi:10.1080/03634523.2017.1388529

Carey, J. (1989). *Communication as culture*. New York, NY: Routledge.

Charland, M. (1987). Constitutive rhetoric: The case of the people Quebecois, *Quarterly Journal of Speech, 73*(2), 133–150. doi:10.1080/0335638709383799

Collins, P. H. (1990). *Black feminist thought: Knowledge, consciousness, and the politics of empowerment*. Boston, MA: Unwin Hyman.

Crenshaw, K. (1989). Demarginalizing the intersection of race and sex: A Black feminist critique of antidiscrimination doctrine, feminist theory, and antiracist politics. *University of Chicago Legal Forum*, 139–167.

DiAngelo, R. (2018). *White fragility: Why it's so hard for white people to talk about racism*. Boston, MA: Beacon Press.

Griffin, R. (2012). Navigating the politics of identity/identities and exploring the promise of critical love. In N. Bardham & M. Orbe (Eds.), *Identity and communication research: Intercultural reflections and future directions* (pp. 51–67). Lanham, MD: Lexington Books.

Griffin, R. A., & Jackson, N. R. (2011). Privilege Monopoly: An opportunity to engage in diversity awareness. *Communication Teacher, 25*(1), 1–6. doi:10.1080/17404622.201.514273

Harris, C. I. (1993). Whiteness as property. *Harvard Law Review, 106*(8), 1709–1795. doi:10.2307/1341787.

Kafer, A. (2013). *Feminist, queer, crip*. Bloomington, IN: Indiana University Press.

Lipsitz, G. (2006). *The possessive investment in Whiteness: How White people profit from identity politics*. Philadelphia, PA: Temple University Press.

Martin, J. N., & Nakayama, T. K. (2006). Communication as raced. In G. J. Shepherd, J. St. John, & T. Striphas (Eds.), *Communication as ...: Perspectives on theory* (pp. 75–83). Thousand Oaks, CA: SAGE.

Marvin, C. (2006). Communication as embodiment. In G. J. Shepherd, J. St. John, & T. Striphas (Eds.), *Communication as ...: Perspectives on theory* (pp. 67–74). Thousand Oaks, CA: SAGE.

McIntosh, P. (1989). White privilege: Unpacking the invisible knapsack. *Peace and Freedom Magazine*, 10–12. Retrieved from https://nationalseedproject.org/Key-SEED-Texts/white-privilege-unpacking-the-invisible-knapsack

Oluo, I. (2018). *So you want to talk about race*. New York, NY: Seal Press.

Rothenbuhler, E. (2006). Communication as ritual. In G. J. Shepherd, J. St. John, & T. Striphas (Eds.), *Communication as ...: Perspectives on theory* (pp. 13–21). Thousand Oaks, CA: SAGE.

Rudick, C. K., & Dannels, D. P. (2018). "Yes, and ...": Continuing the scholarly conversation about immigration and higher education. *Communication Education, 67*(1), 120–123. doi:10.1080/03634523.2017.1392584

Stern, D. M. (2018). Privileged pedagogy, vulnerable voice: Opening feminist doors in the communication classroom. *Journal of Communication Pedagogy, 1*(1), 40–51. doi:10.31446/JCP/2018.09

Witherspoon, N. (2107). Beep, beep, who got the keys to the Jeep?: Missy's trick as (un) making queer. *Journal of Popular Culture, 50*(4), 871–895. doi:10.1111/jpcu.12565

Yep, G. A. (2017). Demystifying normativities in communication education. *Communication Education, 65*(2), 235–240. doi:10.1080/03634523.2016.1143711

Section 4

Actualizing

Chapter 15
Communication Is ... Action

Art Herbig
Purdue University–Fort Wayne

I N OCTOBER OF 2018 A SERIES of bombs were mailed to prominent liberal activists and politicians. Just days after the packages began to arrive, the FBI zeroed in on the alleged perpetrator, Cesar Sayoc (Andone & Crespo, 2018). Much of the arrest was aired live on television, but one part of the process stood out. As agents were covering up Sayoc's van to put it into evidence, the television audience was literally given windows into his thinking. The windows of his van were covered in stickers, photos, and other paraphernalia showing his support for President Donald Trump. The fact that Sayoc's targets had been prominent liberals often targeted by President Trump in stump speeches and tweets alongside the mass of evidence that was covering his van got people wondering: Is President Trump connected to or even partially responsible for these acts of violence? In dismissing the mere thought of culpability, the president's press secretary Sarah Huckabee-Sanders said "there is a big difference between comments made and actions taken" ("Sanders Comments," 2018).

The distinction between words and actions has been a theme of the 45th president's term in office. Following the shutdown of the government in December 2018, the president said, "You can call it the Schumer or the Pelosi or the Trump Shutdown. Doesn't make any difference to me. It's just words" (Qiu & Tackett, 2019, para. 14). "It's just words" was also the excuse Trump gave for his infamous description of sexual assault from the *Access Hollywood* tapes (Nguyen, 2016). Trump's lack of respect for words even extends into the accuracy of his statements. According to *The Washington Post's* Fact Checker Database, the president of the United States lied to the American public an average of 15 times a day in 2018 (Kessler, 2018). Many commentators and pundits have examined the president's constant undermining of journalists and media professionals with his attacks on what the president describes as "fake news," but equally as important as these attacks is the president's belief in an idea that seems to act as a foundation for much of his communication with the American people: Words are not action.

President Trump is not alone in this belief. We can hear it in the title of an old Toby Keith song: "A Little Less Talk and a Lot More Action." You can feel it in critiques of "slacktivism" as lazy or ill-informed. It can function as a catchy T-shirt and as an admonition from someone you respect that you are simply not *doing* enough. Despite its prevalence, the division between "communication" and "action" is a binary that marginalizes the import and influence communication can have. Sticks and stones can break someone's bones, but words can also hurt you.

The goal of this chapter is simple: to advocate that communication is action. For all too long, we have been comfortable with the binary that subordinates theories, questions, ideas, etc. into the realm of the passive while moments of throwing punches, unsheathing swords, or shooting missiles give the impression that something has been "done." While it is equally valuable to critique the gendered associations with being perceived as either active or passive, I have chosen to embrace the idea of action here because of its association with consequences. Choosing how to communicate, what to communicate, or how to interpret communication involves acting, and actions have consequences.

As part of this chapter, I would like to discuss three distinct contexts that exemplify the importance of communication as action. The first has become a communication axiom taught nearly universally throughout the study of communication: "one cannot not communicate." Watzlawick, Beavin Bavelas, and Jackson's (1967) foundational tenet has been a part of a communication education for more than 50 years, but we need to take a moment to reassess their approach as well as the implications of their ideas. Next, I examine the relationship between political correctness and the belief that communication is action. Many in the United States rebel against the notion that we must be politically correct; what can that tell us about them and their relationship to communication? Finally, I will end with an examination of the many forms and ways in which communication media play a role in contemporary discourse. Ultimately, I will use these examples as a means to attempt to break the binary. Communication is action and we must be responsible for its implications.

One Cannot Not Communicate

It is reiterated across communication classrooms: one cannot not communicate (Watzlawick et al., 1967). In their book, *The Pragmatics of Human Communication*, Watzlawick, Beavin Bavelas, and Jackson provide a systemic look at the pervasive nature of communication with clear applications and, as they say in music, that catchy hook. Littlejohn, Foss, and Oetzel (2017) call the book a "classic" (p. 229). Anderson and Ross (2002) write "since the publication of Watzlawick, Beavin, and Jackson's influential *Pragmatics of Human Communication* (1967), many communication theorists have taken most of the theory's claims for granted" (p. 41). According to Griffin, Ledbetter, and Sparks (2015), this theory shows that "Communication is inevitable ... A corollary to the first axiom is that 'one cannot *not* influence'" (p. 167, emphasis in original). However, part of the problem with this central tenet of the study of communication is the ways in which it has become intertwined with *influence and meaning*. In many ways, the pithy nature of sentiments such as "one cannot not communicate" has undermined how we discuss our role in the process of making meaning. To advocate that communication is involuntary also belies the importance of perception and interpretation in the communicative process. So, in order to understand communication as action, we must first step back and try to understand the relationship between action and communication in a very pragmatic way.

In their description of the project they were undertaking, Watzlawick, Beavin Bavelas, and Jackson clearly discuss what they *were* and what they *were not* doing. In their opening chapter, they outline three distinct approaches to communication: syntactical, semantic, and pragmatics. They admit upfront that their work is primarily embedded in the study of pragmatics, which focuses on behavior. According to them, "from this perspective of pragmatics, all behavior, not only speech, is communication, and all communication—even the communicational clues in an impersonal context—affects behavior" (p. 22). Their position is "all behavior in an interactional situation has message value" and "one cannot not behave" (pp. 48–49). The problem with this approach is that by equating communication with behavior we undermine the significance and complexity of meaning. For instance, let me steal a couple of examples from McKerrow (2015):

> In one sense, nothing is "rhetorical" until it is given meaning. It is not the case that death, in and of itself, is rhetorical. It is not the case that what we call a painting is, in and of itself, rhetorical. Death is death; a painting is composed of watercolors or oils with varying texture or strokes culminating in an image. What is rhetorical is how we respond to death, or a painting—the use we make of it in giving it meaning or significance. (p. 155)

If we are to take for granted that finding, assigning, or attempting to understand meaning is central to communication, then we can replace "rhetorical" in the above quote with "communication." By this standard, it is not enough that one behaves. Behavior occurs in the world, but it is the human impulse to make sense of that behavior that makes it communication.

One of the basic assumptions of Watzlawick, Beavin Bavelas, and Jackson's treatise is that interaction can be understood logically, even mathematically. However, in the final chapter, they acknowledge a difference between the relational and existential understandings of individuals. According to them, to understand an individual outside of how they behave in relationships, "we must leave the domain of science and become avowedly subjective" (p. 257). In this subjective space, we find Watzlawick, Beavin Bavelas, and Jackson grappling with how individual interpretation complicates their straightforward assessments, "[R]eality is very largely what we make it to be ... His specific way of 'being-in-the-world,' therefore, is the outcome of his choice, is the meaning *he* gives to what is presumably beyond objective human understanding" (p. 262). Abstract thought and reflection both complicate pragmatics and are essential to understanding communication, but they are also part of an *active* process to attempt to make sense of the world around us. Weick (1995) tells us that this is a constant process and that process might seem involuntary, but it is not.

For this reason, we must embrace complexity over simplicity. Rather than choosing to focus on the ubiquity of communication with laconic sentiments such as "one cannot not communicate," we need to engage the polyvalent nature of interpretation and our roles in the production and reproduction of meaning. It is not enough to focus on behavior as a stimulus, we must understand that behaviors are interpreted in different ways by the multiplicity of individuals involved based on their own knowledge of the world. We must confront those differences. We must understand our role in their existence. In an attempt to manage the many different types of approaches or interpretations that can be created through communication, McGee (1989) wrote that *text construction is now something done more by consumers than by producers of discourse*" (p. 288, emphasis in original). From his perspective, the fragmented associations the people bring to communication shape their interpretations of meaning whether they are evaluating words or deeds.

It is essential that we understand that the assignment of meaning is an active process. Our relationship to or authorship of words, ideas, behaviors, etc. are representative of decisions we make and actions we take even if it happens quicker than we can register. We need communicators that understand that from the words they choose to the ways in which they are interpreting the words, actions, and decisions of others they are taking action. We are not passive bystanders that allow communication to be dictated to us. We are actively engaged with our interpretations of meaning. We are also responsible for attempting to understand the impact and influence of messages both voluntary and involuntary.

Meaning and Impact: Political Correctness

It is sometimes cliché to open an essay or a section of an essay with a definition, but I hope you will indulge me so that I can provide an example of the importance of polyvalent meaning here. According to Merriam-Webster (n.d.), politically correct means "conforming to a belief that language and practices which could offend political sensibilities (as in matters of sex or race) should be eliminated" (para. 1). Eliminated seems like a strong characterization here, but it serves to emphasize an important point about political correctness: It represents a challenge to the status quo. According to a recent survey, most Americans are resistant to political correctness (Montanaro, 2018). In reaction to the same type of data, Mounk (2018)—who identifies as a liberal—wrote that preaching political correctness extends a divide between those who would promote great sensitivity to language and the audience they intend to reach. Self-described liberal softie Stephen Fry (2018) also critiqued political correctness because "it's not effective" (para. 9). Each of these critiques of political correctness privileges addressing the majority opinion as the audience over the potential harms being promoted and caused by certain turns of language to the minority. It belies the influence communication can have and assumes certain people's traditions of meaning or association trump the impact of them. Building on an acknowledgment of the importance of meaning and the fragmented associations people bring to communication, we need to treat what we know as "political correctness" as a chance to create a space for meaning, association, and language to be changed.

The fact is that if at some point you have found yourself lamenting political correctness, you can also likely point to that moment as an expression of your position of privilege. For instance, for years the Fox News network openly proclaimed a "war on Christmas" (Cassino, 2016). Central to the idea was that people had exchanged the more politically correct phrase "Happy Holidays" for "Merry Christmas." While some on the network expressed the concern as a secularizing of the United States (Cassino, 2016), the idea that the continuation of dominant depictions of the time from the end of November to the end of December as *the Christmas season* marginalizes people from a myriad of backgrounds (Given the insistence on "Merry Christmas" as a greeting, it sometimes even feels as if marginalization is the goal.) To go a step further, even the treatment of that time of the year as *the holiday season* privileges the ability of Christians to create the narrative of the time of year. Nevertheless, the idea of "Happy Holidays" representing a threat to Christians creates the idea that their status or position is being threatened. From a belief in "Merry Christmas" to the goal to "Make America Great Again," conservative politicians and media outlets in the United States have worked to reassure people—mostly White, middle-class people—that their position as members of the dominant race, class, sexual orientation, gender bias, or religion is and should be stable while ignoring the damage that can be *done* to others when language excludes or privileges.

One of the most important things one can acknowledge in the face of being asked to be more politically correct is that you are not doing so for you. As an example, in 2013 in the wake of a series of unarmed Black men and children being shot and/or killed by police, but in particular in response to the acquittal of George Zimmerman in the killing of Trayvon Martin, #BlackLivesMatter was born (BlackLivesMatter.com, 2019a). It seems like a simple construct: Black Lives Matter. A logical response would be to say, "of course they do!" However, many across the United States responded with #AllLivesMatter, #BlueLivesMatter, or #WhiteLivesMatter. Responding in this way is the emotional equivalent of seeing someone hit by a car screaming out "I am in pain" and responding "We all feel pain." Clearly, in this moment, one person's pain is more relevant than the other. #BlackLivesMatter is born out of a feeling that Black lives matter less than White li2ves. It is an attempt to create "a world where Black lives are no longer systemically target for demise" (BlackLivesMatter.com, 2019b, para. 4). To respond to that kind of pain and insecurity with #AllLivesMatter is not only insulting, it is an act of communicative violence. It is the kind of communicative violence that, no matter if the person is a family member posting to Facebook, you should hold people to account.

What makes the rebellion against political correctness so vitally important is that it is an attempt to divorce the consequences of communication from the act of communicating. When we conceive of communication as a passive or innocuous pastime, the impact of our words, demeanor, or deeds can be dismissed as inconsequential or faulted as misinterpretation. In either situation, the consequences are not the fault of the actions of a communicator; but instead, the actor is relieved of responsibility for their actions. They did not cause harm—harm happened, and thus they have no reason to evolve or learn from the experience. However, when communication is understood as action, the impact or influence of your actions becomes interconnected with the consequences. We understand that there are consequences for when physical harm is caused by another, but communicative harm is often dismissed as someone being overly sensitive or misunderstanding. More than just individual harm, communicative harms can be seen in structures of oppression and systems of subjugation that are used to dominate entire groups of people. We must be accountable both to and for communication. We must learn from the impact and influence of our words and behaviors. No matter how we communicate, our actions have consequences.

Medium, Media, and "The Media"

If you have read any of my past work, one of the pieces you might have come across is a discussion of "the media" (Herbig, 2012). In that article, I critiqued the ways in which the phrase "the media" has morphed into a discursive character without a voice, a character that can be easily scapegoated. Importantly, in that article, I explore Burke's (1954) description of scapegoating and, for Burke, the process is complete once we have sacrificed the goat. In the short time since that argument was published, we have witnessed increased calls that vilify "the media" as "fake news" or "the enemy of the people" (Johnson, 2018). It seems that some in U.S. public life are trying to sacrifice the goat. Unfortunately, what those calls miss is that "the media" is not a singular thing, entity, or person. It does not have a consciousness or fixed agenda. In fact, there is no "it." Instead, we live in an era of declining media industries where it has become more and more important to recognize the limits and potentials of the medium through which *humans* communicate. The words, ideas, threats, theories, facts, opinions, and more expressed through the plural form of medium—media—cannot be treated as a singular chorus if we are to treat communication as action. Instead, what must happen is we must engage the person or representative from which the message originated and examine the implications of what they have done. In order to do so, we must start by acknowledging the difference between the medium and a person.

One of the most prevalent fears of the modern age is the idea that media are ruining our ability to relate to each other. Whether it is a Public Service Announcement about social media addiction or Putman (2000) lamenting our "bowling alone," the notion that media are hindering our ability to relate is prevalent across much of the rhetoric of the connected world. Nowhere is the communication–action binary more evident than in the public discourses about the role that media play in our lives. However, one of the most powerful reminders about how transitions in media are often met was given to us by Ong (1982). According to Ong, during the transition from an age of orality to a time for literacy, Plato warned us that writing is inhuman and that it weakens the mind. Like reactions to the move from oral to written cultures, evolutions and changes in the different media through which knowledge is transmitted and stored have always been met by anxiety. It is through our engagement with how communication media change our relationship to information that we learn the rules and norms needed to govern how those interactions impact our lives.

One of the central questions that needs to be confronted by the modern communication scholar is: Can we separate the singular "medium," the plural "media," and the discursive character "the media" in our understandings of how humans communicate? As part of this discussion, journalist Katy Tur publicly talked about her role in covering the 2016 presidential campaign (Lopez Torregrosa, 2017). Following a 2015 interview with candidate Donald Trump, Tur became a frequent target of the candidate. "Little Katy" became her Trump-moniker and she became his frequent stand-in for the problems with the "fake news." This ad hominem attack on Tur's character made her subject to physical threats, but those threats have not deterred Tur from confronting indictments of "the media" as a member of the press herself. Tur, like many others, occupies an important space where "the media" can be seen of the vast oversimplification of a myriad of voices that very rarely have the same thing to say.

In fact, our understanding of identity will be central to conversations about media for the foreseeable future. According to Calka (2015), because of modern media "We have more possibilities for identity performances, for connecting with others, for creating, altering, and sharing meaning" (p. 28). This transition from mass to polymediated environments has not just created possibilities and potential benefits, but also connected hate groups and terrorists throughout the world. The need to study the influence of the medium and the role it plays in our lives is unquestionable. Ultimately, however, we must not forget that the medium is a channel for the transmission of messages by humans. Even the most complicated algorithm created to monitor your online activities has real human origins, motivations, and implications. Until the robots come to replace us in apocalyptic struggle for control of a dying planet, media are a space for humans to do the work of communication. They are a public space for action.

Communication as a Field, Not a Discipline

In his opening to the final chapter of his book *Speaking Into the Air*, Peters (1999) exclaims "Communication is a trouble we are stuck with. Other people and other times may be immune from such worries" (p. 263). During the rest of the chapter he discusses the differences between talk or dialogue and touch or time. It is a familiar set of distinctions. Nevertheless, as members of a "field" subjugated to a status of "less than" action, we need to reclaim the notion of what "communication is" to include action and assert the need to take seriously our roles as communicators. We need to grapple with meaning, intention, interpretation, and, in the tradition of Foucault (1972): When we think we are finished, we start all over again. The main problem with "models" of communication is that they normally treat communication as something happening external to a human being, as if communication is somehow "out there." Instead, communication is ubiquitous because we are engaged with it all the time. That engagement is action, even if it is what Lao Tzu (1988) would call *wu-wei*, effortless action. Ultimately, as communication scholars, we have to believe that there will never be a time where we are "immune from such worries;" instead, only opportunities for us to continue to learn and grow from communication.

References

Anderson, R., & Ross, V. (2002). *Questions of communication: A practical introduction to theory* (3rd ed.). Boston, MA: Bedford/St. Martin's.

Andone, D., & Crespo, G. (2018, October 27). Suspect's van—plastered with Trump, Pence stickers—a focus of bomb investigation. CNN. Retrieved from http://www.cnn.com

BlackLivesMatter. (n.d.). About. Retrieved January 22, 2019 from https://www.blacklivesmatter.com

BlackLivesMatter (n.d.). Herstory. Retrieved January 22, 2019 from https://www.blacklivesmatter.com

Burke, K. (1954). *Permanence and change: An anatomy of purpose* (3rd ed.). Berkeley, CA: University of California Press.

Calka, M. (2015). Polymediation: The relationship between self and media. In A. Herbig, A. F. Herrmann, & A. W. Tyma (Eds.), *Beyond new media: Discourse and critique in a polymediated age* (pp. 15–30). Lanham, MD: Lexington Books.

Cassino, D. (2016, December 9). How Fox News created the war on Christmas. *Harvard Business Review*. Retrieved from https://hbr.org

Foucault, M. (1972). *The archaeology of knowledge and the discourse on language* (A. M. Sheridan Smith, Trans.). New York, NY: Pantheon.

Fry, S. (2018, May 17). Personal interview. CBC News. Retrieved from https://www.cbc.ca

Griffin, E., Ledbetter, A., & Sparks, G. (2015). *A first look at communication theory* (9th ed.). New York, NY: McGraw-Hill.

Herbig, A. (2012). Understanding the role of "the media" as a character in political discourse: Revisiting Dan Quayle and Murphy Brown. *Ohio Communication Journal, 50*, 129–149.

Johnson, T. (2018, October 29). Just which outlets are Trump's 'enemy'? By his definition, there are many. *Variety*. Retrieved from http://variety.com

Kessler, G. (2018, December 30). A year of unprecedented deception: Trump averaged 15 false claims a day in 2018. *The Washington Post*. Retrieved from https://www.washingtonpost.com

Lao Tzu. (1988). *Tao te ching* (pocket ed.). (S. Mitchell, Trans.). New York, NY: Harper Perennial (Original work published in the 4th century).

Littlejohn, S. W., Foss, K. A., & Oetzel, J. G. (2017). *Theories of human communication* (11th ed.). Long Grove, IL: Waveland Press.

Lopez Torregrosa, L. (2017, June 10). 'You can't rattle her': Katy Tur on the rise. *The New York Times*. Retrieved from https://www.nytimes.com

McGee, M. C. (1990). Text, context, and the fragmentation of contemporary culture. *Western Journal of Speech Communication, 54*, 274–289. doi:10.1080/10570319009374343

McKerrow, R. E. (2015). "Research in rhetoric" revisited. *Quarterly Journal of Speech, 101*(1), 151–161. doi:10.1080/00335630.2015.994915

Montanaro, D. (2018, December 19). Warning to democrats: Most Americans against U.S. getting more politically correct. NPR. Retrieved from https://www.npr.org

Mounk, Y. (2018, October 10). Americans strongly dislike PC culture. *The Atlantic*. Retrieved from https://www.theatlantic.com

Nguyen, T. (2016, October 9). "This is sexual assault": Anderson Cooper confronts Trump with 2005 tape, and Trump lashes out. *Vanity Fair*. Retrieved from https://www.vanityfair.com

Qiu, L., & Tackett, M. (2019, January 4). The shutdown, according to Trump. *The New York Times*. Retrieved from https://www.nytimes.com

Ong, W. J. (1982). *Orality and literacy: The technologizing of the word.* London, UK: Routledge.

Peters, J. D. (1999). *Speaking into the air: A history of the idea of communication.* Chicago, IL: University of Chicago Press.

Politically Correct [Def. 1]. (n.d.). In *Merriam-Webster* online dictionary. Retrieved January 22, 2019, from https://www.merriam-webster.com/dictionary/politically%20correct

Putnam, R. D. (2000). *Bowling alone: The collapse and revival of American community.* New York, NY: Simon & Schuster.

Sanders Comments to Reporters. (2018, October 25). Retrieved from https://www.c-span.org/video/?453612-1/sarah-sanders-absolutely-ridiculous-blame-president-explosive-devices

Watzlawick, P., Beavin Bavelas, J., & Jackson, D. D. (1967). *Pragmatics of human communication: A study of interactional patterns, pathologies, and paradoxes.* New York, NY: W. W. Norton.

Weick, K. E. (1995). *Sensemaking in organizations.* Thousand Oaks, CA: SAGE.

Chapter 16
Communication Is ... Empowering

Amy Aldridge Sanford
Texas A&M University—Corpus Christi

Kristopher D. Copeland
Tulsa Community College

I N EARLY NOVEMBER IN 1872, Susan B. Anthony cast a ballot in New York supporting Ulysses S. Grant for president of the United States of America. Thirteen days later, on Thanksgiving Day, she was arrested in her home for the crime of voting without the right to vote. In 1998, Lilly Ledbetter received an anonymous handwritten note listing salaries for three of her male colleagues at Goodyear; she noticed that her compensation was nearly 40% less with just a year left until her retirement. Also, in the late 1990s, Lindsay Earls, a high school junior in Oklahoma, was called out of choir practice to take a urine test required of all students participating in extracurricular activities in her school district. She reluctantly complied and continued to submit to more testing when asked, even though she felt that the random testing was intrusive.

People's sense of agency (i.e., the ability to act independently) and power (i.e., the ability to influence others) are challenged every day. Anthony wanted the agency to vote in political elections and the power to influence lawmakers to legally count her vote; Ledbetter desired a fair salary comparable to her peers and to have supervisors who valued equity; and Earls wished to say no to an intrusive urinalysis and to have the support of administrators and school board members who would view the testing as unreasonably as she did. Whether a person is asserting their rights, solving a problem, watching disappointing television news, feeling lost in a corrupt bureaucracy, or sitting in a court of law, a person who feels powerless tends to become hopeless (Gask, 2004) and vulnerable (Morris,

2018). These attributes can lead to feelings of depression, anger, and/or apathy, and can potentially cause a person to bring harm to oneself or another person (Murphy, Stosny, & Morrel, 2005). When a person lacks power and feels devalued, both their nonverbal and verbal communication will suffer (Gardezi et al., 2009). In these situations, communication can be unclear, angry, sad, and/or void of any passion. When a person feels disenfranchised, they tend to make poor eye contact, become silent, and/or are inappropriate with how they turn-take in a conversation. Attempts at dialogue often frustrate the disenfranchised because they feel they never win anyway.

On the other hand, people who perceive themselves to have power often get what they want, which motivates them to participate fully in communicative opportunities. They tend to verbalize their objectives, and the most effective amongst them also do a great job of listening and collaborating in interpersonal exchanges (Olenski, 2016). They keep their shoulders back, make thoughtful eye contact, speak clearly without mumbling, and nod their heads when they like what they hear. Although good communication skills cannot solve all problems, the ability to speak persuasively can certainly *empower* powerful people to feel stronger, determined, and more confident, and in return, lead to claiming one's rights and the rights of others. Although it is true that some leaders use power negatively, empowerment (unlike power) requires that a person feels a sense of responsibility that extends beyond personal interests. When a person uses negative power, it tends to be motivated by selfishness and a need to manipulate situations for their own personal benefit. To be empowered, on the other hand, requires empathy and a heart for the greater good.

The shift from power to empowerment requires that a person be willing to speak for a larger group and to put that group's need before their own individual desires. Anthony, Ledbetter, and Earls all accomplished that purpose. They all fought in court (two of them in front of the U.S. Supreme Court), and unfortunately, all three of them ultimately lost their legal cases. However, each woman persevered because she fought for something bigger than herself. They each sacrificed their reputations, time, and finances. They were empowered and understood the power of communication as well. When the judge in Anthony's trial tried to silence her final statement, she famously retorted: "I will not lose my only chance to speak." After the trial, Anthony continued her advocacy as a prolific lobbyist, speechmaker, and author; she traveled by train to give nearly 100 lectures annually in both the United States and Canada. Similarly, Ledbetter continues to lobby the legislature for equal pay laws and travels the world giving speeches. She often turns down speaking engagements because of her lack of finances. Earls became an attorney and worked in Oklahoma for the Cherokee Nation, of which she is a proud member. Each woman found her voice and was empowered through communication.

Power and agency can turn into empowerment for an individual who desires to fight for something bigger than oneself. A person who does *not* reach empowerment is often fighting solely for self-interests. Empowerment can be honed in many ways throughout a person's lifetime, but the activities of (a) competitive forensics, (b) leadership, and (c) activism have historically proven to be quite effective in developing empathy and a worldview bigger than oneself.

Competitive Forensics

It is advantageous to begin practicing effective communication skills early in life. Oprah Winfrey, Nelson Mandela, Margaret Thatcher, Malcolm X, and Antonin Scalia were all active in speech and debate as students. The lessons they learned as teens and young adults followed them into their very successful careers in media, politics, law, and activism. Competitive forensics (which includes events such as public speaking, debate, and the interpretation of poetry, prose, and scripts) take place across a variety of educational levels, from formative years of late elementary, junior high, and high school to collegiate competition. Presently, more than 3,500 high school students compete annually in the National Speech and Debate Tournament, which has been held since 1931 and is the largest academic competition in the world (Nationals History, 2018). At the postsecondary level, during one recent academic year, there were 14 national, 119 regional, and 9 state tournaments hosted within the United States (Tournament Calendar, 2018). Forensics is big business with many participants.

Scholars have noted a variety of communication, educational, and practical skills that forensic competitors learn, such as public speaking, research, argument development, empathy, and critical thinking (see

Amdahl-Mason & Kapoor, 2018; Billings, 2011; Copeland & James, 2016; Woodall & Blake, 2018). Specifically, students use competition events to build explicit arguments to the audience as to why a topic is important and worthy of examination. Performers receive both written and verbal feedback from seasoned communicators, which allows competitors opportunities to fine-tune their craft and adapt their messages for multiple audiences throughout a competition season.

Competing in forensics can be empowering as one learns to empathize and amplify the voices of people who have engaged in different lived experiences from one's own. For example, a student competing primarily in the Southern Region of the United States recently performed a prose interpretation piece regarding Bayard Rustin, a little-known U.S. Black civil rights activist who helped organize the March on Washington and advised Rev. Dr. Martin Luther King, Jr. When the student introduced the piece, he noted that Rustin, who was openly gay, was almost erased from history. The student embodied Rustin and became a voice for multiple disenfranchised groups. In turn, the piece challenged the audience members' paradigms regarding the U.S. Black civil rights movement. It would have been much more convenient for this competitor to choose a well-known prominent figure in the movement, such as John Lewis, Malcolm X, or Rosa Parks. The piece highlights the necessity of bringing voice to the oppressed and moves beyond the self-interest of a general topic on civil rights. As such, forensics provides a space (often before a person is an adult) to raise social consciousness about important topics and to aid in developing empathy for the Other. Forensics allows students to find their voice and experiment with a variety of ideas and topics. Thus, forensics provides an outlet for students to strengthen empowerment through communication.

Leadership

Leadership is the power or the ability to influence others toward a desired outcome. It is something that is earned; in other words, the ability to lead effectively does not automatically happen with an elected or appointed position. When people look to another for leadership, it is partially because that potential leader has effectively exhibited power and agency and can be empowered by other like-minded individuals to do a greater good for their organization and/or social cause. Leaders committed to the latter will be discussed in greater depth in the next section; this section will focus on leadership in industry, government, and professional organizations.

In addition to effectively exhibiting power and agency, another characteristic that empowered leaders exhibit is likability. In short, a leader must be liked by the people who empower them. This concept has been a foundation of leadership communication literature for decades. In 1984, psychologist Robert Cialdini published the book *Influence: The Psychology of Persuasion*, which sold more than 3 million copies, was translated into 30 languages, and is currently in its fifth edition. Cialdini's theory of influence is based on six key principles, including (a) reciprocity—owing another person a favor; (b) commitment—the need to honor a promise; (c) social proof—doing as others do; (d) authority—obeying a person because of their legitimate power; and (e) scarcity—perceiving that something is in great demand. The sixth and arguably most important principle for leadership is (f) liking. Cialdini (1984, 2008) argued that people are easily persuaded by leaders they like. Dale Carnegie (1936), who was quite well known for his public speaking seminars, made a similar argument half a century earlier when he published his best seller *How to Win Friends and Influence People*. In that book, which sold 15 million copies, Carnegie included sections entitled "Six Tips to Make People Like You," "Twelve Ways to Win People to Your Way of Thinking," and "How to Change People without Giving Offense or Rousing Suspicion."

Empowered, well-liked leaders must have (a) the courage to introduce needed change and (b) the communication skills to persuade others that the change is necessary. Two contemporary leaders have done a great job of achieving these goals: Mitch Landrieu, former mayor of New Orleans, and Michael J. Sorrell, president of Paul Quinn College, a Historically Black College or University (HBCU) outside of Dallas that was near bankruptcy when Sorrell came on the scene. In 2018, *Fortune* magazine included both men on their list of The World's 50 Greatest Leaders (2018).

Landrieu will go down in history as the mayor who led the fight to dismantle four Confederate statues in New Orleans. It all began with a 2015 conversation in a coffee shop with his childhood friend Wynton Marsalis, a world-famous jazz musician and son of New Orleans. During the course of a conversation about the city's upcoming Tricentennial, Marsalis explained to Landrieu how hurtful the city's Confederate statues (which were erected as a result of people mourning the loss of the Civil War) were to the Black community—a community that made up two-thirds of the city's population. Marsalis was convincing, and after their conversation, Landrieu made it a goal to have the statues down by 2018, the year of the city's Tricentennial Celebration (Landrieu, 2018). Although Landrieu felt empowered by Marsalis, he knew he had many more stakeholders to persuade. He needed to be empowered by a bigger audience than just his childhood friend.

Landrieu started his persuasion campaign by seeking the advice of a few close advisers, including his father Moon Landrieu, also a former mayor of New Orleans. He then got in touch with leaders of groups who had empowered him on other projects. They were like-minded and were not difficult to persuade regarding the monuments. They supported the project and the mayor publicly within their groups, in the greater community, and in the media. Empowered by their support, Landrieu gathered a tougher crowd—the Tricentennial Committee, but he brought along top historians to discuss the history of the region and facilitate a conversation about the future direction of the city. Landrieu told the group of his plan to replace the Lee statue with a world-class fountain to be revealed at the Tricentennial. He was met with stares and lukewarm support. They were not ready to empower him. Other groups were ready though—including influential local ministers and other city officials. The committee eventually gave in and city councilors voted 6–1 to remove the statues. On the day that the Lee statue was to come down in May 2017, Landrieu gave a public address in which he stated: "You elected me to do the right thing, not the easy thing, and this is what it looks like." The 20-minute speech went viral. Landrieu was given the JFK Profile in Courage Award in 2018.

In early 2007, Michael J. Sorrell received a telephone call from the president of the board of directors at Paul Quinn College (PQC), who wanted him to serve as interim president at the troubled school. Founded in 1872, PQC was in bad shape in 2007, with 15 abandoned buildings, a history of politicians and presidents stealing from it, 30 days of cash remaining, just a couple hundred students, five eligible graduates, $1 million in dispersed student loans to drop outs, and no admissions policy. The accreditation agency had warned them of an impending probation. Sorrell, a lawyer in the Dallas area known for his calm during crisis, had an affinity for PQC—a few of the alumni he had met playing basketball had become close friends. Additionally, Sorrell had many family members who had attended HBCUs; in many ways, he personally felt indebted to HBCUs. He agreed to the interim position.

Like Landrieu, Sorrell began a difficult transformation by consulting close advisers, including his sister, a public school educator. He also hired his friend of 17 years to be his chief of staff. New on the job, Sorrell communicated with 30 college and university presidents and visited their campuses. Based on that communication, he knew what changes needed to happen to keep the doors open at PQC—the college community needed a shared list of values, a dress code, increased security, admission standards, and donors with deep pockets. They also needed to cancel the very expensive football program. Sorrell already had the support of the board and some alumni who empowered him to make changes. He needed the added support of community members, staff, and students. Those audiences were more resistant. When he spoke to the people in the surrounding community and to some of the staff, they would not commit because they did not believe that he would stay. Eventually, Sorrell dropped interim from his title and was able to convince some local philanthropists to give money to specific projects—like removing the 15 abandoned buildings (some of which had trees growing through them). As more high-profile people started to commit publicly, other people began to empower Sorrell as well. Some staff and faculty members decided to leave PQC during the transformation.

Winning students over took a little more work. Early during Sorrell's tenure as president, a staff member heard him arguing loudly with a male student, who ended up in tears. The staff member comforted the student and removed him from the room. Later, the staff member reminded Sorrell that he had a mother who had a love for him that he never doubted. She went on to tell him that PQC students do not always have the same luxury. From that day on, Sorrell was committed to letting the students know that he loved them in words and deeds. The students liked Sorrell, and they empowered him to make bold moves on their behalf.

Today, a community garden (sponsored by Pepsi) is planted on the land that used to house the football field. The students, staff, and faculty live the mantra "We over Me." Every student who lives on campus is guaranteed a paying job and can easily graduate with less than $10,000 in student loan debt. There are admissions standards, a high retention rate, and a dress code. PQC is a safe place that is accredited at capacity with its student body. They have a waiting list for admission and plans to build new buildings to accommodate the growing student population.

Activism

When a group of like-minded individuals work together to change the status quo in a way that is satisfying to them, they are engaging in *activism* (Sanford, 2014). There have been many great social justice activists throughout history, and there is one characteristic they all have in common—they are/were great communicators who worked well with others. Saul Alinsky, a Chicago-based activist wrote one of the first books for community organizers. In it, he articulated his belief that the single most important attribute of an activist was the ability to communicate well (Alinsky, 1971). Although a talent for public speaking often receives the most attention when it comes to necessary talents for activism (think of great orators like Frederick Douglass or Al Gore), interpersonal and group communication skills are just as important for empowerment and community organizing.

Effective activists are wholly present when in interpersonal conversations, listen more than they speak, return people's messages in a timely manner, show gratitude, seek feedback, and keep their promises. They also possess skills that allow them to conduct meetings, perform specific roles within a group, handle conflict, and encourage others to take necessary actions. Historically, social justice activists prefer flexible roles for participants in social movements, and as a result, will rotate leadership positions. One of the most famous examples of this concept is from the Nashville Student Movement. When the civil rights legend John Lewis cofounded the organization as a college student in the late 1950s, the group chose a central committee that would represent and speak for the larger movement. The chair position rotated so that no one person would own the title. They were focused on group effectiveness, not individual power. They believed that "leaders" should follow the people and that the people can lead themselves.

In 2019, Krysten Sinema became the first Democrat from Arizona elected to the U.S. Senate in more than 30 years and the first out bisexual to ever be elected to the U.S. Senate. Many people believe that Sinema experienced this impossible success as a result of her history of coalition building dating back more than a decade. In 2006, Sinema co-chaired Arizona Together—a coalition fighting against a state amendment that would have banned same-sex marriage and civil unions in Arizona. Sinema knew they needed more than the American Civil Liberties Union (ACLU) and Planned Parenthood to defeat the initiative. The amendment did not recognize unmarried families, and therefore would have outlawed the ability to extend healthcare benefits to any unmarried romantic partner. With that information in hand, Sinema and her allies recruited 50 more groups to the coalition—including teachers, police officers, firefighters, and retired persons. She was empowered by this unlikely coalition, and together they defeated the initiative. Sinema (2009) advises activist leaders to form relationships with people who are different from them and to find common ground.

Conclusion

Good communication skills can gain a person many favors—a dream job, a better price on a car, the best table at a restaurant, etc. Those are all examples of the *power* of effective communication—often referred to as the power of persuasion. To be *empowered* though requires a communicator to care about a cause bigger than oneself. Empowerment is not about a dream job; it is about equity in the workplace. Empowerment is not about a better price on a car; it is about fair global trading practices. Empowerment is not about the best table at a restaurant; it asks that everybody have food security. Scholars of communication have a responsibility to focus on empowerment instead of power within their classrooms, at speech and debate competitions, in their social groups, in their advocacy work, and in their greater communities. The best gift the discipline can give is practitioners who are both empowered and empower others.

References

Alinsky, S. D. (1971). *Rules for radicals: A practical primer for realistic radicals*. New York, NY: Random House.

Amdahl-Mason, A., & Kapoor, P. (2018). Forensics' impact on lived experience of millennials: A phenomenological inquiry. In K. Copeland, & G. L. Castleberry (Eds.), *Competition, community, and educational growth: Contemporary perspectives on competitive speech and debate* (3–14). New York, NY: Peter Lang.

Billings, A. C. (2011). And in the end …: Reflections on individual events forensics participation. *Argumentation and Advocacy, 48*(2), 111–122.

Carnegie, D. (1936). *How to win friends and influence people*. New York, NY: Pocket Books.

Cialdini, R. B. (2008). *Influence: Science and practice* (5th ed.). Boston, MA: Allyn & Bacon.

Copeland, K., & James, K. (2016). "My college education has come from my forensics experience": Discussing the educational benefits of forensics. *Speaker and Gavel, 53*(2), 20–38.

Gardezi, F., Lingard, L., Espin, S., Whyte, S., Orser, B., & Baker, G. R. (2009). Silence, power and communication in the operating room. *Journal of Advanced Nursing, 65*(7), 1390–1399. https://doi.org/10.1111/j.1365-2648.2009.04994.x

Gask, L. (2004). Powerlessness, control, and complexity: the experience of family physicians in a group model HMO. *Annals of Family Medicine, 2*(2), 150–155.

Landrieu, M. (2018). *In the shadow of statues: A White Southerner confronts history*. New York, NY: Viking.

Morris, S. (2018). "The torment of our powerlessness": Addressing indigenous constitutional vulnerability through the Uluru Statement's call for a First Nations voice in their Affairs. *University New South Wales Law Journal, 41*(3), 1–40.

Murphy, C. M., Stosny, S., & Morrel, T. M. (2005). Change in self-esteem and physical aggression during treatment for partner violent men. *Journal of Family Violence, 20*(4), 201–210. https://doi.org/10.1007/s10896-005-5983-0

Nationals History. (2018). In *National Speech and Debate Association*. Retrieved from https://www.speechanddebate.org/nationals/

Olenski, S. (2016, March 29). Five communication skills that make good leaders great. *Forbes*. Retrieved from https://www.forbes.com/sites/steveolenski/2016/03/29/five-communication-skills-that-make-good-leaders-great/#248a423f7ae9

Sanford, A. A. (2014). Feminist students' perceived barriers to feminist activism in the Heartland. *Iowa Journal of Communication, 46*, 204–224.

Sinema, K. (2009). *UNITE and conquer: How to build coalitions that win—and last*. San Francisco, CA: Berrett-Koehler.

Tournament Calendar. (2018). In *Council of Forensic Organizations*. Retrieved from https://www.collegeforensics.org/tournaments/2018-01/

Woodall, A., & Blake, S. (2018). Soul sharing: Forensics as a cultivator of empathy and worldview development. In K. Copeland, & G. L. Castleberry (Eds.), *Competition, community, and educational growth: Contemporary perspectives on competitive speech and debate* (pp. 219–230). New York, NY: Peter Lang.

The world's 50 greatest leaders. (2018, April 19). *Fortune*. Retrieved from http://fortune.com/longform/worlds-greatest-leaders-2018/

Chapter 17
Communication Is ... Reification

Katherine J. Denker
Ball State University

Kendra Knight [1]
DePaul University

C OMING OF AGE (IN A SCHOLARLY SENSE) within the field of interpersonal communication, we were introduced to most critical concerns and critical research via other areas of the field. The work of organizational and rhetorical scholars has long championed the issues of power and marginalization (e.g., Ashcraft, 2005; Deetz, 1992), but most of us who developed within the confines of interpersonal communication encountered scholarship grounded largely in psychologically based frameworks that aligned with postpositivist traditions (Stamp & Shue, 2012). Even today, critical interpersonal research reflects only a fraction of the field (Moore & Manning, 2019; Suter, 2016). This is concerning as interpersonal research offers a key site to attend to the microdiscourses that situate power and resistance in our day-to-day interactions and help reinscribe norms and expectations onto ourselves and our relationships. Understanding communication as reification creates a space for us to explore, examine, and offer opportunities to attend to these ideas differently.

To suggest that communication *is* something requires a sedimenting of ideas. In this chapter, we put forth just one of the many ideas that authors in this volume offer. As the reader, it is up to you to evaluate the veracity of these claims—do they have the support that you would like? Do they offer backing to the claims that you would expect? By endorsing any of these claims and sending them forward, in either your own writing

---

1   Thank you to Sarah Vitale for help with work on reification.

or maybe even class discussion, you are helping to solidify the reality of a particular prescription as to how communication is understood. We are sure that you have seen this before: As a group of your colleagues bite into a new reading, or engage in a new theory, you start to see more of the world and our communicative interactions from that lens. As an idea is rearticulated, recreated, and restated, it starts to gain more ground, both in a theoretical discussion and in our social reality. It is from this framing that we propose the claim that communication is reification, or a site in which we construct the more abstract as real. Communication is a making of social worlds (Pearce, 2007), wherein ideas that are viable but not absolute gain greater purchase as they are taken up and reasserted in interaction. To define reification in interpersonal communication, we argue this can be understood as the communicative process by which we make something, typically more abstract, more concrete and/or real.

To articulate our vision of how communication is reification, we first situate our use of reification within and against the Marxist conceptualization of the term. Next, we examine sites of reification in interpersonal communication, as well as the possibility and role of resistance in the communication process. Finally, we broaden our lens for reification and offer instances—including an extended example—that speak to reification as both possibility and problem before offering suggestions for moving forward and wrapping up.

Reification Defined

Our definition and framing of reification both derives and diverges from work within the Marxist conceptualization. Marxist work on reification comes from Marx's framing of alienation, shaped further through Lukacs' discussion of reification. In Marx's (1988) original conceptualization of alienation, he offered four sites of (the workers') alienation—generally from his product, the ways of production, his self, and finally from other workers. This early conception is then taken up by Lukacs (1963) who expands on Marx's original idea and initial framing. In Lukacs' framework, alienation from the object that individuals create—thus removing themselves from their connection to work—is only partial. Yet when we see reification in communication we speak to more totalizing norms that are reproduced and shape our understanding. Lukacs argues that we fail to recognize the social relationships behind things. Similarly, if we understand communication as reification we can note the ways in which the discourse that we privilege also helps solidify social systems and power structures that we might not often attend to.

Our conceptualization of reification diverges from Lukacs and other Marxist thought in three main ways. First, in Marx's conceptualization, alienation and later reification mostly create a site of struggle or estrangement between the worker and capitalist. Though others can also be estranged, that is not the focus. By contrast, in looking at communication as reification through the interpersonal lens, our focus centers on the interpersonal or close relationships as a site for reification rather than that of the more distant organizational or political estrangement. Second, our perspective views individuals as retaining some agency in their lives and as not totally removed from their own power. In Marx's framing of reification, the individual is removed (in terms of their power) from the system and unengaged with the production, where as we see individuals actively engaging in the discursive constructions that are the site of reification, thus wielding power. Like Giddens (1984), we argue that reification occurs via discursive moves that treat properties of the social world as given or real in the same sense as natural phenomena. We acknowledge that individuals are often not aware of or able to problematize the ways in which they are recreating normative values and beliefs in their conversations; however, the possibility for engagement and strategic choice is there. Finally, Marxists argue that the capitalist system gives birth to alienation, which grows from the divide between the individual and the product, shaping all of the normative systems around the pursuit of profit. Though we would agree that capitalism authors normative relations around objectified terms, other norms (e.g., misogyny, heteronormativity) may function removed from the constraints of capitalism.

Discourse shifts and is reestablished in ways that better support arguments. Just as Manning and Stern's (2018) conceptualization of the interpersonal panopticon both draws on and modifies Foucault's (1995) original conceptualization, we, too, acknowledge these differences and move ahead in our framework. However, as academic fields and even subdisciplines of communication offer distinct conceptualizations of terminology, we turn next to define our framework. Moving from Marxist philosophy and returning to a communication-based conceptualization; we draw on scholars across "areas" of our field to best situate how communication is reification, illustrated through interpersonal communication exemplars and concluding with a case study.

Interpersonal Communication as a Site of Reification

Within the field of interpersonal communication, we take reification to mean the space in which individuals in dyadic interactions discursively reinscribe and/or resist definitions, norms, and beliefs in ways that offers power to, and discipline of, the individuals, the relationship, and those in the relationship. In interactions both the resistance and reinscription of norms and power structures can function as a location of reification in discourse as scholars have suggested that when individuals attend to one discourse at the expense of the other it is often an attempt to inscribe another norm in the place of what was first suggested (Baxter, 2011; Kinser & Denker, 2016). Turning first to the possibility of reinscription, we discuss further the ways that discursive reification acts to reestablish existing power structures.

Individuals, relationships, and families do not operate in a vacuum, but instead function as part of larger systems being shaped by—and shaping—the goals and norms of these systems. Research in the field of communication has often illustrated that norms are reinscribed through recursive process. Earlier work in the field of organizational communication spoke to the duality of structure, offering that "the structural properties of social systems are both medium and outcome of the practices they recursively organize" (Giddens, 1984, p. 25). Similarly, Poole and McPhee (2004) stated that "when we draw on structural rules and resources to act within a social system of practices, we also keep that system going" (p. 175). Thinking of the normative value associated with good mothers, Buzzanell et al. (2006) illustrated the ways that working mothers reestablished the requirements of second-shift labor and mothering behaviors of working mothers as enactment of good mothering, both granting legitimacy to the ways in which they parent and work, but also trapping them in discursive structures that normalized gender imbalance and overwork.

Similarly, in the parental discussion of teenage daughters and purity rings, parents reinscribe the norm that young girls lack sexual agency, reifying the norms of parental protection and women as objects of sexuality (Manning, 2014). At the intersection of the home and organizations, we see discourse reified through the discursive spillover of managerial norms that bleed into household interactions (Denker & Dougherty, 2013). Discourses—at the micro, meso, and macro levels—provide templates for understanding and thus guide behavior and interaction. At the same time, discourses are the *outcome* of social practices because actors reproduce discourses in invoking them.

Communication also reifies when individuals discursively *resist* a conceptualization offered by a relational partner, or about a relational type, and instead bolster other frameworks. In ignoring, negating (Baxter, 2011), or disqualifying (Deetz, 1992), individuals turn from one source of power to another. In the resistance of one relational norm in our discourse, we often turn to and reify other norms. This is illustrated in the ways in which working mothers discussed familial feeding practices "strategically pitting" norms off each other in an attempt to avoid material erasure (Kinser & Denker, 2016). Though some of these discursive turns relied on the norms of individualism, which can be seen as harmful to families, these turns allowed working mothers to resist the norms that are often used to frame them as responsible for family meals. Beyond supplanting discourse in interactions through voicing alternatives, individuals can also resist reification of a discourse offered by their relational partner through silence. What is not said can be an important and forceful resistance against reinscribing expectations. The importance of attending to the silence in communication was explicated in Clair's (1998) conceptualization of the voice/\ silence framework. Here, we see that silence can marginalize and oppress members of society, but it can also express protection, resistance, and defiance if it is selected by the individual as a discursive move.

Often, further understanding of a framework can be established by conceptualizing what it is not. Communication as reification does offer a site where we start to solidify and trade in known understandings of concepts. However, those conceptualizations should not be thought of as permanent or immutable. As individuals help to reify discourse they are firming up the frameworks or norms that exist within these conversations, but these discourses are still moveable. Through affirming the discourse of family first we might be reifying a pronatalist discourse, but we might also be adding small nuances to the idea of family first in the conversation. Further, in framing interpersonal communication as reification, we do not argue that the interpersonal communication is an agent in and of itself. Rather, interpersonal interactions exist within a culture ripe with norms and larger discourses that have infiltrated our day-to-day lives. Therefore, it makes sense that after individuals' interactions offer discursive constructions, likely shaped through larger discourses, which normalize and shape power relationships as these discourse are carried forward they then become a site of reification. Suggesting that communication can become a site of reification requires that we clarify the difference between big Discourse (at the cultural level) and smaller discourse (at the level of interaction). It is the smaller interactional-level discourse that we attend to here, and the space where we see those in relationships reproduce and reify larger Discourse.

By exploring instances where communication is reification, you can see how power is solidified through the naming and reinforcing of communicated ideas in ways both helpful and harmful. Reified meanings both enable and constrain. They open up possibilities for action by creating a jointly understood symbol system within which interlocutors can act. They simultaneously limit possibilities by centering certain meanings and banishing others to the margins (Baxter, 2011), sanctioning certain social practices and levying penalties against others (e.g., Schrodt, Baxter, McBride, Braithwaite, & Fine, 2006), and directing the allocation of goods and resources (Dougherty, Schraedley, Gist-Mackay, & Wicker, 2018; Giddens, 1984). Sometimes reification is helpful in advancing social change, as in the case of codifying and building the idea of sexual harassment (Wood, 1992). Though certainly sexual harassment existed prior to the term, not until the codification of the term in everyday language did we have a tool (i.e., a symbolic resource) to assess and address the limitations that individuals were feeling in organizations. On the other hand, instances of reification allow for the continuation of problematic norms. When we look at early work on conflict in interpersonal communication, and specifically the terminology of nag–withdraw patterns (Watzlawick,

Beavin Bavelas, & Jackson, 1967), we see a form of gender-based discursive disciplining, as nagging, a term often reserved for women, recreated a pattern in our interpersonal relationships that limited the way we could understand conflict. Renaming the phenomenon as demand–withdraw (Gottman & Levenson, 1988) offered more inclusive terminology, which then opened up relational possibilities as well as scholarly approaches to its study.

Moving forward in exploring the possibility for more critical theoretical conceptualizations within the field of interpersonal communication, researchers need to attend to both the ways in which communication as reification calls us to explore concepts further as well as the ways in which communication as reification limits our understanding. As researchers, we need to continually interrogate the ways that social scripts both come to play in our interpersonal relationships, as well as the ways in which we privilege discourses and help extend these norms. One helpful standpoint for interrogating these discourses further can be found in the promise of critical interpersonal research (Manning & Denker, 2015; Moore & Manning, 2019). Through the lens of critical interpersonal research, we can attend to reification in its dualistic nature, the both/and. The discursive reinscription exists as both possibility and problem. When couples recreate discourse of family first, they strengthen and help shore up their relationships, but the needs of the individual are swept under the rug, possibly normalizing inequitable gender relations in service of the overall family (Denker, 2013). Framing interpersonal interactions as reification offers a site for theory to move us forward. This provides possibilities in examining romantic relationships, families, and friendships in new ways.

Application/Demonstration

To demonstrate communication's reifying nature in action, consider research from Knight and Wiedmaier (2015) on emerging adults' talk about their casual sexual relationships and experiences during college. Knight's research (e.g., Knight, 2014) has found that college student participants make sense of casual sexual involvements—such as friends with benefits relationships—in a variety of ways. Yet one of the most compelling descriptions of student participants is that friends with benefits relationships are a viable alternative when students are "too busy for real relationships." Even within just this single utterance, the discerning communication researcher can identify two discourses being reified.

The first discourse pertains to what constitutes a "real" relationship. By contrasting friends with benefits to "real" relationships, the college student speaker reifies an understanding of real relationships as containing certain qualities, including but not limited to, romantic interest, psychological intimacy, and perhaps sexual monogamy or commitment. Scholars in a range of subareas within interpersonal and family communication have articulated how reified discourses of "realness" elevate and laud certain relational or family structures, while marginalizing others. The marking of friends with benefits relationships as less than "real" does similar discursive work to sort relational involvement along socially constructed lines demarking (il)legitimacy.

But what of the former part of the utterance, the remark that the participant is "too busy"? Is such an utterance reifying? At face value, this utterance can be accepted as merely a representation of the psychological and material realities facing the relational member. And certainly, an image of a college student who is too busy for a relationship fits with our understanding of contemporary university life and the attendant demands on students' time. However, our argument in this chapter is that to see communication as reifying is to interrogate the social world that communication is making and remaking.

What world is being made or remade when a student says they are too busy for a *real* relationship? Knight and Wiedmaier (2015) claimed that such relational talk remakes a world operated according to the "ideal worker norm" (Williams, 2000)—a world wherein workers are expected to be unencumbered by personal and familial commitments, so as to be completely available and utterly devoted to their career and employer. This is a world that has been discursively remade for generations by early career professionals who delay childbearing in order to focus on launching careers, but Knight and Wiedmaier argue that when used by college students the notion of being "too busy" for relationships reinscribes the norm of ideal work in a new context, an earlier life stage, one of prefamily formation, thus expanding its discursive power and reach.

This example shows us what is gained by examining communication's reifying properties. First, it underscores the world-making nature of communication. Communicating in and about relationships is not a matter of representing relational partners' thoughts and motives, but is about creating social and relational realities. Second, it encourages us toward the crucial social level of analysis, concerning the implications of communicative acts for power structures in our social world. Whose interests are advanced by a sedimenting of these meanings? Whose interests are marginalized? Knight and Wiedmaier's (2015) critical argument was that reifying the ideal worker norm keeps the onus of work–life management on the individual, releasing organizations and public policy makers from the responsibility of valuing and promoting workers' whole selves, and notably their lives outside of work. It also marginalizes individuals by framing noncommitted relationships in emerging adulthood as disposable or falsely inconsequential, and dehumanizes relational partners as insignificant.

Conclusion

Through our daily discourse, communication, especially at the interpersonal level, offers a site in which we construct the more abstract as real. Consider, for example, the ways in which you have accepted frameworks for your own interpersonal relationships that have continued to define your interactions, your conception of self, your definition of the relationship, and your view of your relational partner. At times these definitions and norms have been helpful for building and maintaining your relationships, yet we are sure that you can also think of instances in which the recreation of these discursive frames have operated to limit your relationships or yourself. Such is communication's reifying power.

As communicators, each of us is engaged in the process of making and remaking social worlds, identities, and relational realities. As communication scholars, we are called to attend to the ways this meaning making operates, and the ways in which power and resistance work in all areas of our discourse. We believe that analyzing communication for its reifying properties offers one avenue to achieve this. And doing so realizes a potential, not only for critique, but for speaking a different social world into being.

References

Ashcraft, K. L. (2005). Feminist organizational communication studies: Engaging gender in public and private. In S. May & D. K. Mumby (Eds.), *Engaging organizational communication theory and research: Multiple perspectives* (pp. 141–170). Thousand Oaks, CA: SAGE.

Baxter, L. A. (2011). *Voicing relationships: A dialogic perspective.* Los Angeles, CA: SAGE.

Buzzanell, P. M., Meisenbach, R., Remke, R., Liu, M., Bowers, V., & Conn, C. (2006). The good working mother: Managerial women's sensemaking and feelings about work–family issues. *Communication Studies, 56,* 261–285. doi:10.1080/10510970500181389

Clair, R. P. (1998). *Organizing silence: A world of possibilities.* Albany, NY: State University of New York Press.

Deetz, S. A. (1992). *Democracy in an age of corporate colonization: Developments in communication and the politics of everyday life.* Albany, NY: State University of New York Press.

Denker, K. J. (2013). Maintaining gender relations during work-life negotiations: Relational maintenance and the dark side of individual marginalization. *Women and Language, 32,* 11–34.

Denker, K. J., & Dougherty, D. (2013). Corporate colonization of couples' work–life negotiations: Rationalization, emotion management, and silencing conflict. *Journal of Family Communication, 13,* 242–262. doi:10.1080/15267431.2013.796946

Dougherty, D. S., Schraedley, M. A., Gist-Mackay, A. N., & Wicker, J. (2018). A photovoice study of food (in)security, unemployment, and the discursive-material dialectic. *Communication Monographs, 85,* 443–466.

Foucault, M. (1995). *Discipline and punish: The birth of the prison.* New York, NY: Vintage Books.

Giddens, A. (1984). *The constitution of society.* Berkeley, CA: University of California Press.

Gottman, J. M., & Levenson, R. W. (1988). The social psychophysiology of marriage. In P. Noller & M. A. Fitzpatrick (Eds.), *Monographs in social psychology of language, No. 1. Perspectives on marital interaction* (pp. 182–200). Clevedon, UK: Multilingual Matters.

Hochschild, A. E., (1983). *The managed heart: Commercialization of human feelings.* Berkeley, CA: University of California Press.

Kinser, A. E., & Denker, K.J. (2016) Feeding without apology: Maternal navigations of distal discourses in family meal labor. In F. Pasche Guinard and T. M. Cassidy (Eds.) *Mothers and food: Negotiating foodways from maternal perspectives* (pp. 11–27). Bradford, ON: Demeter.

Knight, K. (2014). Communicative dilemmas in emerging adults' friends with benefits relationships: Challenges to relational talk. *Emerging Adulthood, 2,* 270–279. doi:10.1177/2167696814549598

Knight, K., & Wiedmaier, B. (2015). Emerging adults' casual sexual involvements and the ideal worker norm. In A. Martinez & L. Miller (Eds.), *Challenging social norms and gender marginalization in a transitional era.* Lanham, MD: Lexington Books.

Lukacs, G. (1963) *History and class consciousness*. London, UK: Merlin Press. Retrieved from: https://www.marxists.org/archive/lukacs/works/history/index.htm

Manning, J. (2014). Paradoxes of (Im)purity: Affirming heteronormativity and queering heterosexuality in family discourses of purity pledges. *Women's Studies in Communication, 38*, 99–117. doi:10.1080/07491409.2014.954687

Manning, J., & Denker, K. J. (2015). Doing feminist interpersonal communication research: A call for action, two methodological approaches, and theoretical potentials. *Women and Language, 38*, 133–142.

Manning, J., & Stern, D. M. (2018). Heteronormative bodies, queer futures: Toward a theory of interpersonal panopticism. *Information, Communication, and Society, 21*, 208–223. doi:10.1080/1369118X.2016.1271901

Marx, K. (1988). *Economic and philosophic manuscripts of 1844 Karl Marx*. (Martin Milligan, Trans.). New York, NY: Prometheus Books.

Moore, J., & Manning, J. (2019). What counts as critical interpersonal and family communication research? A review of an emerging field of inquiry. *Annals of the International Communication Association, 43*, 40–57. doi:10.1080/23808985.2019.1570825

Pearce, B. R. (2007). *Making social worlds: A communication perspective*. Malden, MA: Blackwell.

Poole, M. S., & McPhee, R. D. (2004). Structuration theory. In S. May & D. K. Mumby (Eds.), *Engaging organizational communication theory and research: Multiple perspectives* (pp. 171–195). Thousand Oaks, CA: SAGE.

Schrodt, P., Baxter, L. A., McBride, M. C., Braithwaite, D. O., & Fine, M. A. (2006). The divorce decree, communication, and the structuration of coparenting relationships in stepfamilies. *Journal of Social and Personal Relationships, 23*, 741–759.

Stamp, G., & Shue, C. K. (2012). A review of research trends over the past 20 years in family communication research. *Handbook of Family Communication* (2nd ed., pp. 11–28). New York, NY: Routledge.

Suter, E. A. (2016). Introduction: Critical approaches to family communication research: Representation, critique, and praxis. *Journal of Family Communication, 16*, 1–8. doi: 10.1080/15267431.2015.1111219

Tracy, S. J. (2005). Locking up emotion: Moving beyond dissonance for understanding emotion labor discomfort. *Communication Monographs, 72*, 261–283. doi:10.1080/0363775050020674

Watzlawick, P., Beavin Bavelas, J. H., & Jackson, D. D. (1967). *Pragmatics of human communication: A study of interactional patterns, pathologies, and paradoxes*. New York, NY: W.W. Norton.

Williams, J. (2000). *Unbending gender: Why family and work conflict and what to do about it*. New York, NY: Oxford University Press.

Wood, J. T. (1992). Telling our stories: Narratives as a basis for theorizing sexual harassment. *Journal of Applied Communication Research, 20*, 349–362. doi:10.1080/00909889209365343

Chapter 18
Communication Is ... Service

Adam W. Tyma

University of Nebraska—Omaha

Service—To serve, to help, to aid, to direct

T HE ABOVE IS A COLLECTION OF synonyms that came to mind when I
asked myself, "What is 'service'?"

I have been working through this question for a while now. What *is*
communication? Yes, we can break it down into a modeled process—think
Shannon and Weaver (1963), the transactive model, Monroe's motivational
sequence—that is measurable and predictable. Yes, we can contemplate
it though different philosophical houses considering how symbols are
used (semiotics, social constructionism, deconstruction). We can even
throw it all out the window and argue that it is innate. Each of these gets
at aspects of what *it* is. In the next few pages, I suggest that "communication" may not be a state of being but, rather, a perfect incompleteness,
continually in the process of happening-ness.

I am tackling the idea of "service" in the monastic sense or as a "calling." When I look up the definition and etymology of "service," the first
two definitions (as a noun) offered are "the action of helping or doing work
for someone" followed by "an act of assistance."[1] This sounds wonderful.
As a verb, the first two are "perform routine maintenance or repair work"
and "supply and maintain systems for public utility and transportation
and communication." Oddly enough, each of these align with aspects of

---

[1] Google Search, "definition of service," conducted June 7, 2019.

the communication discipline (think of terms of art like "sensemaking," "meaning coordination," "critique," or "analysis"). However, for the etymology of the word, we see the Latin *servus* ("slave") moving to later Latin *servitum* and old French *servise* ("slavery"), finally becoming the old English *service*, pointing toward religious devotion or a form of liturgy.[2] Keep these ideas in mind as we progress through this conversation.

The following is the conversation I have been having with myself over the past couple of years about this very topic. I began capturing my thoughts in earnest while sitting on a boat between Washington State and Canada. It ends while watching the snowfall in Omaha, Nebraska. The following mantra seems to best capture where this conversation is going for me: service through insight, through production, through advocacy. In turn, this will help organize the overarching argument that communication, at its core, is service. I start my work on understanding how and why communication is service and why this has been sticking with me for so long. The first part of this chapter offers my rough thoughts in various locations. The second part is me trying to bring it all together through the three ideas mentioned above, connecting it with other ideas within the discipline, and seeing if it all makes sense in the end.

The Collection of Thoughts

5/28/17—Spencer Spit State Park, San Juan Islands, WA

In the communication discipline, we work to do this. All of the branches—from media to communication studies to rhetoric to performance—and all the myriad ways we signify them, work to do all of this. We serve.

"Service" is both noun and verb, subject and predicate. It is the describer of the thing and the thing itself. Hall reminds us that identity is both product and process, and we are always in the process of becoming (Hall, 1996). The same can be argued with the signifier "service" and of "communication." Perhaps what we may find here is that these actuations of the word "communication" exist at the intersection of the two ontologies—one *is* the other.

---

2   This comes from a quick search on Google for "etymology of service."

I propose an argument, followed by a question. The argument is that communication *is* service and service *is* communication. This entanglement is not unique to the discipline, but it *is* quite pronounced. Shepherd (2000) argues as such when he looks at the etymology the word "communication" and begins to see the origins aligning with terms of "giving" and "serving" (p. 30) the community and the collective. The purpose of this chapter is to explain this particular discursive articulation and, once it is as identified as it can be, wrestle with another philosophical/methodological sign: pedagogy. I propose that, somewhere in this discursive milieu, we can locate the core of what communication is. This will best be done by identifying and articulating each of the concepts: communication, service, and pedagogy. Then, like a Venn diagram, figure out the overlapping parts and interrogate that intersection.

But why ...

Why do this? Why am I wrestling with this? There is often this discussion of communication as an "applied discipline," "needs to be applied," or "we cannot be seen as credible if we are not applied." On the other side of that discussion "we are extensions of Socrates," "we explain the human condition through our use of symbols," or "without a link to our ontological roots, we are nothing." I often see this happening when graduate students, wrestling with their place within the discipline, hit a wall during a seminar. However, any of us who have studied the history of the discipline as a profession, from the days of communication or rhetoric being buried within college English departments to SCA to NCA and now established as truly our own, we see that these questions still extend from perceived and never-resolved "inadequacies." Let's explore this identity crisis first to get at the inevitable realization that we are, as a discipline, both/and/all/"yes."

6/21/17—Crane Coffee, 60th and Center, Omaha, NE

Communication is ...

In 2006, Shepherd, St. John, and Striphas invited scholars in the field to, in a series of short essays, to complete the sentence "Communication as ..." This collections of essays explored the various aspects of the communication discipline, not through the traditional lenses and labels—interpersonal, group, mass, org, etc.—but through the question and central tropes that are explored, challenged, and considered. It is really the first attempt I could find since *Ferment in the Field* (Gerbner & Siefert, 1983) that has collectively examined "who we are." Since reading *Communication as ...*, I have been working to understand our discipline and, one step further out, what communication is at a philosophical level. I think we can approach this question through three different lenses: political, academic, and existential.

Political: The discipline is in a unique political position. It is actually quite rare that those of us in the academy who study the communicative process itself are part of the political conversation in society. The vast majority of us do not run for office, join campaign teams, or even do more than the occasional TV spot. Often, we are on the back end, studying the results and scraps of such discourse. Why are the scholars and the researchers, the teachers of the discipline, not more connected to political discourse? Yes, the occasional letter to the editor or "radical" class lecture or protest rally happens, but what about message crafting at-the-moment? One of the foundational pillars of communication is the art and practice of political persuasion. Read Socrates, see commentary on how to be the strong citizen. Read Aristotle, learn the ways to speak effectively in front of the Senate. Read Cicero, work to be a strong and democratic leader. It is curious that a discipline that places rhetoric as one of its foundational elements does not encourage its practitioners to become involved with politics. If you were to survey a group of communication scholars and practitioners in a setting—say, the lobby at a conference—would you find that the majority of them started their exploration of the discipline through activities like forensics, speech, or debate? Chances are that you would. I know I did. Those sanitized spaces let us develop those ancient skills without getting our hands dirty ... beyond losing a round and facing the ridicule of the ballot. Yes, we train the future politician ... at least, we hope they listen to us, but *we* do not engage the political world. We have our avatars—our token representation—but what about the rest of us? Why is that?

Academic: What are we? Social scientists? Essayists? Philosophers or futurists? Critics? Humanities scholars? Why play the binary? The "this or that?" Go back far enough, and we are all of the above and then some. We are both/and. If you follow the Western traditions (whatever that actually means today), go to our Greek "roots" and both consider the nature of the universe *and* design how argument is created *and* exist within a political world *and* work to measure and understand the natural world. All of this is recognized as foundational to the communication discipline. This myriad discourse constructs the reality that we exist in now. We have been exploring and explaining both the process and product of the communicative act/phenomenon for near 3,000 years (and, again, that is only the Western traditions), yet we appear to be at a point where universities, colleges, and other educational bodies see us as expendable, simply serving the general education part of the program of study. Have we positioned ourselves out of the essential curricula? Is the ability to communicate—to formulate an idea and deliver it to an audience—been declared "basic" or fall under the "well, they should have learned that already" category? Have we "serviced" ourselves into quiet extinction, recognized as only the "public speaking" instructors or public relations skills presenters to the next graduates of that recognizable field?

Existential: So, who are we? The previous questions and comments get us here. At a time when the academy is under continued attack from multiple fronts, when a diversity of voices—once a hallmark of our chosen vocation—is being constricted to guarantee funding, jobs, even physical locations to hold class, when teacher-scholars do not feel free to voice their political, religious, and philosophical foundations because they might either be found to be "too left," "too right," "too radical," or "not radical enough"—at that time (which is right now) any discipline needs to ask this question. "Who are we?" This question ultimately led me to this analysis.

We are scholars of the human condition in its brilliant myriad forms and expressions. Because the discipline was viewed under the moniker of philosophy, we have worked to understand what, how, and why we are who we are. We *serve* the greater good through inquiry, measurement, and critique. If you collect the variety of communication theory textbooks and essays that have been published over the years, we start to see a convergence of definition. Whether you examine Griffin, Littlejohn, Lucas, McQuail, Anderson, Campbell, Burell and Morgan, Craig, Deetz, Baran and Davis, or whatever approach aligns with your own positionality, a common thread emerges: *Communication is both a product and a process. The discipline works to understand the phenomenon that is communication.*

However, we cannot stop there. What good is the study of a thing if you do not actuate on a thing? Knowledge for its own sake is not knowledge at all—it is simply information. *Knowledge* happens when information is applied. Therefore, by our very nature, we are an applied discipline. I would contend, however, that we need to reconsider what is often viewed as "applied."

3/2/18 through 3/10/18—Mumbai, India

I am spending this week working with faculty from Balhk University, Mazar-e Sharif, Afghanistan. Our role is to continue the conversation that has been going on with both Balhk and Kabul University since 2009 through multiple grants from the U.S. State Department that will ultimately lead to the formation of Communication Studies and Journalism departments on those campuses. In particular, the Communication Studies academic units might be the first departments in that part of the world that actually focus on the communication discipline. What an amazing opportunity ... and I am completely overwhelmed. It might be here that I am actually and fully understanding what is meant by "service."

For starters, our (the faculty team that I am part of) purpose is to prepare these faculty—who do not have the Western privilege for the most part to have the advanced training the team has—to get them at least ready enough for, as our team lead says, "teach day 1." What this looks like on paper, and what it actually becomes in reality, are oceans apart. How does someone who has been immersed in particular aspects of their discipline take that knowledge and transform it in such a way that someone who does not have the same immersion can be ready to teach it? It is more than just a "class in a can"—it is a whole discipline, one that (particularly with communication studies) is rarely if ever even discussed or taught in the region. Are we serving them or setting them up for failure? When we challenge the Afghans own belief structures on race, gender, or class by the very existence of those ideas within the discipline that we adhere to, how are we serving them? It is in the asking of these questions of myself, particularly before I joined the team (which I was hesitant to do for a host of reasons) that "service" really came to me.

Now that I have had time to come back and reflect on what I experienced in India, and through working with the faculty from these two universities that simply want to offer the best they possibly can to their students, "service" starts to reveal itself to me in a bigger sense. The connection to a more secularized view of "monastic" service is starting to be revealed. Consider that we (the team) started this project as a way to help this particular group any way we could. Near-immediately, we realized that we needed to get rid of the notion that this Westernized way of understanding communication as "universal" needs to be done away with. This is not true at all. We talk about it within intercultural communication theory and studies, but we really do not get it. Once we shed that skin, we can truly serve. We can truly communicate.

9/11/18 through 9/12/18—Home office, Omaha, NE

Pedagogy: The intersection between the communicative act/process/ phenomenon and teaching (as a praxis) is not new to the discipline. Any of the Socratic dialogues, Platonic insights, Aristotelian measurement and modeling, and a myriad of others all point towards the intersection of the communicative act (whether it is oration, argument, critique, etc.) and being taught the particular thing. Currently, one of the key areas that Communication explores *is* the teaching act. Through the communicative act, we are informing on (or, to put it another way, *teaching* about) the world around us. The use of symbols to encapsulate ideas—the connection of those symbols and ideas to our daily action and interaction—all are taught realities.

Because the discipline works to understand the communicative phenomenon, those in the discipline have to help others understand all aspects of it as well. Is this not, then, teaching? If it is at the core of our philosophical construct, is it not, then, pedagogy? We are teaching ourselves about "ourselves" at every level, from the intrapersonal statements and moments we take to the group/mass moments that occur all around us. We are observing, commenting, interrogating, measuring, and critiquing. Then, we are bringing those observations, comments, results, and critiques back around to both ourselves and those that we serve.

Our pedagogy *is* our discipline. This is the reality we exist in. We start with questioning. We end with teaching. Then we start again.

The Three Ideas: Insight, Production, and Advocacy

Looking through the headings above, the circle does come back to service (see opening discussion), so I might be onto something here. The headings also demonstrate an intersection between these ideas. Does this mean that "service" becomes a dominant artifact for consideration? I think so. Communication creates and critiques the spaces we exist in. By that very fact, the discipline serves all aspects of those spaces—of our spaces.

In my classes, from an introductory course to a graduate seminar, we always start at the beginning, the foundational premise (at least for me) of Communication. When I move into fundamental aspects of the discipline, before diving into the various lexicon and jargon that causes the first glaze to form across my students' eyes, I try to explain that Communication, as a field of study and discipline, is working to understand the process and product of the communicative act. We work to understand the ideas as a complete phenomenon, from the initial thought and moving out in whatever directions the act takes.

From there, we move to how we create that understanding, and finally how we use that understanding. It is from there that three words emerge that signify the idea of service: insight, production, and advocacy. The remainder of the chapter explores what has been mentioned thus far and funnels it through these three words.

Serving through insight: Insight, at its core, is the recognition of inner wisdom. Etymologically (as discussed earlier), the word starts to show up in 16th-century Franco-Germanic languages, extending from a potential Latin root. Five hundred years later, we are still considering what insight truly is. However, if the premise that communication works to understand the act and phenomenon of meaning-making through symbols, the creation of use of those symbols points near-directly to the human condition and the process itself. In other words, through insight, we serve those who communicate. This search for insight is at the core of how the communication discipline has existed and evolved over time. We have always searched—some argue for a truth, some argue for *the* truth, and others simply want to understand just a little more. This is where communication really moves into the realm of philosophy—an attempt to better understand the human condition through interrogating the phenomenon of symbolic usage. It is argued the communication creates reality. That language/discourse/words have the power construct the world around us. It is this insight that forces us to recognize and confront the construction of our own realities.

This insight is found in the Socratic dialogues, where citizens were forced to confront their own internal and external spaces through questioning how those spaces are created and performed. It is found in the first studies into mass communication, exploring how specific mediated messages might affect audience through government-funded research (granted, the direct effect model developed here was quickly discounted, but the search for insight was there). The search for insight is also seen in the explosion of speech communication as a discipline starting in the 1950s, when scholars began establishing the study of symbolic usage across new fields of study: interpersonal relationships, familial structures, and organizational spaces. It is seen today at the intersection of communication as a discipline with other disciplines of study, all working to better understand this space we occupy. Communication serves by offering an ontologic and epistemic paradigm that can be nuanced, massaged, and developed to better see the world we inhabit.

Serving through production: How do we produce? How does that production serve communities, peoples, organizations, individuals, families? The term "production" is often aligned with media creation of one form or another. Courses are taught around media production. Departments in media companies are named this kind of production or that kind of production. We often do not consider the writing of the essay, the delivery of the speech, the development and performance of a lesson plan, the advising of the student, or even the informed answering of a question as production—yet I contend that we should. In all of these cases, we are encoding the insights we have constructed, discovered, uncovered, come across, and accepted into these products. Those who practice the communication discipline engage in, depending on your epistemological positioning, the production of knowledge *or* the production of lenses *or* the production of critique to best understand the realities that exist around us. We gift (to use Young's parlance in this collection) these products to those that we serve as a way to ensure that we all understand these worlds we exist in.

If *production* is part of this service, then there is an ethical responsibility to use all of what we have learned through our interrogations of communicative (and, by extension, human) phenomenon to ensure that the limiting, marginalizing, coercive, or caustic realities created through past productive moments are not repeated. When I teach media research methods, film theory, and even an introductory journalism course, Laura Mulvey (1975) always arrives in the conversation, along with the Bechdel test or what has been coined the "Sexy Lamp" test. Each of these tests, applied to any mediated scripted text, easily and painfully demonstrate the positionality of women (and, really, anyone who does not identify as a heteronormative White male) is objectified through the very production values that are taught within our media production labs and courses. We produce reality. Which reality do we advocate for? How do we decide? What do we produce through our service?

Serving through advocacy: Service is more than considering the human condition or offering knowledge about the human condition. Service is acting to better the human condition. It is this action that transforms into advocacy. Regardless of the area of the discipline that we each work from and through—at the end of the day, we are advocating for an idea, a position, a discovery.

Communication is in a unique position to do such a thing. Aristotle taught that rhetoric is the act and art of persuasion (side note: does that mean that we *all* are rhetoricians?). We analyze and critique the message from creation to consumption and beyond. We understand all aspects of it. We should ask ourselves if the next study we are going to engage in, the next project we are going to take on, or the next questions we are going to ask *actually* serve society? Communication, at its root, is a communal act. It needs a community. Even at the level of intrapersonal communication—because it involves language—language only exists in order to exchange ideas and coordinate activity. Therefore, language assumes community. Community leads to, well, the communicative act. When we design that next study, lecture, class, model, or theory, we need to remember that we are not just informing publics of our results, we are advocating for more than a position. We are advocating for those who implement our ideas, who internalize our findings into their own praxis. It is at this moment, where advocacy and production and insight intersect, that we recognize that communication is truly service.

Where we are now ...

What started on a boat during a cool May morning ends here, in front of my computer at home, more than 2 years later. The communication discipline is not a throw-away discipline. It is not "the folks that teach that General Education class that everyone is required to take." It is not a service in the Latin sense, as a collection of thinkers, only good for the menial labor. We are the discipline embodied. Those who engage the questions of how we create our realities through the symbolic exchange that we are involved with at any given moment are both practitioners and scholars of communication. If our goal is to understand the human condition, to bring that knowledge to others, and to advocate for a better reality through the act, then we truly are serving the greater good. In that sense, communication is service—and "to serve" is the infinitive definition of communication.

References

Gerbner, G., & Siefert, M. (Eds.). (1983). Ferment in the field: Communications scholars address critical issues and research tasks of the discipline. *Journal of Communication, 33*(3).

Hall, S. (1996). Introduction: Who needs identity? In: S. Hall & P. Du Gay (Eds.), *Questions of cultural identity* (1st ed.) pp. 1–17. London, UK: SAGE.

Mulvey, L. (1975). Visual pleasures and narrative cinema. *Screen, 16*(3), 6–18. doi:10.1093/screen/16.3.6

Shannon, C. E., & Weaver, W. (1963). *The mathematical model of communication.* Champaign, IL: University of Illinois Press.

Shepard, G. J. (2000). Communication as an interpersonal accomplishment of communication. In G. J. Shepard and E. E. Rothenbuhler (Eds.), *Communication and community.* pp. 25–35. London, UK: Routledge.

Shepard, G. J., St. John, J., & Striphas, T. (Eds.). (2006). *Communication as ... perspectives on theory.* Thousand Oaks, CA: SAGE.

Chapter 19

Communication Is ... Voice

Mohan Dutta

Massey University

I N THIS CHAPTER, I WILL OUTLINE the nature of communication as voice, attending to the role of voice as the basis of inequality as well as an anchor for structural transformations (Dutta, 2004a, 2004b). Voice, the public expression of opinion in ways that matter, as communication lies at the heart of processes of marginalization, constituted by overarching socioeconomic inequalities and, in turn, reproducing these inequalities. The hegemonic formations of communication are integral to the reproduction of inequalities globally, embedding in themselves the logics of erasure. The erasure of the voice(s) of the margins is integral to the reproduction of the hegemonic logics of capitalism and colonialism. Technologies of communication, framed as solutions to poverty, underdevelopment, absence of democracy, absence of technology, are often disseminated to communities at the margins, with the work of communication configured as the dissemination of modernist tools of growth and development. The paradox of voice lies in the deployment of voice-based interventions for empowerment, participation, and engagement that reify the very structures of neoliberal[1] capitalism that fundamentally

---

1   Neoliberalism is a political economic formation based on the principle that the free market, left to itself without state intervention, is the basis for solving local, national, and global challenges. Under neoliberalism, private capital is privileged, with minimization of tariffs and trade barriers, weakening of labor unions, minimization of welfare programs, and privatization of public resources.

erase subaltern[2] voices and displace subaltern communities from their spaces of livelihood.

The marking of a community, people, collective as without voice or without the capability for voice forms the basis of communicative colonialism, formed as a solution to the problems of the colonized spaces that have been rendered voiceless. The erasure of voice is integral to the reproduction of knowledge claims, constituted within the networks of colonialism. The (neo)colonial enterprise is built upon the erasure of sites of articulation from the subaltern margins. What then are the communicative processes through which subaltern voice is erased? The subaltern, marked as a trace, as without a voice, is incorporated as a category to be targeted, as the object of technocratic neocolonial interventions. The dominant framework of communication knowledge, embedded within the logics of Whiteness and intertwined with the agendas of capitalism, render as normative the claims originating from institutions, organizations, and structures that serve as the instruments of colonialism. Simultaneously, the voices from subaltern spaces, marked as illegitimate, primitive, and traditional, are strategically erased, paradoxically through the deployment of the very narrative of empowerment. Interventions, developed in elite networks of expert power anchored in neoliberal capitalism, are directed at subaltern communities to bring about change. Particularly salient are expert-designed projects of engagement, participation, and dialogue, embedded in elite logics of technocratic control deployed to promote capital through the incorporation of the subaltern. Digital technologies of capital, formulated as e-engagement, participatory democracy, smart participation, deliberative platforms form the futuristic version of the neoliberal engagement industry, performing the veneer of participation to precisely erase subaltern voice. The erasure of subaltern voice is tied to the subaltern being cut off from access to structures of mobility, depicting the interplay of communicative and material inequalities.

Communication infrastructures for voice are critical to addressing the challenges of inequalities across sites and spaces (Duran et al., 2010). That those who are cut-off from pathways of mobility are also rendered

---

2   Subalternity refers to the condition of being erased from dominant discursive spaces and resources.

voiceless points toward the transformative role of voice in challenging the immobilities. Drawing from the key tenets of the culture-centered approach that centers subaltern voice as an anchor for structural transformation (Dutta, 2004a, 2004b, 2008), I will outline the roles played by voice infrastructures as anchors to resisting and transforming inequalities at local, national, and global levels. Moreover, the contexts of global challenges from the increasing global inequalities to the disproportionate burdens of climate change being borne by the poor offer the contexts for conceptualizing voice as a basis for generating alternative knowledge claims and building struggles at the global margins. Amid the accelerated project of global neoliberal transformation in different forms and textures of neoliberalism, voice offers an anchor to transformative change. Through the presence of the voices of the marginalized in global discursive spaces, material transformations are realized. Alternative imaginaries of local, national and global organizing based on communicative equality are placed as counterhegemonic anchors. Voice offers the basis for collective organizing and raising demands at the global margins, bringing about fundamental transformations in how societies are organized. Drawing from cases of raising voice from across the globe, the chapter will attend to the ways in which voice transforms unequal material formations.

Communicative Inequalities and Structures

That communicative inequalities, inequalities in the distribution of communicative resources (such as traditional media that carry voices, communication campaigns, digital media, face-to-face meetings, consultations), mirror structural inequalities is one of the key conceptual threads of the culture-centered approach (CCA). Drawing from subaltern studies theory (Guha, 1997), the CCA interrogates the processes that produce erasure of voice(s) (Dutta, 2008; Zoller & Dutta, 2009). Subalternity as the condition of erasure, is marked by ongoing processes of communication that shape the forms, rules, and roles of communication in interactions, spaces, and discursive sites. These forms, rules, and roles of communication in hegemonic structures erase subaltern articulations through their assumptions about the role of communication in interactions. The material inequalities in distribution of economic opportunities is constitutive of inequalities in access to communicative opportunities, particularly opportunities for voice. Moreover, the erasure of subaltern voices from sites and spaces of decision-making is tied to the reproduction of material inequalities. In this sense, inequalities in distribution of communication both constitute material inequalities in distribution of opportunities for well-being, and are produced by these material inequalities. Take for instance, the systematic absence of infrastructures for voice among African American communities in the United States amid their everyday negotiations of Whiteness. The materiality of police atrocities and murders of African American communities is constituted amid the absence of communicative infrastructures for African American voices in the White mainstream, continually erasing the narrative accounts of racism and violence. Similarly, consider the erasure of communicative infrastructures for indigenous voices in the United States, which forms the backdrop of the material practices of violence and erasure by the settler-colonial U.S. state, as evidenced in the recent example of neocolonial occupation of indigenous land for the Keystone XL pipeline. The everyday struggles of the poor with housing and hunger is constituted amid the lack of communicative infrastructures for the poor where the voices of the poor can be heard in ways that matter (Dutta, Hingson, Anaele, Sen, & Jones, 2016; Gordon & Hunt, 2019).

Subaltern Bodies and Erasure

Erasure of voice is intrinsic to the production, mapping, and circulation of the subaltern body (Dutta, 2018). The subaltern body emerges in hegemonic communication as the body to be mapped, managed, and incorporated into the circuits of capital and colonialism, while her voice is systematically erased from opportunities of articulation. Communication here is mapped and configured as information, to be strategically formulated and disseminated to the subaltern recipient. The overarching history of communication within the dominant framework of persuasion reflects this ideology, with information as a tool for transforming recipient communities into sites of modernization. The "science" of communication therefore has worked to develop the effective tools of communication that generate positive outcomes in targeted communities, mostly devoid of dialogic possibilities for listening to subaltern voices. Consider for instance the framing of indigenous engagement in science communication that parochially constructs engagement as a tool for disseminating science (designed by experts in largely neoliberal institutions, embedded in networks of profiteering) to indigenous communities (Kulis, Wagaman, Tso, & Brown, 2013). Similarly, consider the arrogance and paradox inherent in climate change adaptation outreach that targets indigenous communities to teach them about the science of climate change, erasing the extensive body of indigenous knowledge on climate, environment, and indigenous principles of adaptation (Jackson, Tan, Mooney, Hoverman, & White, 2012).

Informatization. Information, conceptualized as message disseminated through strategic channels to target audiences, works as an instrument for generating change in individual-level beliefs, attitudes, and behaviors (Dutta, 2008). Communication as information is disembodied, targeted at the individual removed from her sociocultural context, community ties, and from the structures that constitute her everyday negotiations (Dutta, 2005). The individualization of communication forms the basis of effective messaging, with the subaltern recipient configured as the target audience to be deciphered, scripted, and then targeted through information. Effective audience analysis through the fixing and deciphering of the characteristics of the target audience therefore is the key to the formulation of effective messages that would lead to the "desired behavior change" in the subaltern population.

Disconnected from the overarching structures that constitute well-being and from the logics of capital that fundamentally threaten the well-being of many subaltern communities across the globe, the individualized target population is the subject of communication packages that she is bombarded with. In this framework, communicative inequalities are constructed as inequalities in the distribution of communication channels for disseminating information, devoid of the structural contexts of inequalities and integral to the perpetuation of a colonial approach to communication. That subaltern communities are devoid of knowledge and therefore to be enlightened through effective messages forms the basis of hegemonic communication. The solution to communication inequalities as the dissemination of newer technologies of dissemination (note for instance the narratives of digital inequalities) creates new market opportunities, incorporating the subaltern through promises of enlightenment and participation. Consider for instance the wide array of digital interventions targeting subaltern communities that position technologies as giving voice to the communities. Similarly, consider the wide range of app-based interventions that are designed for subaltern communities, projected as giving them tools to move out of poverty.

Postcolonial critiques and multicultural appropriation. Postcolonial critiques of the top-down framework of communication have been incorporated into the hegemonic structures of communication, with emerging cultural approaches positioning themselves as frameworks for addressing difference (Dutta, 2018). Postcolonial critics, themselves often elites in postcolonial societies, often remain oblivious to the inequalities in distribution of political and economic resources within postcolonial societies. The turn to culture is positioned as enabling difference, with difference itself becoming a market category. References to cultural intelligence serve as the new instruments of capital, gathering cultural knowledge to shape new techniques of penetration, management, and profiteering. Extracted from the spaces of everyday negotiations and contestations, culture is a marketable category, measured through specific indices of cultural participation. Constructions of hybridity incorporate the postcolonial other into celebratory narratives of globalization, writing over the inequalities that constitute communication within postcolonial societies. References to cosmopolitan movements celebrate specific forms of postcolonial mobility (of the upper class, typically educated postcolonial subject) in culturalist accounts, erasing the voices emerging from the margins of postcolonial formations. For instance, in postcolonial celebrations of Indian hybridity in global cultural circuits (consider for instance accounts of global Bollywood, flows of Bollywood celebrities and products), voices of indigenous communities, Muslims, and dalits (lower caste untouchable Indians) are violently erased.

Similarly, the politics of class that constitutes the inequalities in access to spaces and pathways of mobility within postcolonial spaces is erased from the articulations of cultural hybridity. The subaltern as a category is utilized to depict erasure, while simultaneously failing to recognize the historical and ongoing struggles of subaltern groups for voice. The argument that "because a subaltern has been heard, she no longer is a subaltern" is thrown in superficially to disengage from, much less offer solidarity with, the ongoing struggles for subaltern voice and sovereignty. The recognition of the erasure of the subaltern on one hand individualizes subaltern agency, and on the other hand, remains oblivious to the many subaltern movements and struggles across the Global South and the South in the North seeking to create collective registers for subaltern voice for a transformative politics. For instance, in the context of Indian social movements, ongoing organizing of indigenous communities against land grab is a key site for resistance to the accelerated expansion of neoliberal capitalism.

In another strand of work, culture shapes intelligent program development and communication design. Broadly categorized as the cultural sensitivity approach, this turn to culture in communication treats culture as an aggregation of static characteristics that can then inform effective message design. The power is very much held by the hegemonic communicator and the structures he or she is working within, with knowledge being located within the institutional settings from which communication emerges. From communication campaigns targeting subaltern communities (such as healthy eating campaigns designed by experts embedded in Whiteness targeting Maori communities, pushing *Pakeha* ideology of healthy eating) to culturally sensitive communication in clinical encounters (such as cultural training for providers and nurses on cultural characteristics of specific communities), culture emerges as a category for effective management, to be scripted into strategies that lead to effectiveness as defined by the hegemonic actors. Paradoxically, the treatment of culture as a category to drive effective communication often continues to keep the inequalities intact, failing to recognize the agentic capacities of subaltern participants.

Voice and participation as tools of erasure. Voice is a key element of contemporary neoliberal transformations, amid the global resistance to neoliberalism (Rastogi & Dutta, 2015). International financial institutions (IFIs) such the World Bank and International Monetary Fund regularly deploy voice-based projects. Participation is the key to these projects, incorporated into the frameworks of the structural adjustment programs of privatization and opening up of markets driven by these IFIs. New information technologies, positioned as technologies of empowerment, are disseminated to subaltern communities, with programs designed around skills building and creating access to technologies. The overarching control on these voice projects are held by the IFIs, with voice emerging as a tool for legitimizing the neoliberal project. Individualized empowerment is framed as a solution to development, with market-based offerings promoted through the technologies of capital.

Worth noting here is the absence of infrastructures within the hegemonic sites of global capital where subaltern voice would be heard and through the process of being heard, would lead to transformative change in the organizing processes of neoliberal capitalism. The new engagement industry throws in the rhetoric of dialogue and participation to incorporate the subaltern voice into the trajectory of global capital. Global foundations, private corporations, and public–private partnerships see new market opportunities in voice technologies, with the dissemination of these technologies framed as empowerment. The category of empowerment is itself colonized, registered in the language of the market and participation in market-based processes. These new communication technologies of participation work to incorporate the "new subaltern" as the frontier of transnational capitalist profiteering.

Technologies of empowerment. The neoliberal transformation of the globe is achieved through technologies and techniques of empowerment that position themselves as solutions to poverty and dispossession (Sharma, 2008). Paradoxically, the very technologies of capital that reproduce impoverishment are framed as solutions to poverty. Consider for instance the structural adjustment programs (SAPs) and their later versions, the poverty reduction strategy papers, that have been pushed by the World Bank as solutions to poverty, framed in the language of poverty alleviation, while these programs have actually worked to consolidate power and control in the hands of private capital, push for free market reforms that have displaced communities from their sources of livelihood, and systematically attack state-based welfare programs. The turning of the subaltern into a consumer of the technologies of capital is achieved through the narrative of empowerment. Programs of empowerment run by global networks of NGOs bring new market opportunities for technology corporations, incorporating subaltern bodies as sites to be profiteered from. Projects such as voice-based digital training programs for youth in urban slums present themselves as emancipatory tools for voice while co-opting participation of the youth within the structures of technology corporations, and in doing so, building new market opportunities for global technology corporations.

Similarly, the turn to "Smart Cities" as the basis of big data governance through e-participation and digital deliberation incorporate participation into authoritarian structures of control, actually working to erase participation. Consider for instance the proliferation of e-deliberation and e-participation in the Asian "Smart City" Singapore, where an authoritarian regime works systematically through techniques of control to erase democratic spaces and subaltern voices. Paradoxically, digital platforms projected as platforms of participation are deployed as platforms of surveillance and control. When culture-centered voice infrastructures emerge within such contexts of neoliberal authoritarianism, such as in the example of the "No Singaporean Left Behind" advocacy campaign created by the poor in Singapore (Tan, Kaur-Gill, Dutta, & Venkataraman, 2017), various techniques of repression are deployed through state structures to control, manipulate, and erase the infrastructures.

Culturally Centering Voice

In the backdrop of the erasure of subaltern voices through the very techniques of participation and engagement, the culture-centered approach (CCA) foregrounds the agentic roles of subaltern communities in their struggles for voice. Communicative inequalities are constitutive of and constituted by structural inequalities (Dutta, 2004a, 2004b, 2008). What then are the opportunities for equalizing access to spaces/infrastructures for voice? Noting that voice is intertwined with listening and that the realization of voice is made possible through listening, subaltern struggles depict their work of/with communication for recognition and representation, based upon rules and norms that emerge from subaltern contexts (Carvalho, Pinto-Coelho, & Seixas, 2016). Beginning with the question "who shapes the rules and processes of communication?" the CCA explores the communicative infrastructures for voice that emerge from within subaltern communities in their everyday struggles (Dutta, Anaele, & Jones, 2013). An ongoing commitment to building communicative equality shapes the recursive processes of community participation, shaping through community voice the distribution of communicative resources and opportunities.

Salient to these struggles is the collective articulation of subaltern resistance as a feature of voice, alongside the role of voice in shaping a politics of solidarity. Through their voices, subaltern communities offer alternative imaginaries of organizing that challenge neoliberalism and the expansionist logics of global hypercapitalism. The architectures of listening disrupt hegemonic categories of communication, transforming theories of communication. The recognition of communication as voice interrupts the hegemonic position of academic theorists of communication in the Global North, putting forth openings for thinking through, living with, and practicing communication differently. In this section, I offer three examples of the roles played by voice as communication, incorporating the concepts of voice as communicative right, voice as collective, and voice as solidarity. These key principles of voice I argue position it in resistance to neoliberal capitalism, anchoring it in principles of communicative equality (Dutta, 2015).

Voice as communicative right. The concept of communicative right reflects the right to having one's voice be heard in ways that are meaningful (Dutta, 2008). The anchor to meaning lies in the lived experiences of subaltern communities, with its embodiment in the realization of desired actions and outcomes. The unequal distribution of communicative right is tied to the hegemonic formations of communication, with the nature and role of communication being shaped by those in power. Voice as a communicative right resists and transforms this power differential by situating the right to define what is meaningful communication in the hands of subaltern communities. The communicative resources, infrastructures, and platforms emerge from community voice, with community members participating in defining and building these resources. In other words, community members voice their understanding of communication, work collectively in challenging hegemonic structures that erase communicative rights, and seek pathways of communication in being heard (Salsberg, Macridis, Garcia Bengoechea, Macaulay, & Moore, 2017). For instance, in their struggles against state violence, threats to dignity by the police–military apparatus, and state-led privatized projects of development, indigenous communities in Eastern India communicate through their drums, songs, dances, and blowing of conches. Communication as collective expression is formed in community members coming together to sing and dance, and through these performances expressing their resistance to the onslaughts on their dignity. Similarly, in subaltern movements for water rights among indigenous communities in Latin America, community-wide meetings emerge as spaces for articulation within, and street performances and blockades emerge as spaces for voicing the demands for water rights to the local, national, and global structures. In our collaborations with communities experiencing hunger, the communicative right to voice forms the basis of activist interventions developed by the poor that talk back to neoliberal structures, disrupting the ideology of the "lazy poor" circulated by such structures to minimize welfare policies (Dutta, Anaele, & Jones, 2013). Consider for instance the voices of foreign domestic workers working in precarious conditions, often under conditions of bonded labor and/or labor trafficking (Dutta & Kaur-Gill, 2018), in Singapore. Amid an authoritarian framework of state control, where scholars within the dominant institutions undermine the capacity of a rights-based framework by incorrectly and selectively discounting such frameworks as Western (see for instance Koh, Goh, Wee, & Yeoh, 2017), the very articulation of rights to decent labor conditions emerge as disruptions, embedded in the right to voice.

In their struggles for communicative rights, subaltern groups participate in communicative spaces that are constituted by local cultural logics and draw on local knowledge, and simultaneously strategically deploy hegemonic tools of communication in hegemonic spaces to disrupt neocolonial capitalism. The concept of voice as a communicative right is also tied to the redistribution of communicative opportunities within subaltern communities, attending to the ways in which inequalities within community spaces create sites of erasure. The framework of culturally centering the communicative right to voice therefore continually asks, "Who is missing from this discursive space?" "Whose voice is being erased from this discursive space?" seeking to continually democratize communicative spaces and to achieve communicative equality. The reflexive interrogation of power and the plays of power in silencing voices of the margins within community spaces is anchored in a commitment to communicative equality, the ongoing creation of communicative opportunities for the margins through the everyday work of reflexivity.

Voice as collective. Decentering the individualizing logics of communication, voice as collective attends to the collective formations and spaces that form the basis of struggles for recognition and representation (Basu & Dutta, 2009; Kapoor, 2009). The large majority of subaltern social movements across the globe depict the transformative role of collectivization, with the collective offering an anchor to the struggle. It is through their organizing into a collective, subaltern communities express their voice(s). The organizing into a collective is a key ingredient in the struggle for recognition, cocreating spaces within communities for voice. These spaces within communities are built on normative ideas and principles of communication that are embedded in community norms (Duran et al., 2010). By coming together as collectives, subaltern communities articulate strategic identities that enable them to make claims and seek structural transformation. The formation of the collective as a space for voice further opens up the question of opportunities of participation within the collective. The recognition of the power inequalities within communities therefore is tied to struggles for democratizing communicative rights.

Voice as solidarity. The violence embedded in hegemonic structures of global capital strategically erases voices from the subaltern margins when they are articulated (Dutta, 2018). These voices from the subaltern margins are threatening to the hegemonic structures. The presence of subaltern voices within/into hegemonic discursive spaces/sites on one hand, invites techniques of erasure through claims of civility based on hegemonic norms, and on the other hand, invites the violence of state–private–civil society networks, often through the deployment of the police and the military (Padel & Das, 2010). Consider for instance the large-scale deployment of state violence to catalyze extractive projects of development that expel subaltern communities from their spaces of livelihood; this expulsion from spaces of livelihood is situated within the violent erasure of subaltern voices from spaces and sites of deliberative democracy (Dutta, 2015). Solidarities with subaltern voices collectivize the struggles for voice, working hand-in-hand with subaltern agency to seek structural transformation. Particularly salient here is the role played actively by global civil society in erasing voice through the co-option of voice architectures at the global margins. Consider for instance the role of e-platforms of digital land acquisition and participation created by global technology giants in Bangalore, India, through partnerships with the state and civil society (Benjamin, 2007, 2010). Presented as opportunities for voice, such platforms co-opt and erase sites of political participation in the everyday life-world of the city that are accessible to subaltern communities of squatters, landless workers, and small-holding farmers, instead turning land acquisition into the hands of capital and the aspiring middle classes. The technologies of voice and participation thus deployed under the language of democratic empowerment work precisely to erase subaltern agency and participation.

In this backdrop, the struggle of subaltern participation is one of building networks of solidarity that monitor these hegemonic infrastructures of communication (returning the gaze as surveillance of power) and at the same time displace the arguments from the sites of technology-enabled decision-making into the everyday networks of face-to-face participation, community meetings, *gheraouts* (surrounding the offices of local government), and street protests. Subaltern voice emerges in the very conversations on where voice infrastructures ought to be located, moving voice infrastructures into the hands of subaltern communities. The work of the academic and activist communities therefore is one of collaborating with subaltern communities to locate voice infrastructures in the hands of subaltern communities.

Solidarity here is expressed in the embodied work of "standing beside" subaltern communities and in lending one's privilege in coconstructing infrastructures for subaltern voice. The role of the academic as an active listener is transformed into cocreating infrastructures for subaltern voice. The presence of subaltern voices in hegemonic discursive spaces resist the policies and pathways of development that displace and expel subaltern communities (Dutta, 2018). To challenge the co-optive capacity of global capital through the very techniques of voice and participation calls for ongoing forms of solidarity that access these structures, decode their rules and norms, and cocreate communicative strategies of disruption. Given the likelihood of structures to respond with violence when subaltern voice is registered within hegemonic discursive spaces, the work of solidarity translates often into sustaining relationships that sustain the possibilities for voice. This is embodied in the work of the academic placing herself/himself alongside the subaltern struggles for voice, directly resisting the tools of control deployed by dominant structures. Solidarity draws on the courage and the conviction to stand by subaltern struggles, especially when the state-corporate nexus deploy a variety of techniques of repression from threatening to fire, to setting up false disciplinary cases, to disciplining academic working within neoliberal institutions. To sustain these spaces of solidarity also translates into collectivizing within to resist the onslaught of authoritarian managerial-bureaucracy within the neoliberal university. Through solidarity, academics stand with other academics that are targeted by authoritarian techniques for committing to listening to subaltern voices.

Socialist futures. The hegemonic formations of communication have been historically embedded within global capitalism (Dutta, 2015). The promotion of communication as tools for modernization and development are embedded in the role of communication in capitalism (Dutta, 2018). These ideological roots of communication as an instrument of global capital is systematically obfuscated from the discussions of theories of communication. The social scientific studies for instance of media effects, persuasion, and influence carry within them the capitalist (neo) colonialist visions of modernization, based on linear concept of growth as an instrument of development. The overarching emphasis on growth then is tied to the conceptualization of communication as an instrument of changing individual values, beliefs, and attitudes. The struggles of organizing expressed by subaltern voices seek to undo these capitalist logics, instead suggesting pathways for communication in re-distributing wealth, income, and opportunity (Dutta, 2008, 2015; Smith, 2013).

The commitment to socialist futures however is fundamentally based on, first and foremost, the redistribution of communicative opportunities. The CCA offers a framework for inverting communicative inequities through the decolonization of communication as community ownership of communicative resources and infrastructures. Noting that the resistance to inequalities ought to be fundamentally rooted in the communicative capacity of voice among subaltern communities, the CCA seeks to explore the distribution of communicative infrastructures for voice in subaltern communities. These infrastructures are built on the recognition that subaltern communities are creative participants in agentically exploring opportunities for collective well-being, thus cocreating openings for the generation of subaltern knowledge claims (Dutta, 2004). Such knowledge claims not only disrupt the hegemonic structures of knowledge but also carve out spaces of healing and wellness through collective journeys of voice, democracy, and participation. The democratization of knowledge thus is embedded within the democratization of communicative opportunities. Through the presence of subaltern voices as expressions of agency, dominant structures constituting inequalities are challenges and transformed.

Conclusion

In this chapter, I explored the role of communication as voice. Whereas on one hand, the erasure of voice is key to the perpetuation of structural inequalities, on the other hand, voice offers the promise of resisting and transforming structures. In the project of transforming local, national, and global inequalities communication is voice. It is through the voicing of articulations that transformative seeds of change are cocreated, embodied, and sustained.

References

Basu, A., & Dutta, M. J. (2009). Sex workers and HIV/AIDS: Analyzing participatory culture-centered health communication strategies. *Human Communication Research, 35*(1), 86–114.

Benjamin, S. (2007). Lifestyling India's metros: the elite's civic reform. *Ensuring Public Accountability Through Community Action*, 179–208.

Benjamin, S. (2010). Manufacturing neoliberalism: Lifestyling Indian urbanity. In S. Banerjee-Guha (Ed.), *Accumulation by dispossession: Transformative cities in the new global order* (pp. 92–124). New Delhi, India: SAGE.

Carvalho, A., Pinto-Coelho, Z., & Seixas, E. (2016). Listening to the public–enacting power: Citizen access, standing and influence in public participation discourses. *Journal of Environmental Policy and Planning*, 1–19. doi:10.1080/1523908X.2016.1149772

Dewhurst, K., Munford, R., & Sanders, J. (2017). Making a claim for services: Supporting young people's engagement with services. *Aotearoa New Zealand Social Work, 29*(1), 4.

Duran, B., Harrison, M., Shurley, M., Foley, K., Morris, P., Davidson-Stroh, L., ... Andrasik, M. P. (2010). Tribally-driven HIV/AIDS health services partnerships: Evidence-based meets culture-centered interventions. *Journal of HIV/AIDS & Social Services, 9*(2), 110–129.

Dutta, M. J. (2004a). The unheard voices of Santalis: Communicating about health from the margins of India. *Communication Theory, 14*(3), 237–263.

Dutta, M. J. (2004b). Poverty, structural barriers, and health: A Santali narrative of health communication. *Qualitative Health Research, 14*(8), 1107–1122.

Dutta, M. J. (2005). Theory and practice in health communication campaigns: A critical interrogation. *Health Communication, 18*(2), 103–122.

Dutta, M. J. (2007). Communicating about culture and health: Theorizing culture-centered and cultural sensitivity approaches. *Communication Theory, 17*(3), 304–328.

Dutta, M. J. (2008). *Communicating health: A culture-centered approach.* Malden, MA: Polity.

Dutta, M. J. (2012). Hunger as health: Culture-centered interrogations of alternative rationalities of health. *Communication Monographs, 79*(3), 366–384.

Dutta, M. J. (2018). Culturally centering social change communication: subaltern critiques of, resistance to, and re-imagination of development. *Journal of Multicultural Discourses, 13*(2), 87–104.

Dutta, M. J., Anaele, A., & Jones, C. (2013). Voices of hunger: Addressing health disparities through the culture-centered approach. *Journal of Communication, 63*(1), 159–180.

Dutta, M. J., Hingson, L., Anaele, A., Sen, S., & Jones, K. (2016). Narratives of food insecurity in Tippecanoe County, Indiana: Economic constraints in local meanings of hunger. *Health Communication, 31*(6), 647–658.

Dutta, M. J., & Kaur-Gill, S. (2018). Mobilities, communication, and Asia| Precarities of migrant work in Singapore: Precarities of migrant work in Singapore: Migration, (im) mobility, and neoliberal governmentality. *International Journal of Communication, 12,* 19.

Gordon, C., & Hunt, K. (2019). Reform, justice, and sovereignty: A food systems agenda for environmental communication. *Environmental Communication, 13*(1), 9–22.

Guha, R. (1997). *Dominance without hegemony: History and power in colonial India.* Cambridge, MA: Harvard University Press.

Jackson, S., Tan, P. L., Mooney, C., Hoverman, S., & White, I. (2012). Principles and guidelines for good practice in Indigenous engagement in water planning. *Journal of Hydrology, 474,* 57–65.

Kapoor, D. (2009). Participatory academic research (par) and people's participatory action research (PAR): research, politicization, and subaltern social movements in India. In *Education, participatory action research, and social change* (pp. 29–44). New York, NY: Palgrave Macmillan.

Koh, C. Y., Goh, C., Wee, K., & Yeoh, B. S. (2017). Drivers of migration policy reform: The day off policy for migrant domestic workers in Singapore. *Global Social Policy, 17*(2), 188–205.

Kulis, S., Wagaman, M. A., Tso, C., & Brown, E. F. (2013). Exploring indigenous identities of urban American Indian youth of the southwest. *Journal of Adolescent Research, 28*(3), 271–298.

Padel, F., & Das, S. (2010). *Out of this earth: East India Adivasis and the aluminium cartel.* New Delhi, India: Orient Black Swan.

Phillips, L. (2011). *The promise of dialogue: The dialogic turn in the production and communication of knowledge.* Amsterdam, Netherlands: John Benjamins.

Rastogi, R., & Dutta, M. J. (2015). Neoliberalism, agriculture and farmer stories: Voices of farmers from the margins of India. *Journal of Creative Communications, 10*(2), 128–140.

Salsberg, J., Macridis, S., Garcia Bengoechea, E., Macaulay, A. C., & Moore, S. (2017). Engagement strategies that foster community self-determination in participatory research: Insider ownership through outsider championship. *Family Practice, 34*(3), 336–340.

Sastry, S. (2016). Long distance truck drivers and the structural context of health: a culture-centered investigation of Indian truckers' health narratives. *Health Communication, 31*(2), 230–241.

Sharma, A. (2008). *Logics of empowerment: Development, gender, and governance in neoliberal India.* Minneapolis, MN: University of Minnesota Press.

Smith, L. T. (2013). *Decolonizing methodologies: Research and indigenous peoples.* London, UK: Zed Books.

Tan, N., Kaur-Gill, S., Dutta, M. J., & Venkataraman, N. (2017). Food insecurity in Singapore: The communicative (dis)value of the lived experiences of the poor. *Health Communication, 32*(8), 954–962.

Walters, K. L., Beltran, R., Evans-Campbell, T., & Simoni, J. M. (2011). Keeping our hearts from touching the ground: HIV/AIDS in American Indian and Alaska Native Women. *Women's Health Issues, 21*(6), S261–S265.

Walker, S. C., Whitener, R., Trupin, E. W., & Migliarini, N. (2015). American Indian perspectives on evidence-based practice implementation: Results from a statewide tribal mental health gathering. *Administration and Policy in Mental Health and Mental Health Services Research, 42*(1), 29–39.

Zoller, H., & Dutta, M. J. (2009). *Emerging perspectives in health communication: Meaning, culture, and power.* New York, NY: Routledge.

Contributors

Tony E. Adams is Professor and Chair of the Department of Communication at Bradley University. He has published more than 60 articles and book chapters and has (co) authored and/or (co)edited six books, including *Narrating the Closet: An Autoethnography of Same-Sex Attraction* (Routledge), *Autoethnography* (Oxford University Press), and the *Handbook of Autoethnography* (Routledge). He is a coeditor of the *Writing Lives: Ethnographic Narratives* book series (Routledge) and founding coeditor of the *Journal of Autoethnography* (University of California Press).

Ahmet Atay is Associate Professor of Communication at the College of Wooster. His research revolves around media and cultural studies, and critical intercultural communication. He is the author of *Globalization's Impact on Identity Formation: Queer Diasporic Males in Cyberspace* (2015) and the coeditor of eight books. His scholarship has appeared in a number of journals and edited books.

Christina S. Beck currently serves as Professor and Associate Director for Graduate Studies in the School of Communication Studies at Ohio University. In addition to publishing multiple journal articles and book chapters, she has authored or coedited five books, including, most recently, the *Routledge Handbook of Communication and Bullying*. In 2014, she established the National Communication Association Anti-Bullying Project as part of her NCA Presidential Initiative. She is currently conducting research at the intersection of popular culture and health communication.

James G. Cantrill is the head of the Department of Communication and Performance Studies and Director of General Education at Northern Michigan University. Over the years, he has developed a reputation as an international expert on environmental communication, was instrumental in the creation of conservation psychology as a distinct disciplinary focus in the social sciences, and has served as a consultant for organizations such as the U.S. Environmental Protection Agency, Parks Canada, and the government of Brazil.

Kristopher Copeland currently serves as Provost: West Campus at Tulsa Community College. His research has been published in *Communication Studies, Disability and Society,* and *Speaker and Gavel.* He recently coedited a book, *Competition, Community, and Educational Growth: Contemporary Perspectives on Competitive Speech and Debate,* which was published by Peter Lang.

Katherine Denker is an Associate Professor at Ball State University. Her work centers on issues of power and voice in both the interpersonal and instructional context, with a further focus on couples' coconstructions of work–life concerns. Her work has appeared in multiple book chapters as well as in journals, including the *Journal of Family Communication, Women and Language, Computers in Human Behavior,* and *Communication Teacher.*

Autumn Edwards is a Professor in the School of Communication at Western Michigan University. Her primary research interest is human–machine communication. She is codirector (along with C. Edwards and P. Spence) of the Communication and Social Robotics Labs and editor of *Human–Machine Communication.*

Chad Edwards is Professor of Communication in the School of Communication at Western Michigan University. His primary research is in human–machine communication. He is a Past President of the Central States Communication Association.

Deanna L. Fassett is Professor of Communication Pedagogy at San José State University, where she serves as a department chair and mentor to future teachers. Her scholarship works to open spaces for educators to explore and enact communication and/in instruction as equitable, inclusive, intentional, and just.

Lynn M. Harter is Professor in the School of Communication Studies at Ohio University and Director of the Barbara Geralds Institute for Storytelling and Social Impact. Her scholarly interests focus on the communication construction of possibility as individuals and groups organize for survival and social change. She is committed to engaged scholarship and working with community members to explore salient social challenges and develop narrative-based interventions.

Tiffany Hecklinski is a PhD student in Health Communication at IUPUI. As a long-time instructor in communication studies focusing on public speaking and persuasion, her career path changed after surviving stage III colorectal cancer. Prior to her PhD work, she served as a communication consultant with the University of Michigan Health System and as an instructor at Ball State University in Indiana.

Art Herbig is a wannabe Jedi who settled for Doctor (sans TARDIS). His current powers include critical rhetoric, documentary production, and ethnography. He uses those skills to study issues of memory, identity, gender, class, and power. Art has directed two films, coedited two books, and authored numerous articles and chapters. By bringing together media production and academic writing, Art also attempts to merge the worlds of scholarship and popular discourse.

Kendra Knight is Assistant Professor in the College of Communication at DePaul University in Chicago. Her research is focused on how individuals in (primarily close) relationships communicate relational boundaries and responsibilities, particularly in moments of strain or uncertainty. Dr. Knight has examined these questions in three intersecting contexts: casual sexual relationships, relational conflict and transgressions, and the negotiation of the work–life interface.

Benny LeMaster is Assistant Professor of Critical/Cultural Communication Studies in the Hugh Downs School of Human Communication at Arizona State University. Their scholarship explores the performative, discursive, and material constitution of identity with particular focus granted to queer and trans of color experience at the intersections of class, ability, and embodiment. Their pronouns are they/them/their.

Jimmie Manning is Professor and Chair of Communication Studies at the University of Nevada, Reno. His research focuses on meaning-making in relationships. This research spans multiple contexts to understand how individuals, couples, families, organizations, and other cultural institutions attempt to define, support, control, limit, encourage, or otherwise negotiate relationships. He explores these ideas through three contexts: relational discourses, especially those about sexuality, gender, love, and identity; connections between relationships and efficacy in health and organizational contexts; and digitally mediated communication. His research has been supported by funding agencies such as the National Science Foundation and Learn & Serve America and has accrued over 30 journal publications in outlets, including *Communication Monographs, Journal of*

Social and Personal Relationships, and *Journal of Computer-Mediated Communication.* He recently coauthored the book *Researching Interpersonal Relationships: Qualitative Methods, Research, and Analysis* (SAGE) and has another solo-authored book, *Qualitative Research in Sexuality & Gender Studies* (Oxford University Press), forthcoming.

Mark P. Orbe is Professor of Communication and Diversity in the School of Communication at Western Michigan University, where he also holds a joint appointment in the Department of Gender and Women's Studies. His teaching and research center on the inextricable relationship of culture, power, and communication.

Sandra Petronio is the creator of Communication Privacy Management Theory and is the Founding Director of the IUPUI Center for Translating Research into Practice. Dr. Petronio is a Professor in the Indiana University (IUPUI) Department of Communication Studies and the IU School of Medicine. She is recognized nationally and internationally for her work in privacy management.

Anji L. Phillips is Assistant Professor of Television Arts, and advises radio, television, and film projects in the Department of Communication at Bradley University. Dr. Phillips conducts media research at the intersection of mass/niche, and political communication with an emphasis in both new and traditional media. Telling a good story well is at the heart of her media projects, and how she advises her students to create content.

William K. Rawlins is a Stocker Professor in the School of Communication Studies at Ohio University. He has published extensively about the unique challenges and dialectical tensions of communicating in friendships across the life course. His ongoing research addresses the role of friendships in accomplishing the well-lived life for individuals and communities, and the role of dialogue and narrative in coauthoring viable and edifying identities with others. Lately, Bill also has been embodying musical performances and compositions to address the aesthetics of interpersonal and relational communication, music as communication, and the musicality of social life and interpretive inquiry.

Robert J. Razzante is a doctoral candidate at the Hugh Downs School of Human Communication at Arizona State University. His engaged scholarship seeks to transform conflict involving the intersections of culture, privilege, and marginalization.

Amy Aldridge Sanford is Professor of Communication and Associate Provost for Academic Affairs at Texas A&M University–Corpus Christi. She specializes in leadership, gender, nonprofit, diversity, qualitative research, and pedagogy, and her research has been published in numerous academic journals, book chapters, newspapers, and national newsletters. Her book *From Thought to Action: Developing a Social Justice Orientation* is available from Cognella.

Deanna Sellnow is Professor of Strategic Communication and Assistant Director/Chair of the Communication Department in the Nicholson School of Communication and Media at the University of Central Florida. She has also taught as a tenured professor and assistant provost for transformative learning at the University of Kentucky and a tenured professor and director of the public speaking fundamentals program at North Dakota State University, as well as a visiting professor at the Chinese University of Hong Kong. Dr. Sellnow conducts research in two major areas. The first focuses on strategic instructional risk and crisis communication in a variety of contexts (e.g., natural disasters, health epidemics/pandemics, biosecurity, terrorism, and agricultural biotechnology). The second focuses on rhetoric and persuasion in mediated popular culture texts (e.g., entertainment media, advertising, social media). She has conducted funded research for the United States Geological Survey (USGS), the United States Department of Agriculture (USDA), the Department of Homeland Security (DHS-National Center for Food Protection and Defense), and the Centers for Disease Control and Prevention (CDC). Her work is published in several books, as well as in national and international journals. She has presented her research across the United States and in many countries around the world, including Canada, China, Czech Republic, Denmark, Egypt, England, Germany, Hong Kong, India, Indonesia, Ireland, Italy, Japan, Senegal, Singapore, Spain, Sweden, Turkey, and Vietnam. She has also served as President of the Central States Communication Association, of which she was inducted into the Hall of Fame in 2018. She is past-editor of *Communication Teacher,* sponsored by the National Communication Association, and current editor of the *Journal of Communication Pedagogy,* sponsored by the Central States Communication Association.

Timothy L. Sellnow is Professor of Strategic Communication in the Nicholson School of Communication and Media at the University of Central Florida and currently serves as Director of Graduate Programs. He has also taught as a tenured professor at the University of Kentucky and North Dakota State University, as well as a visiting professor at the Chinese University of Hong Kong. Dr. Sellnow's research focuses on biosecurity, precrisis planning, and strategic communication for risk management and mitigation in government, organizational, and health settings. He has conducted funded research for the Department of Homeland Security, the United States Department of Agriculture, the Centers for Disease Control and Prevention, the Environmental Protection Agency, the United States Geological Survey, and the World Health Organization. He has also served in an advisory role for the National Academy of Sciences and the Food and Drug Administration. He has published numerous refereed journal articles on risk and crisis communication and has coauthored six books on risk and crisis communication. Dr. Sellnow's most recent book, coauthored with Matthew Seeger, is entitled, *Communication in Times of Trouble: Best Practices of Crisis Communication and Emergency Risk Communication.* He is also past-editor of the *Journal of Applied Communication Research,* a publication of the National Communication Association. Dr. Sellnow is a recipient of the National Communication Association's Gerald M. Phillips award for Distinguished Applied Communication Research and the Nicholson School of Communication's Excellence in Teaching Award.

Patric R. Spence is an Associate Professor in the Nicholson School of Communication and Media at the University of Central Florida. His primary areas of research are crisis communication and human–machine communication. He is the current editor of *Communication Studies.*

Danielle M. Stern is Associate Professor of Communication at Christopher Newport University, where she teaches courses in media studies, gender, and intersectionality. Her research engages the role of intersectionality and social justice in transforming popular culture and pedagogy. Her more than 20 scholarly articles have been published in *Information, Communication and Society; Women's Studies in Communication; Text and Performance Quarterly; The Communication Review; Sexuality and Culture; The Popular Culture Studies Journal;* and *Women and Language,* as well as in various edited books.

Adam W. Tyma is Associate Professor of Critical Media Studies in the School of Communication at the University of Nebraska at Omaha. He also is the current Graduate Program Chair for the master's program in the School of Communication and the coordinator for the Visual Communication and Culture minor. He teaches courses that focus on media theory and culture, media literacy, visual culture, critical and cultural theory, computer-mediated communication, media consumption, and popular culture. Dr. Tyma has refereed published work in the *International Journal of Communication, Journal* *of Communication Inquiry, Communication Teacher,* the *Basic Communication Course Best Practices: A Training Manual for Instructors* (edited volume), *Communication Perspectives on Popular Culture* (edited volume), conference proceedings for the *Alta Conference on Argumentation* and the *Association for Internet Researchers,* and state-level communication journals. He also has developed book projects working to understand the future of media studies (*Beyond New Media*) and the homebrewing subculture (*Beer Culture in Theory and Practice*). In addition to publishing, Dr. Tyma has developed the Media Literacy Education Project (MLEP), a service-learning program that creates curriculum for after-school programs at the fifth- to eighth-grade level. He also likes to brew beer, sail, and lift heavy things.

Quaquilla Rhea Walker is a Lecturer of Communication Studies in the School of Communication at Northern Arizona University. Her research is in communication, technology, and social justice, having participated in conference panels and publications in these areas. She earned her PhD in communication from Northwestern University with a master's degree in engineering management, and a BA in mathematics and physics from North Central College. She has taught at Northwestern University, Robert Morris University, DePaul University, Saint Xavier University, University of Minnesota Morris, and presently at NAU intertwining social justice and social media in all of her communication courses. She additionally has a work background in computer software systems and management at AT&T.

David Westerman is Associate Professor in the Department of Communication at North Dakota State University. His primary research foci includes technology and how people communicate through and with it.

Stephanie L. Young is Associate Professor of Communication Studies at the University of Southern Indiana. She specializes in visual rhetoric, popular culture, autoethnography, and issues of race, gender, and sexuality. She has published in several scholarly journals, including *Women's Studies in Communication* and the *Journal of International and Intercultural Communication.* She is also the cohost of the podcast Pop Culture Pizza Party.

Index

CPSIA information can be obtained
at www.ICGtesting.com
Printed in the USA
LVHW080054270623
750838LV00002B/2

9 781516 578207